Christianity
and
Islam:

THE STRUGGLING
DIALOGUE

Edited by

Richard W. Rousseau, S.J.

VOLUME FOUR

MODERN THEOLOGICAL THEMES:
SELECTIONS FROM THE LITERATURE

Scranton: Ridge Row Press
(Imprint of University of Scranton Press)

© 1985 by Ridge Row Press
(Imprint of The University of Scranton Press)

ISBN 0-940866-03-X
SAN 223-1123

Library of Congress Catalog Card Number 84-62715

Distribution:

University of Scranton Press
Chicago Distribution Center
11030 S. Langley
Chicago IL 60628

PRINTED IN THE UNITED STATES OF AMERICA

CONTENTS

GENERAL INTRODUCTION

This study of Muslim-Christian relations differs somewhat from the previous three volumes in this series.[1] The dialogue between Christians and great religions of the East is between two cultures and religious traditions that have not known each other very well in the past and are now seriously engaged in the explorations and conversations brought on by the rapprochements of a shrinking world. Dialogue between Christians and Jews, for all its difficulties, is proceeding reasonably well and is beginning to delve into some central issues. The dialogue between Christians and Muslims, however, is much more difficult. There is the weight of centuries past, with its military conflicts and commercial rivalries between Christian Europe and the encircling world of Islam. In the present there are tensions over oil and the world wide conflicts over Muslim minorities in Christian countries and Christian minorities in Muslim countries. And there are even tensions in those countries where the proportions of Christian and Muslim population and power on the national level are roughly equal.

In attempting to assess the present dialogic relation between Islam and Christianity, one discovers at least two major levels. The first is that of politico-religious discussions and acceleration in various countries. So it is necessary to include in this book, as opposed to the other three, essays which chronicle the efforts, at times desperate and military, to work out relations on a national level.

On the more traditional second level are the actual attempts at religious/theological dialogue between representative Christians and Muslims. These have been both successful as beginnings and disappointing as solutions.

In the following introductory pages, then, we shall first examine each chapter briefly to grasp its main ideas and message and then, in a last section, attempt a more theoretical and summary synthesis of where the Muslim-Christian dialogue is today.

---

1) *Modern Theological Themes: Selections From the Literature Series: Volume One: Interreligious Dialogue: Facing the Next Frontier, Ridge Row Press, 1981; Volume Two: Christianity and the Religions of the East: Models for a Dynamic Relationship, RRP, 1982; Volume Three: Christianity and Judaism: The Deepening Dialogue, RRP, 1983, all edited by Richard W. Rousseau, S.J.*

i

"Christianity and Islam"

CHAPTER ONE: WILFRED CANTWELL SMITH

In this essay Smith proposes to examine the presuppositions underlying interactions between two major world religions: Christianity and Islam. He sees four such basic presuppositions: 1. The Classical Christian one: "Islam is a Christian heresy;" 2. The Classical Islamic one: "Jesus is an important member of a long line of prophets beginning with Adam and culminating in Muhammad;" 3. The Classical 19th century one: "Christianity is one religion and Islam another;" and 4. The new approach which he describes in the essay.

The first point made by this new approach is that just as Zarathustra transcended the history of Zarathustrianism, so, in world religious history, the roles of Jesus and Muhammad transcend the history of Christianity and Islam.

The second point concerns "church": a. "church history" needs to be changed to a study of religion in a particular modern culture or country; b. the church must be understood as an impetus or nucleus rather than a form; and, c. the Western church has to be understood as a whole made up of two sub-sectors rather than of two distinctly separated parts.

The third point is that even the division between Christians and Jews has to be put into a similar wholistic context.

The underlying reason for all this is that both Islam and Christianity have been dynamic movements, changing with new times, new places, new cultures, that is, both of them are in a continuous process of transcending themselves. Both have for centuries participated in, "a larger context constituted in significant part by the other." The Crusades, for example, need to be understood as a crisis in this Islamic-Christian complex. Both Islam and Christianity contributed to the development of Scholasticism. Both circulated and lived on similar tales of self-denying asceticism and piety. The idea of God has been central in both.

To the objection that despite all this, the Christians remain Christians and Muslims remain Muslims, the answer given by Smith is that today both are moving beyond this extended participation in a common historical context to a new period of theological convergence. One very preliminary suggestion that he makes along this line is the following: Since the figure of Christ is influential in Islam, though conceptualized differently, "Who is to say that the movement stemming from Jesus (and before) is not to be traced as much outside the explicitly Christian church as within."

To sum up, it is possible, to argue, says Smith, that Christians have always been muslims, that is, that they have consecrated themselves to God's word and truth and Muslims have been christians, that is, that they have been followers and reverers of Christ. Muslim-Christian relations he concludes, must be approached in terms of "a single complex of which the two parts are different but not discrete; they are to be understood as elements of a dynamic whole."

Introduction

CHAPTER TWO: JACQUES LANFRY

This essay is based on Lanfry's report to the Seminar on Islamic-Christian Dialogue held in Tripoli in 1976 and which has ongoing significance. After explaining that Jews were not included in the Seminar because Islamic-Jewish relations were at their tensest in centuries, he takes up the obstacles between Christians and Muslims. Lanfry then spends a good bit of time examining the obstacles that Christians must overcome in order to dialogue productively with Muslims. He begins with Muslim perceptions of past Christian errors and prejudices. Thus, for example, Muslims see Christians as persistent and deliberate obstacles to the development of their civilization. Western colonialism and imperialism are understood as a kind of continuation of the Crusades. Many Muslims also feel that the paramount importance of Arab scientific and philosophical contributions to the medieval West have been acknowledged by only a handful of Christians. It is true, he concedes that not all of these problems were intentional; geographical separation and linguistic unfamiliarity were also important in creating and perpetuating the chasm. For centuries Christians as well have been disposed to judge Islam on the basis of only some of the followers, not always the most representative. Finally, the silence of Christians about Muhammad disturbs many Muslims. They revere Jesus and cannot understand or appreciate why Christians tend to disparage Islam's prophet.

The Second Vatican Council and the Secretariat for Non-Christian Religions have urged Christians to overcome their prejudices against Islam as a religion "of fatalism, legalism and fear, of laxism, fanaticism and opposition to progress." Muslims, they say, obey God out of love rather than fear; and sincere efforts are underway in all parts of the Islamic world to overcome static structures.

Another misunderstanding of Muslims by Christians, according to Lanfry, is that no distinction between church and state exists in Islamic countries. Though many of these are obviously not western style democracies, it is wrong to conclude that there is no room in Islamic society for anyone who is not Muslim.

Christians have tried hard to overcome these prejudices. The Vatican Council itself took strong steps and various structurers have been established to pursue dialogue. Christian scholars have worked hard at deepening their knowledge of the world of Islam and of Islamic religious experience. New initiatives and dialogues have sprung up on the local level. And a general theology of non-christian religions has been developing rapidly in which Islam of course plays a major role. Proselytism has been discouraged in favor of personal witness.

Turning then to Muslims, Lanfry lists a number of Muslim attitudes towards Christians which they find equally difficult to accept: that Christians are atheists deserving of hell; that the Christian Scriptures are "inauthentic;" that the only reason Christians are interested in dialogue now is fear of the threat of such common enemies as materialism and communism; that both

"Christianity and Islam"

Western churches and individual Christians are too often identified with the policies and actions of Western governments.

Lanfry concludes by asking both Christians and Muslims why they should not prefer those schools of thought internal to both of them that favor encounter and dialogue with each other. There are centuries of accumulated problems to overcome as well as the tensions of the present day, but he is confident that dedication to a common God will somehow help all to overcome their difficulties in order to fulfill His common purposes.

CHAPTER THREE: MAURICE BORRMANS

Written to be delivered first to the Muslims then to the Christians attending the Congress of Tripoli in 1976, this essay concentrates on areas of agreement, acknowledging that much remains to be said further about areas of disagreement.

It is divided into two main parts: "A Common Heritage," and "Areas of Convergence." The first deals with areas of religious or doctrinal rapprochement between Muslims and Christians and the second deals with their common response to the many problems of the world today.

The first area of religious rapprochement, then, is their ways of knowing God. Both recognize the world as created and acknowledge in Creator. God's existence is argued and the existence of "original sin" recognized. At the same time, they acknowledge that God also makes himself known through revelation.

They also give similar answers to the great questions of human life. They both believe in the oneness of God, reaffirmed over and over again in their Scriptures and official statements. Both praise the greatness of God, the benevolent Creator and admire his deeds in creation and in history.

Both recognize a divine providence which benevolently oversees our lives. They see in God one who judges sinfulness strongly but who nevertheless pardons and is merciful. Therefore they see God as worthy to be praised and glorified.

Both believe that God has spoken in history at various times through prophets. They both recognize Abraham and Moses. They do differ over the criteria by which to recognize definitive prophecy. Christians see its fullness in Jesus; Muslims, while acknowledging Jesus' greatness, see in Muhammad the apex of prophecy. Each should not ask too much of the other in this area. The same could be said with regard to the sacred books.

Both acknowledge a divine day of judgment, when the good will be rewarded and the evil punished. Thus both accept an abode of reward and an abode of punishment. Because of this fidelity to God, the great, the one, the saver, both "submit" to him, or, accomplish true "islam" as did Abraham and Moses. This shows itself in prayer, fasting, almsgiving and righteous acts which correspond to God's will for humankind. In this, then, all men and women are believers.

In the second part, Borrmans turns to the challenges to both Islam and

iv

Christianity from the modern world, challenges which most appropriately should be faced together. Faith is after all a commitment to service as well. Love of the living God leads both to protect life wherever it is threatened. Love of a just God leads both to fight against all forms of discrimination, whether sexual, racial, cultural, religious or national. It leads also to opposition to economic injustice and maldistribution of wealth. The love of a God who freely creates leads both to support the values of freedom everywhere, for God can be truly worshipped only by a truly pure heart. Love of a God of peace leads both to support world peace and the resolution of conflicts.

Vatican II's "Church in the Modern World" has touched on all these major issues: human dignity, human community, the values of human action, the dignity of marriage and the family, cultural development, economic justice and world peace.

In conclusion, Borrmans says that believers today can "prove the effectiveness and real credibility of their faith in God" by living lives filled with justice, freedom and fellowship. All who strive in this way will be brought joy and peace.

CHAPTER FOUR: MOHAMMED TALBI

Though this paper is older than the others in this collection and has seen various versions, both oral and printed, it is so remarkable a survey of Muslim attitudes towards dialogue that this outweighs other considerations.

Mohammed Talbi begins by stating his premise, namely that in this rapidly developing 20th century, Islam cannot afford to remain a spectator. He sees dialogue as something supported by Islamic tradition and as necessary for a reestablishment of Islam's connection with the world at large. This dialogue must begin with an explanation of various misconceptions about Islam.

One of the difficulties of dialogue with and by Islam today is the difference in educational level and knowledge between Christian and Muslim representatives at various conferences. Qualified Islamic partners from third world countries are hard to find, whereas, after centuries of discussion, conflict and refinement, there are many qualified Christian representatives available. It is no solution, says Talbi, for Islam to react to this situation by withdrawing into itself. Such frontiers are easily breached these days; the upheaval cannot be escaped and must be met head on.

Some of the conditions then which he sees as fruitful for Muslim-Christian dialogue are the following: 1. an avoidance of polemics and proselytism on both sides; 2. the recognition that arguments no longer bring about conversion; 3. a realization that the apostolate for both sides is a deepening of faith and a living witness to it; (even jihad should be interpreted this way); 4. a recognition of the fact that the ways of salvation are pluralistic and that good faith and sincerity are the essential prerequisites for all.

Talbi than turns to the purpose of this dialogue. He says it is to remove barriers between Muslims and Christians and "to increase the amount of Good in the world by a free exchange of ideas." All believers should work together to face the great and perennial problems of mankind as well as the major questions of the 20th century. It might be helpful, therefore, to study together the legacy of spiritual values found in all religions.

As for specific theological points of dialogue between Islam and Christianity Talbi suggests the following as some that would be useful to pursue: hidaye (guidance), lutf (protection-help), tawfiq (assistance-direction), dalal (the trial of going astray), human liberty, a transcendental God, religion and science.

There are certain subjects, however, which may have to be postponed: Jesus and Muhammad; the nature of the Christian Bible and that of the Qu'ran.

Though there may be some limits to the scope of the dialogue for the present, there are no limits to its purpose, concludes Talbi, which is to stir people up and make them open to new ideas. Complacency on either side is neither desirable nor possible in the light of the great challenges to all religions today. This could be especially helpful to Muslims who need to recapture their dynamic, ongoing sense of revelation. The best tradition is the one that knows how to grow.

Where will all this lead us then? No one can say. It is an adventure on which to embark. God's help, light and guidance will be with us. Dialogue is not going to solve all problems. Many disappointments will occur, but it is essential that we become open to deeper insights into the mysteries of the Kingdom of God.

CHAPTER FIVE: PENELOPE JOHNSTONE

This essay is a survey of the state of Muslim-Christian relations in Britain. It begins with the background of the some of the 1,250,000 Muslims presently in Great Britain. Most are Indians and Pakistanis rather than Arabs. A few are African. Most came after 1945 and especially after the 1947 partition of India.

The British Government has tried to provide services such as language training and health aid. Muslims themselves have not only built mosques in several large cities but have also developed such infrastructures as the Islamic Foundation, the Muslim Educational Trust and the Union of Muslim Organizations. Since the 1944 Religious Education Act's multi-faceted approach to religiously mixed student bodies did not prove fully satisfactory to all, Islamic religious instruction is now generally provided after school hours.

As far as Church schools are concerned, they seem divided in their approach to Religious Education: some favor witnessing to Christianity before Muslim students, others are reluctant to give up proselytizing.

British Churches do not necessarily separate their "religious" from their "social" concerns. The Anglican Church has developed a variety of interfaith agencies and many local Anglican churches have "outreach" programs for Muslims. The Roman Catholic Church has not developed an explicitly interfaith agency, though a number of Catholic organizations are involved in such activities. The Roman Catholic Bishops, trying to better inform Catholics about the various religions in the country, especially Islam, have

Introduction

publicly acknowledged that Britain is a multi-racial, multi-cultural society and that all should be "sensitive to the particular religious needs of ethnic minorities." One religious Order, the Little Sisters of Jesus, is dedicated to working among Muslim communities.

Other Christian Churches such as the United and Reformed and the Methodist, have also set up working groups in this area. A number of interfaith organizations have been established: the World Congress of Faiths, the National Interfaith Conference: Jewish, Christian and Muslim and other smaller groups.

Some study and educational centers have also developed, such as the Birmingham Centre for the Study of Islam and Christian-Muslim Relations. This last is a joint venture by Muslims and Christians to explore the living traditions of the two faiths in Europe and elsewhere. There is a small research centre at Oxford called the Farmingham Institute.

Interfaith relations in Britain, then, according to Johnstone, need to be seen "in the wider context of the post-conciliar Catholic Church, the growth of the ecumenical movement, the pluriform nature of post-colonial Britain, the changing circumstances in which they live and the varied, constantly changing, attitudes of those around us."

CHAPTER SIX: MARAWI REPORT

This communication from the Joint Catholic-Protestant Consultation on Christian presence among Muslim Filipinos held in Marawi in 1978 is a helpful summary of formal issues that rises above the confused tangle of Muslim-Christian problems in the Philippines.

After a disclaimer that the 26 participants do not speak as official representatives of their denominations but as Christians seeking a solution to the hatred and oppression that have marked Christian-Muslim relations in the Philippines, they address the first part to Muslims.

In this first section they express repentance for the tragedies of the past and ask to be accepted for themselves even though they do not come bearing ready-made answers. They say that they seek a dialogue with the Muslims of the Philippines, acknowledging that they have much to learn even in their own tradition. They express the hope that they will be able to face oppression together and achieve a status where freedom of conscience will be possible for all. They conclude this section by also expressing the hope that God in his compassion will support solidarity and help to overcome obstacles.

The second part is addressed to Christians. The following is a summary of the attitudes they suggest are needed by Christians to improve their presence among their Muslim brothers: a. a serious respect for Islam; b. a repudiation of coercive missions and arrogant proselytizing; c. a common front against social, economic and political challenges; d. a serious attentiveness to Muslim expression of grievances; e. a respect for Muslims by public officials, educators and media persons; f. a sense of shame for past injuries done to Muslims, and, finally, g. a need for Christians to work together in helping Muslims.

"Christianity and Islam"

CHAPTER SEVEN: JOSEPH KENNY

Slightly more than half of the population of Nigeria is Muslim, concentrated in the northern half, while the remainder, mainly in the south, is Christian.

Under the British, says Kenny, Christian missionaries were at first naively confident of converting Muslims. They kept contact with the Emirs of the North in order to be able to preach to the pagans there. Because of northern Muslim hesitation to accept Christian or even government schools, an educational disparity developed between North and South which is only now beginning to be overcome. Muslims in the South attended Christian schools and even opened their own.

While the South was maneuvering for independence from Britain, the North was resisting and suggesting that only Islam could provide a unifying bond. Political opposition in the North also came mostly from Christian groups. In 1959, when the North was granted self-government, real pluralism and tolerance of Christians was slow in coming. Yet when independence did come in 1960, the mood, both North and South, was to make it work, to "bridge the gap." There were mutual appointments of Christians and Muslims and other gestures of cooperation. Tensions arose, however, when Christian missions expanded their work in the North with great success. Islamic crusades were conducted and political promotions in the North went only to leaders who cooperated with the Northern government and there were counter movements by Christians. Thus pressures began for the government to take over church schools and tensions with the Ibos of the North finally resulted in their expulsion.

When Yakubu Gowon (1966-1975) came to power, he divided the nation into 12 states, which included a division of the Eastern region. This was the occasion of the civil war. Though in the North the situation took on a religious overtone, the Federal Government, mainly Christian, fully pleased neither Christians nor Muslims. National solidarity during the civil war generally reduced religious tensions. The Catholic Church had the opportunity to develop a Northern constituency for the first time and a vocation boom followed, including the indigenization of the episcopacy.

Universal primary education was introduced in 1975, with religious education made mandatory. There were protests in the South by Muslim students about various slights to their religion, most of which were remedied. Religious polemics, both North and South, continued as a problem.

Rapid political change, the ouster of Gowon in 1975, the assassination of his successor, Murtali Muhammad in February, 1976 and the appointment of Obasanjo, a Baptist, as head of state, with a Muslim really administering the country, all produced religious tensions.

The Muslims next demanded Shari'a courts for all aspects of life, even going so far as to suggest that the Shari'a should be made the law of the land, with Islam the state religion. This was defeated by the constituent assembly in 1978. But many aspects of the Shari'a were introduced at the state level.

Introduction

There were attacks on Christian establishments and the army had to intervene. In the transition to civilian rule in 1979, however, religious issues were kept strictly in the background.

Against this politico-cultural background, efforts at Muslim-Christian dialogue were being made. Protestants, for example, developed what they called the "Islam in Africa Project," aimed at peaceful relations based on positive and accurate understandings of Islam. But this Project failed since it was not responsible to any church for its theological position. Study Centers and University lecturers on Islam helped improve relations.

Roman Catholics, after Vatican II, organized meetings between private individual Catholics and Muslims. They also established a Dominican study center on Islam. Courses on Islam were offered in Catholic schools and seminaries. High level relations, however, were not particularly good and more was accomplished at informal levels like hospitals.

Muslims initiated ecumenical gestures more often and more strongly in the Yoruba South than in the North. Relations between Muslim scholars and Christian scholars and their institutions have generally been good.

As for the future, dialogues will have to be extended beyond a few formal meeting places to a larger number of interested individuals. Politically, Christians fear that Muslim power is becoming predominant on the Federal level. Christian schools, for example, are being renamed with Muslim names. Muslims often remain suspicious of dialogue itself and of the influence of Christian schools in the South. The good will of many on both sides, however, is a hopeful reason for meaningful dialogue and improved relations in the future.

CHAPTER EIGHT: PRO MUNDI VITA STAFF

This essay is the fourth part of a massive fifty page report on "The Muslim-Christian Dialogue of the Last Ten Years (1968-1978). Its sub-title is "Opportunities and Limits of Organized Dialogue." It begins with some analyses of the makeup and characteristics of recent dialogues. Whereas Christian participants have been largely academic or ecclesiastical figures, Muslim participants included many governmental officials. Whereas many of the initiatives for dialogue have come from the Christian side, few have come from the Muslim side. Shiite Muslims have been underrepresented. Some ideological groups on both sides were not represented. And, finally, some of the colloquia were double monologues, others, genuine dialogues.

Among the themes taken up by such dialogues have been the following: the Christian-Muslim dialogue itself; such religious activities as prayer, charity, etc.; the response of believers to the challenges of the modern world; the irreducible differences between Christianity and Islam such as attitudes towards Muhammed and Jesus.

The meetings were usually prepared by joint commissions and the responsibilities for presentations were equally divided. Sometimes they tried to deal with too many topics, thus leaving little time for interpersonal dialogue. Though the discussions were free and open, they did not always reveal that religious sensibilities were very different. At Cordoba, it was possible to be at each other's liturgies; at others this was more difficult.

On balance these dialogue meeting reports agree that: a page has been turned and that past conflicts are seen as past; polemics have been put aside and genuine conversations have taken place; genuine understanding and respect have been shown; there has been an awareness of the shared religious convictions of the "sons of Abraham"; the conclusions of one meeting can serve as the agenda of the next; since 20th century economics and demography offer many more opportunities for contacts between Muslims and Christians, they also require better relationships; attitudes are more flexible and all need to protect spiritual values against materialistic and Marxist challenges.

There are difficulties, of course, that need to be dealt with: dialogues need to be specific; they need to go beyond the level of "official representatives" to the wider bodies of believers; there must be patience with changing long-standing prejudices on both sides; they must be protected from ideological and political misuse; they need a spirit of impartiality; all must learn how to listen; personal outlooks need to be transcended.

Two different kinds of dialogue need to be envisaged for the future: the first kind, large congresses, with a different audience each time, led by a nucleus of specialists; and, the second kind, a great number of workshops for specialists dealing with in-depth scientific research, on all levels: local, regional and national. All this should proceed on the basis of an agreed charter of understanding that includes mutual recognition and respect. They should be well prepared on all levels, including the technical and procedural. Topics should include key religious and theological points.

The spirit of such dialogues, then, is that of "seekers of his Face," giving witness together "for the glory of God." Three simple virtues are needed: "how to keep silent, how to listen and how to be moderate." Both sides can find support in their Scriptures for such attitudes.

The report concludes by noting the fact that after thirteen centuries of difficult confrontation, these dialogues, for all their shortcomings, represent a remarkable achievement. This is only the beginning of a new period. The lesson is clear: "only by engaging in dialogue can one learn how to do it." Reality demands an acceptance of differences, but there is hope for long term success through vigorous discussion which then leads to grass roots awareness and acceptance.

CHAPTER NINE: EMILIO GALINDO AGUILAR

This essay by Aguilar is a report on the Second International Muslim-Christian Congress held at Cordoba from March 21st to 27th, 1977. It brought together about 200 participants from 20 countries. Many Arab countries sent official delegations and it had the full support of the Spanish Episcopal Conference. The main theme of the Congress, determinedly maintained on a high academic level was "Positive Esteem for Muhammad and Jesus in

Christianity and Islam." Though there was a certain amount of advance apprehension about this theme, others were more optimistic. It had been agreed that both Muhammad and Christ would be treated by Muslim and Christian scholars from the point of view of their respective faiths. More lectures were to be devoted to Muhammad because of the greater need for Christians to know about Muhammad. The welcoming address by Cardinal Tarancon of Cordoba was of great importance to all concerned. In his speech he expressed the support of the Spanish bishops for their efforts as well as his understanding of the Congress as a working session expressing mutual respect and love. He emphasized the need for Christians to show respect for Muhammad and acknowledged Muslim values. He highlighted two of Muhammad's concerns: his faith in God and his desire for justice.

In the course of the Congress, the following points were made concerning Muhammad: 1. He is a great historical figure and his life as a prophet must be studied by Christians; when Dr. Gregorio Ruiz then went on to say that though Christians could accept Muhammad as a sociological prophet and as a biblical prophet, but not as a revealing prophet, there were many objections raised by the Muslim members. This carried over into the next day and was concluded by Fr. Basetti-Sani of Italy who, in speaking on "How can I recognize as authentic Muhammad's prophetic mission?" said it was because Islam had to be brought into the history of salvation; 2. Muhammad is an exemplar and model of virtues; 3. Muhammad was a politician and the founder of a political community; 4. Muhammad's religious message and popular devotion to him; 5. Muhammad and Christianity.

The Congress then discussed Jesus beginning with 1. the Qur'anic portrait of Jesus; 2. Christian reactions to the Islamic presentation of Jesus. This too provoked strong debate in which calls were made for a search for common ground; 3. the universal message of Jesus according to Christianity.

Apart from the sixteen main papers, a number of communications on specific topics were presented. There were two moments of prayer for the participants, on Friday a Salat in the ancient Mosque of Cordoba and, on Saturday, a Eucharist in the Cathedral/Mosque.

Aguilar concludes that the Congress was a successful and authentic religious encounter; honest yet friendly. Progress was made in the relations between Christianity and Islam. Also a certain number of practical lessons were learned for the benefit of future congresses.

CHAPTER TEN: JOHN TAYLOR

John Taylor reports in this essay on the international meeting held in Sri Lanka in 1982 on the theme of "Christians and Muslims Living and Working Together." This was held ten years after the WCC sponsored international Christian-Muslim meeting held in Lebanon in 1972. Intermediate meetings, in the 70's had raised, for further clarification, the different roles of Christians in different political situations, here in the majority, there in the minority. There had also been raised the question of joint ventures in the area of social justice and development. The Mombasa Conference, (cf. Chapter 12), also recommended an international conference on "Christians and Muslims Living and Working Together." So preparations and consultations went on through 1979-1981 and Sri Lanka was chosen because both Christians and Muslims are in a minority there.

Attending were thirty Christians from 26 countries, including six Roman Catholic Bishops. Muslim participants came from 22 countries. The discussions were substantive and though overly formal at times, quite productive.

Papers were presented on "Working Together in Relief and Rehabilitation;" "Refugees;" "Planning and Realizing Community Development;" and "Religious Minorities."

This introductory, background material is followed by the full text of the Conference Report. It states, for example, that both parties agreed to discuss the central theme in a world threatened by materialism and loss of faith, as well as by injustices and violations of human rights. The participants realized that many obstacles still lie in the way of fuller cooperation in these areas by Christians and Muslims, and some of these obstacles were presented by both sides.

It was then recommended that a Joint Standing Committee be established by the World Muslim Congress and the World Council of Churches to study these problems and work out through seminars and various groups ways of dealing with them.

With regard to refugees, it was recommended that this was an area whose scope and urgency made it ripe for Christian-Muslim cooperation without proselytism.

With regard to minorities, it was agreed that the religious rights of minorities in many countries both Christian and Muslim were being violated and that efforts should be made to remedy this.

The text of the main report is followed by a report from the WCC delegates to the Conference spelling out specific conclusions and recommendations for further action in these areas by the WCC and its member Churches. These recommendations follow the structure of the main report. The final section is a full list of the participants.

CHAPTER ELEVEN: LUCIE PROVOST

Provost in her essay says that since Vatican II a whole series of Roman Catholic texts, some conciliar, some papal, have spelled out a doctrine of dialogue that is well worth analyzing for a number of reasons.

The first principle stated by the Council is that Christians have an obligation to know something of other religions and to enter into dialogue with them. The foundation proposed is the Incarnation itself: just as God the Father entered into a dialogue with humanity through his Son, so Christians should take the initiative in developing a dialogue to others.

This vision begins with the image of a circle of Christendom, with the other religions related to the center, but gradually expands in the late 60's and 70's

Introduction

to address a pluralistic world, where "fellow citizens have a different faith."
With regard to Islam, a similar progression can be found. "Esteem" for
Islam is expressed by Paul VI based on the faith of Muslims and their pillars of
belief and practice. There are warnings at that time against being too quick to
simply identify Christianity and Islam and indications that its search for God
is incomplete, yet other documents speak clearly of a "common faith in the
Almighty."

This faith can express itself in a common witness, even the witness of
martyrdom, as demonstrated by the Muslim martyrs of Uganda in 1875. Pope
John Paul II, in 1979, speaks of Muslims as "obedient towards God," and
"servants of God." He also establishes parallels between statements in the
Bible and those of the Qur'an on man and creation. At times he adopts a
universalistic mode of speaking which echoes Jesus' praise of the Centurion
of Capharnaum. He even criticizes Christians for not living up to their own
ideals as many in Islam live up to theirs. The comparison shifts from content
of faith to moral conduct, where omissions and failures are not confined to
any particular religion.

The Practice of Dialogue: There is a similar evolution, says Provost, in the
language related to the practice of dialogue. In the mid 60's there were
expressions of respect and esteem for Muslims and the need for mutual
efforts towards social justice and moral values. But this moves to the level of
recognizing and developing mutual spiritual trends. Pope John Paul VI
pointed to "the profound roots of faith in God in whom your Moslem fellow
citizens also believe."

At the same time, the Pope does not diminish the duty of Christians to
"give the reason for the hope that is in them." Though this affirmation of faith
has been supported for other African or Asian religions after the Council, it is
only at Ankara in 1979 that Pope John Paul II said the same for relations with
Islam, namely that these words, (I Pet 3:15-16), are "the golden rule for the
relations and contacts that the Christians must have with his fellow citizens
who have a different faith."

This new implication of moving ahead together, of emulating and encouraging one another, recalls, she concludes, the saying of the Qur'an, "He had
surely made you all one people; be emulous then in good deeds. To God shall
you all return." (Q 5.48).

CHAPTER TWELVE: WORLD COUNCIL OF CHURCHES STATEMENT

This is a brief report of the WCC sponsored Conference on "Christian
Witness in Relation to Muslim Neighbors" held in Mombasa in 1979. The
meeting was made up of 100 Christians from 40 countries, including 25 Roman
Catholics and some Orthodox.

The Conference, very specifically, recommended the following to member
Churches and to all concerned:

1. That Christian attitudes towards Muslims be improved and that there be
a positive evaluation of the "renewal" movement in the Muslim world;

2. That there be further encouragement and development of a variety of study centers dealing with Islam;

3. That there be ongoing efforts to reconcile differences between Christians and Muslims including the establishment of a mediating commission;

4. That joint Christian and Muslim Commissions oversee international human rights and religious freedom and that special care be exercised concerning interfaith marriages;

5. That theological reflection and discussion continue apace, including major international consultations;

6. That, finally, the possibility of mutual Muslim-Christian witness to the world continue to be explored.

SYSTEMATIC ANALYSIS

Muslim-Christian dialogue is not as far along as other dialogues. History explains a good bit of the reasons why. From the days of the original Islamic imperial surge, reaching to the Pyrenees in Spain and briefly penetrating France, through the drawn out frustrations of the Crusades, the gradual decay of the Islamic powers, the colonial era and, in these latter days, the OPEC and Iranian revolutions, the Christian West and the Islamic East have been antagonists.

Yet just as Christianity transcends even the Crusades so Islam transcends even OPEC and there are a number of encouraging developments between them. As opposed to other dialogues, however, a number of these developments have to be described as pre-dialogical, a situation where a number of conditions have to be met and problems alleviated before genuinely religious discussions can take place.

This pre-dialogical situation can be divided into a theoretical and a practical segment. The theoretical tries to clarify the broad ideological conditions that make Muslim-Christian dialogue seem feasible and the practical tries to overcome the social, economic and political tensions between Christians and Muslims in various parts of the world so that true dialogue can have a solid foundation on which to build.

THEORETICAL PRE-DIALOGUE

This theoretical pre-dialogue can take a "religious studies" form where both Islam and Christianity are examined and compared as world religions. In this context, they are seen as dynamic movements that need to change with the times. This active growth, then, would lead them on a convergent path towards each other, where Christians will continue to submit themselves to God and Muslims will continue to revere Jesus. This viewpoint thus sees them as elements of a dynamic whole where dialogue and mutual understanding are essential for future growth.

It can also take a more "psychological" form where Muslims are asked to overcome their historic prejudices against Christians and Christians are asked to overcome their long-held prejudices against Muslims. To take only two examples: Muslims perceive Christians as believing that there is no tolerance of other faiths in Islamic countries because there is no distinction there between Church and State, whereas Christians perceive Muslims as believing that the Christian Bible is religiously inauthentic.

There is also a more "theological" form. First, Christians are encouraged to see connections between Christianity and Islam in several major faith areas: God, Creator and Revealer; Providence and Judgment; Prophecy and Submission to God through Prayer; Fasting, Almsgiving and Righteousness. Furthermore, Christians are reminded that with the challenges against religion in the modern world, with the threats to life, with the ugliness of discrimination, with the pain of economic injustice, that both Christians and Muslims need to work together to try to deal with these major challenges.

Second, Muslims as well are encouraged to see a number of religious areas of convergence: Jesus and Muhammad, the Bible and the Qu'ran, Muslim objections such as the paucity of trained Muslim scholars to engage in dialogue are met with a number of encouraging arguments, namely that despite the past, polemics and proselytization are avoidable and, that despite the difficulties, Islam cannot afford to remain a spectator in this rapidly developing 20th century.

Though obviously dialogue will not solve every problem, it needs to be seen as an ongoing adventure of discovery into the mystery of God's plans for mankind.

PRACTICAL PRE-DIALOGUE

If historical tensions and theological misunderstandings are seen as the "rock," then the socio-cultural and political conditions of a number of countries can be seen as the "hard place" between which fall Muslim-Christian relations in reality.

This is of course an extremely complex subject and the three essays that deal with it in this present volume only scratch the surface. Suffice it to say then, that in broad terms, it is a problem of religious minorities: Muslim minorities in Christian countries and Christian minorities in Muslim countries. In Great Britain, for example, the underlying tensions are dealt with both by law and by a multi-faceted group of organizations and institutions that try to meet the needs of the many Muslim Indians and Pakistanis now there. In the Philippines, where Muslims are a relatively isolated minority in the Archipelago, relations are barely above the stage of military truce, with armed clashes still occasionally happening. Nevertheless, many attempts are being made on several levels to better relations. Finally, in Nigeria, we find a situation of near equality between Muslim (Northern) and Christian (Southern) populations. Once again, relations are stormy and it is taking all the ingenuity of a combination of Federal and State efforts to bring about civic peace. Despite these difficulties, religious dialogue between Muslims and Christians continues to grow.

"Christianity and Islam"

RELIGIOUS DIALOGUES: INTERNATIONAL CONFERENCES

In a report on "religious" dialogues during a ten year span (1968-1978), a number of points are made about both their shortcomings, the content of their discussions and their accomplishments. Among their shortcomings have been the fact that while most Christian participants were academic or ecclesiastical, many Muslims there were government officials and the ideological groupings on both sides were not always included. Topics dealt with were the dialogue proper, responses to an unbelieving world and what were perceived as irreconcilable differences.

One of the most important such conferences of the past decade was that of Cordoba in 1977. This tackled the core of the dialogue. It's theme was "Positive Esteem for Muhammad and Jesus in Christianity and Islam." Despite the optimistic intentions, however, the record of that Conference shows how deep are the wounds and how delicate are the sensitivities on this theme.

Finally, in 1982 in Sri Lanka, interest turned towards cooperation between Christians and Muslims in meeting the threats of a materialistic, secularistic world and its challenge to human rights. In this context, refugee problems and the rights of minorities were given extended consideration.

OFFICIAL POSITIONS

As for the official positions in all this, there has been progress and development. In Roman Catholic circles of the 60's, for example, along with exhortations to openness to other religions, there could be found an image of Christendom as the center of a circle with other religions on the periphery. This vocabulary has gradually grown to include the images of a religiously pluralistic world. As for Islam, there has been progression beyond statements of esteem for Christians to the acknowledgment of parallels between the Bible and the Qu'ran and the exhortation to Christians to be encouraged in their own religious commitment by that of Muslims and an invitation to join them in meeting the new challenges of this century.

The World Council of Churches in its 1979 Report, besides exhorting Christians to study Islam more sympathetically and to work harder to overcome differences, also asks for common efforts in support of human rights, religious freedom and mutual witness in both the national and international levels.

CONCLUSION

It is obvious that while much has been accomplished in recent years in improving Muslim-Christian dialogue, much yet remains to be done. This sobering fact, however, should not cause us to lose sight of the forest for the trees. Given the fact of some 13 centuries of estrangement, war and confrontation between the Muslim and Christian worlds, these dialogues, for all their shortcomings, represent a remarkable achievement. As for the future, we must all leave it in the hands of God, the Compassionate, the Merciful.

Introduction

Richard W. Rousseau, S.J.
University of Scranton

Note: For reasons of accuracy, each author's critical apparatus has been preserved unchanged or with only minor changes.

I

Interpreting Religious Interrelations: An Historian's View of Christian and Muslim

BY WILFRED CANTWELL SMITH

Muslim-Christian 'encounter'? 'relations'? 'interinvolvement'? For the past fourteen centuries a large part of the population of the world has been constituted of two major groups, called Christians and Muslims respectively. The interaction between these two groups has been and continues to be historically significant; also, theologically (on both sides). The purpose of this present essay is to propound a new framework for seeing the history of that relation more truly, understanding it more adequately; or at least, to wrestle with an attempt to forge such a construct; or at the very least, to suggest that the presuppositions with which we have tended in the past to view the mutual impingement are open to improvement.

It is offered in homage to Professor Slater, colleague and friend, as dealing, however inadequately, with issues in which he has been interested; and as touching on matters of which he will recognize the seriousness.

All will doubtless agree that the conceptual categories that we bring to the task determine in some measure our perception of the world. This is so perhaps especially of what has gone on in the historical process. Past and present developments are seen and interpreted within a context constituted

Wilfred Cantwell Smith is McCulloch Professor of Religion and Chairman, Department of Religion, Dalhousie University, Halifax, Nova Scotia. This essay is from Sciences Rel./Studies in Religion. 6/5, 76-77. pp. 515-526 and is reprinted by permission of the publisher.

"Christianity and Islam"

by our foundational ideas. The matter is a two-way process, however. If we are intelligent, alert, and open, what we learn, though in part a function of what we presuppose, yet in turn modifies these basic conceptions. To study the history of religion is hardly serious if it does not continually induce a revision of one's deepest categories.

In the case of Islamic-Christian interrelation, one may suggest four basic ways of conceiving the matter:

(i) To say: 'Islam is a Christian heresy,' is to formulate the situation in classical-Christian terms (e.g., John of Damascus);

(ii) To say: 'Jesus is an important member of a long line of prophets, beginning with Adam and culminating with Muhammad,' is to formulate it in classical-Islamic terms:

(iii) To say: 'Christianity is one religion, and Islam another,' is to formulate it in classical nineteenth-century terms.

(iv) The most fruitful and responsible way to formulate the issue in the light of present-day knowledge and current sophisticated sensibilities, and particularly in terms of world history, the religious history of our race, is a question not yet answered. To it, I address this paper.

I will suggest that a proper elaboration of the fourth stance will include more of both the first and the second, of course in revised form, than the third was either able or willing to do. One may note, in passing, that there have been secular sub-developments of the first formulation: for example, Gibbon's dubbing of the so-called Muslim creed as an eternal truth and a necessary fiction; or modern Western scholarship's analysis of Islam as largely derivative historically. (This last might also include Jewish scholarship showing it as derivative from Judaica.) I will in a moment touch on a modern development of the second. And I will quite supersede the third by suggesting that we may better understand what has happened by discerning the history of the two movements as sub-facets of a transcending complex in which both have participated. But that is to anticipate.

I begin by making three points, which may seem at first irrelevant to the matter at hand; or at least, innocuous. Yet they may serve, by way of detour, to illustrate what is involved, in a neutral and instructive fashion.

The first has to do with Zarathushtra, and the ancient Iranian religious complex surrounding him. It is quite evident, so soon as one reflects on the point, that the role in the religious history of humankind of Zarathushtra and of his milieu is a very different matter from the development of what modern Western scholars, and now even some Parsis, call 'Zoroastrianism.' This last is a relatively small fact today and with a relatively narrow history. On the one hand it incorporates a great deal (some of it of much value, certainly of much significance) that does not derive from Zarathushtra. (Why should it?— unless you happen to be a nineteenth century Protestant Christian of the type that believes that the reality of any religion is, ought to be, the teaching of its so-called founder.) On the other hand, and more important for our present purposes, the 'influence' of Zarathushtra and ancient Iran, if we may use that

2

inadequate word 'influence,' has in historical fact been prodigiously operative in religious movements outside the one that self-consciously crystallized around his memory. Notions of cosmic conflict dualism, Heaven & Hell, the Devil, angelology, and much else, which he did not necessarily originate but to which his inspired preaching contributed force, have played a role in Jewish, Christian, Islamic, and other movements, of massive proportions, across half the world. Not merely the impingement of these component ideas and orientations on a substantial phase of, for instance, Christian history, but their almost central significance during that phase, are now well known.

The point here is that modern awareness of the religious history of the world means that in understanding that history we cannot interpret it to ourselves in terms simply of erstwhile categories of thought (specifically, of disparate and independent entities called 'religions') constructed on the basis of radically less knowledge than is ours, both of data and of historical change. The history of several centuries of Christian religious life was, we now know, what it was, in substantial relation to the fact that ancient Iranian religious orientations were what they were. In other words, a true understanding of the religious history of either ancient Iran or of the later Christian Church requires that each be understood in the context of both. The boundaries, in time and space and conceptuality, that we used to erect around given systems, turn out to be postualtes of doctrine rather than facts of history.

My first point, then, is that the role of Zarathushtra and ancient Iranian world religious history radically transcends the history of the explicit Zarathushtrian or Parsi community. I shall presently suggest that in somewhat comparable ways the roles of both Jesus and Muhammad in world religious history radically transcend the boundaries of the Christian Church and the Islamic *ummah* respectively.

My second starting point concerns the concept 'Church History,' which illustrates another important principle. An earlier position among Christians saw the Church as an entity not merely reified but reified divinely; and therefore an object of historical inquiry. It was envisaged as an idea in the mind of God and as injected as a corporeal reality into human history in the first century A.D. and having a tumultuous but essentially identifiable history since. I do not know how many of my readers will agree that the waning of this theological postulate has been followed by a waning of 'Church History' as a topic, as something distinct from general Western history. In the traditional seminary curriculum, it was a fact worthy of notice that a student could prepare for his (not often in those days, her) Church history examinations, so far as the mediaeval period was concerned, by studying general mediaeval history books, which gave excellent portrayals of Church developments; the seeing of these in context was helpful for their understanding, and such students did well on the exams. When they got into the modern period, however, one could not do that any more. Especially in the United States case I think it is beginning to be widely recognized, at least among younger intellectuals, that what is needed, even in order to understand Christian developments in that land, let alone in order to understand social and human developments, is a history of religion in America. Ecclesiastical history is in this case too narrow to be illuminating; even self-illuminating, we are finding. With the theological postulate gone, I suppose that Ph.D.'s in Church History will cease, within a measurable time, to be given?

Beyond this, however, is the fact that a history of the Church tended to take for granted the Church as a form; whereas the historian—not of the United States in this case, but of the classical Mediterranean world—must deal with the fact that Christians produced a Church, historically, and with the fact that Christian faith has apprehended the world in ways that *inter alia*, have made a Church for them significant, holy. This is something that no other religious group on earth has done, at least not in quite the same fashion. There was a time when the idea of a Church, even the ideas of the Church, the form, the Sacraments, and all were held to be bequeathed; whereas now we recognize that historically they were constructed. What was bequeathed, if one likes, from Jesus—as, in comparable although not in the same fashion, from the Buddha—was an impetus, around which those who received it and responded to it creatively constructed, and have continued creatively to construct across many lands and across many centuries, a dynamic historical movement. Far from taking either the movement, or the forms in which it has creatively crystallized itself, for granted, the historian must take nothing for granted and must see it as his or her task to study and to interpret the emergence of those particular forms. Students, rather than taking the Church for granted and studying its history, should surely sit there gaping that there is a Christian Church at all, and has been now for twenty centuries. The history of the Christian Church is a sub-facet, albeit a fascinating one, of the history of religion in the Western world.

There is, of course, the further point that until recently Protestant Church histories tended to omit, or at least to underplay, Roman Catholic developments since Trent (of course!), while for Catholics the history of the Church has (equally 'of course') been the history of what others call the Roman Catholic Church. Germane to our particular problem in this essay, also, is the transition—in recent memory—of a history of Protestant-Catholic relations, from a two-entity matter to something more complex but holistic. Would most not agree that a study of this relationship has moved from envisaging two bodies, essentially distinct but in some sort of interaction with each other across a boundary that was nonetheless still felt to separate them, towards a recognition that it has been a history, rather, of the Western Church as some sort of whole with two sub-sectors whose relations with each other were in principle no more important than, nor prior to, the development of both in relation to the rest of the society and the rest of the world?

Some have even been arguing lately, in persuasive Hegelian anlysis, that the dialectic of religion and secularism in Western society is itself best seen as an integral development in which neither sector can begin to be understood separately or on its own terms. Several theologians as well as various secular

An Historian's View of Christians and Muslims

sociologists have been moving towards this kind of view. Certainly an historian of the non-Western world can hardly fail to see Western secularism as a sub-facet of specifically Christian history; indeed, of specifically Western Christian history. It is a whimsy of mine that the first really penetrating history of Western secularism will be written by a *Religonsgeschichtler*. More gently: Where else in a modern Faculty of Arts is one likely to find a good course on the history and understanding of Western secularism, than in a Department of Religion?

The third preliminary issue that I would raise is that of so-called Christian-Jewish relations, in the historical dimension of this issue; or the post-Emancipation concept of a 'Judaeo-Christian' tradition. Most Christians are more familiar with the issues here, than with the comparable ones further East, such as those that might come under a rubric of Christian-Muslim relations. Much, of course, can be said on the Jewish-Christian matter; I wish to draw attention here to only one point, in itself by no means novel. The movement, in world religious history, that begins in Palestine in Old Testament times and moves into modern Western religious life, may be interpreted (so far as over-all schematic pattern is concerned) in any one of three major ways. A choice among these three interpretations is usually made on grounds of religious *a priori* more than of historical analysis. The options are to categorize this large sweep of developments in terms of:

(i) Ancient Israel up to the first century A.D. (or: 'C.E.'), continued essentially by the history of the Jews since then; with the Christian movement as an offshoot from this;

(ii) Ancient Israel continued by the Christian Church, with the Jews from the first century A.D. onwards an offshoot or aberration (the orthodox Christian view);

(iii) Ancient Israel, followed by a bifurcation in the first century into two branches, each continuous with what went before but each, also different from that and from each other.

My suggestion presently will be that the situation is more complex; that once one has taken serious note of the Eastern Church, Semitic-speaking and especially once one has taken serious note of the Islamic fact, one may think rather of a trifurcation: East, West, and Centre.

This brings us, then, to our topic of consideration: the scope and significance of Christian-Muslim; or Muslim-Christian, relations (part of our problem is illustrated by the fact that something depends on how you state it: Christian-Muslim; or Muslim-Christian; or again, Islamic-Christian, or Christian-Islamic; and so on).

As those who chance to know my previous writings will recall, I have more than once observed that what used to be thought of as a static and fixed entity called the religion of Islam gives way on careful inquiry to being seen as the ongoing process of Islamic history, a divine-human complex in motion; and that even that, on fuller understanding, is recognized as not self-contained but as the Islamic strand in the religious history of human-kind. Muslims, in their own way, have long known this last fact. The same, of course, is true in the Christian case. As we have just remarked, it is no longer tenable to interpret the Church as something whose form, whose idea, whose ideas, whose Sacraments, whose existence were bequeathed to it by Christ, were sent down from Heaven. It emerged, rather, as a movement—an enormous movement of the human spirit. It was constructed. Into it have gone components from Greece, from Rome, from Palestine, from the person of Jesus, from that of Saint Paul, from paleolithic times (an example of this last is the practice of burial), from Zarathushtrian, from mediaeval Europe, and so on. So far as originality is concerned, on the other hand: there has been originality every morning.

Furthermore, every morning, into both the Islamic and the Christian movements, has gone some measure of transcendence; of grace; a divine component suffusing the human; or sustaining the human, or challenging it, or at least mingling with it. Both these movements, the Christian and the Islamic, have been *movements:* dynamic, ever-changing, reacting with new days, new centuries, new geographic and social and economic and philosophic and human contexts. That is: each of them has participated, every moment, in a larger context far transcending itself. (This context has been divine at one end, mundane, historical, social, at the other.)

The point to which I am working up, via these platitudes, is that each of these two movements has, for fourteen centuries now, participated in a larger context constituted in significant part by the other. For our present purposes, my thesis is that both Christian history and Islamic history are to be understood in significant part as each a sub-sector of a history of human religiousness that is in principle, of course, world-wide and history-long, but for our present purposes must be seen as at least a context of development that we may call Islamo-Christian history.

The Crusades have long been seen as an event in the history of the West, of Christendom. More recently, in striking ways, they have begun to be studied as an episode in Islamic history. No one, however, I will suggest, can in our day be thought to have an adequate grasp of the Crusades, especially as a happening in specifically religious history, unless he has apprehended them—and the Spanish Inquisition, their eventuating culmination—as a crisis emerging in the joint history of the Islamo-Christian complex.

To take another example, less painful. Western historians of thought used to be conscious of Christian scholasticism. They then moved on to a recognition of the 'influence' on that, of Arabic scholasticism; both Muslim and Jewish. (The word 'influence' here is in quotation marks, for I use the term somewhat disparagingly. 'Influence' is a concept derived from astrology, not from either natural science or the study of human history.) A third step is taken, a truer understanding attained, when one moves on from these first and second approximations to a truer historical apprehension. In this, one sees Islamic thought and Jewish and Christian, more or less in that order so far as beginnings go, participating historically in a Mediterranean movement of thought called scholasticism.

Another example is Scripture. Christians have had a Bible; Muslims a Qur'an. In this case the chronological order is reversed from the scholastic case; those who atomize would say that the 'influence' in this case was the other way 'round. A better interpretation, I am suggesting, is that, when seen on a world scale, Jews, Christians, and Muslims may all be understood, and understood more tellingly, as participating historically in the religious phenomenon of Scripturalism—initiating their participation in the Scripture movement at somewhat different stages in its dynamic development, with interesting and important differential results; but the phenomenon of Scripture in no one of the cases can be so fully and accurately understood as when apprehended in all. The concept and form 'written revelation' are historical.

Another example, into which I shall not go here (I have been writing a chapter on it in a book on which I am currently working) is the case of certain motifs in stories of self-denying piety depicting a person's turning his back on the material world to find salvation in a strongly ascetic spirituality. It is possible to demonstrate specific borrowings of popular tales which circulated in only superficially different forms in the various communities. Common throughout, and not only in these tales, is a certain fundamental ascetic orientation with a dualist world-view in which piety consisted in turning away from the mundane in renunciation towards a quite other world of spiritual reality and salvation. This mood of piety, emerging rather late in the history of civilization, was for many centuries remarkably widespread across the Eurasian land mass, and during those centuries Chinese, Indians, Near Easterners, and Europeans largely participated in it, in Buddhist, Hindu, Islamic, Jewish, and Christian ways. This orientation to the world gave way in due course to once again a more monistic, 'this worldly' orientation. Western Europe made this second transition somewhat earlier than did Eastern Europe, though both were Christian; and China earlier than India. Yet eventually all groups have indeed made it. A much more this-worldly chapter in religious history has begun, and we are now in the midst of it, both Muslims and Christians. The history of both our communities participants in that new phase.

Finally, let me touch on a matter near the core of each so-called religion: the idea of God. This idea has been more dominant, more central, in the Islamic case than in the Christian. Yet even the most Christophile or most Christocentric could hardly deny that the idea of God has been decisive for the Church. I should not wish to make the naive mistake of confusing God with the idea of God. Nonetheless it would be difficult to deny that the idea of God has played a central role both in Islamic and in Christian history; and by this I mean in the spiritual life, the moral action, the community practice, and every other facet of both Muslim and Christian being. The theologian might wish to recognize the justice of this observation by saying that God has mediated Himself to Muslims and Christians through, *inter alia*, their idea of God. I myself will say this in a forthcoming work. Here I wish only to press this point: that the Christian idea of God, to take that instance, in its course over the centuries has been a part of the world history of the idea of God on earth, the historian can now see; Christians receiving from, contributing to, and participating in that total history.

A serious, sensitive study of the idea of God in human history has not yet been written; someday this will be a mighty work. Both Muslim and Western thinkers have tended to take the idea for granted. I say this despite the library of volumes discussing it as a problem. Even our Western irreligious have tended to suppose that the idea of God is 'of course' something that religious people will affect—whereas in the light of a global perspective we now know that this is by no means obvious. The idea of God is one particular religious form. It is one that has had in certain areas and over certain centuries enormous import, and is prodigiously and exquisitely interesting. In any case, it is something Muslims and Christians have shared in common; and the history of neither can be fully or adequately understood in isolation.

In fact, a time is perhaps coming when both Islamic and Christian history will be seen as sub-aspects of what is by all odds one of the world's greatest movements of the human spirit: the theist. Indeed, I hardly see how either a theist or an atheist could disagree with such a thesis.

There is neither space, nor probably need, to develop this argument further. Clearly it could be elaborated in many directions. Conspicuous differences between Christian and Muslim on almost any point could be partly matched by in some fashion comparable differences within the Christian, and within the Muslim, communities. It is turning out to be the case that the comparative history of religion is a requisite perspective for seeing differences between centuries almost as much as between traditions. Let us move, however, to another level.

For some might respond: This is all very well; yet surely you do not dispute the fact that after all, Christians have not been Muslims, and Muslims have not been Christians. Now oddly enough, I do dispute this so-called fact; or rather, I suggest that the historian has a good deal less evidence for this view than the theologian has had conviction. And indeed, I will even suggest that the *modern* theologian maintains the traditional dichotomy more from momentum than from considered theoretical analysis. The *history* of the two movements may indeed be discerned in terms of a transcending historical complex in which both have participated, each in its own fashion. Nonetheless, the historian of *religion* should not, these objectors might hold, stress this historical level so much, to the neglect of the theological, where the dichotomy has surely been acute. My case will end, accordingly, with the contention that theology itself is moving to a point where the convergence is discernible, and may well become inescapable. It hardly behooves a Christian to discriminate too sharply between the historical and the theological level—if it indeed be in history that God acts.

Of course, the theological argument even minimally is. more elaborate, subtle, comprehensive than is appropriate or possible here. Two or three volumes, rather, are in order; or two or three generations of sustained reflection, including collaborative reflections between the groups. The historical argument too would of course be massive, if pursued at any length; but in that case I have felt that mere suggestive indications might serve, whereas theology is not so open to mere titillation.

Reserving more serious wrestling for other more voluminous occasions, however, let us here call on a few quips from, as it were, the outside to suggest that theologians as well as historians may or must find themselves engaged in new vistas. The quips constitute no argument. They are proffered as suggesting, rather, one or two directions along which an argument might conceivably go; or along which, at least, traditional reasons for not going may perhaps today be challenged.

For clarification, it is perhaps requisite to insist that I myself am not saying, nor even suggesting, that Christian theologians should adopt positions like those adumbrated in these various 'quips.' Some of the positions do not, moreover, represent my own theological views (as the wording, in certain cases, I trust makes clear). What I am saying is that in our day an alert theology ought to be able to give a reasoned judgement on issues such as these considerations raise. Linguistic analysts are asking of theologians much less trenchant questions.

That Christians have not been Muslims, Muslims not Christians, is less clear than one might suppose.

The figure of Christ is not missing in Islam. To be sure, it is presented and treated differently there from in the Christian Church. Yet the presentation and treatment of that figure have differed within Western Christian circles, too; from sect to sect and from century to century. We return here to my trifurcation theme: the branching out, into differentiated substreams, of the movement continuous with what went before in Palestine, and reacting in large part to the person of Jesus—East, West, and Centre. The 'Centre' movement from Palestine continued as the Jews. The other two emerged as the Christian movement. There was a period during which for a time this was in turn divided historically into three areas, roughly comparable in numbers and momentum, and geographically: (from left to right) Latin-speaking, Greek-speaking, and Semitic-speaking. The former two I lump together as having given us the present Church. The Eastern movement used to appear in one chapter in Church History textbooks under the heading 'The Oriental Heresies,' a way of dismissing them. Yet of course each of the diverse developments regarded the others as heretical. Historically (and even nowadays theologically?) there is not much point in saying simply that the East was wrong, the West right. Each of the movements developed: dynamically, creatively, constructively. And each in its own way. The West constructed its metaphysical Christologies, which have proven vastly productive; the Semitic world never quite understood these (and the basically Greek categories in which they were articulated), and presently most of the religious movement memorializing Christ but thinking in Semitic languages adopted another metaphysical framework for its religious life which we call Islam. At this point, the Western Church said, they ceased to be Christian. Those who joined the new interpretation and formulation of ultimate truth held, however, that they now understood and honoured Jesus Christ better. Western Christians have never really paused to consider that view.

One might imagine, perhaps a bold spirit posing some such question as this: Is it conceivable (theoretically conceivable) that if Jesus came back to earth to-day, he might perhaps say, 'The Muslims have understood me better than have Christians'?

I leave the reader to ponder that. Worth pondering is, at least, how one would go about answering it. Until a century ago, Western Christians assumed that the Christological formulations of the Western Church were right. We now know that they were historical. (They were attempts to formulate in words—words expressing concepts then available to them or new ones that they could excogitate—what they saw and felt and interiorly knew.) Let me leave my above question aside and go on to ask rather a second and third question, as follows:

What could an objective, secular, historian say on the first question?

Indeed, what can an historian of religion say on it?

Let us consider a possible fourth question. If a choice between 'yes' and 'no' answers about Christians' and Muslims' interpretation of Christ can be made only on priorly articulated positions of faith, on particularist options, does this mean that for a modern man the questions, and especially the positions propounded, and particularly the choice between them, are inadequately conceived? As I argued in my *Questions of Religious Truth* on a comparable question ('Is the Qur'an the word of God?'), a strong case can be made that they probably are: the positions are inadequately formulated, and the choice is inadequately conceptualized. In particular, the either/or polarity is undue.

Let us try to answer our question for the historian of religion. And might one speculate whether this would be the answer of a modern sophisticated theologian as well? One possible religionsgeschichtliche answer could be imagined perhaps to be: The human person Jesus made an enormous impact on the imagination and spirit of many of those about him; around His memory, inspiration, example, teaching, impact, crystallized a mighty and continuing movement. In the Western Church, He became a symbol: of eternity, of the world, of oneself; of the relation of humankind to ultimacy (of God and man, and of God in man, and of man in God). And it is not even that He became such a symbol, as a full person, for that was not too well-known; rather, a few stories about Him, legends, snatches of data—and a living impetus transmitted from generation to generation. At work, the historian of religion would maybe say, was also the continuing openness of men and women to transcendence.

In the Eastern world, the story was in some ways similar, in some ways different. There, too, his memory was cherished, his teaching honoured, his example idealized. A different religious and metaphysical construct was

10

An Historian's View of Christians and Muslims

framed, however. Those affected formulated their vision, their experience, their awareness, in diverging ways. Into their articulations went fewer components from Greece and Rome, as one might expect; more from the Palestinian or Semitic heritage. The metaphysical and the humanist elements were less; the idea of God, and of moral imperatives, were emphasized more. After a few centuries a conceptual framework from Arabia, supplied by an Arab preacher named Muhammad, was adopted. Within that new framework (not fully new; not so new as some have supposed) the populace—hundreds of millions of them—claimed and still claim to be following Jesus, but following Him in devotion to God. Now it is true that by this move community between East and West was broken. (It was already precarious.) The Thirty Years War in northern Europe, and current events in our own day in northern Ireland, show that Catholics and Protestants, for instance—each of whom claim to be followers of Christ—do not necessarily constitute a community, either; even though the historians call them both Christians. The recognition of a community of faith beyond differences of doctrinal formulation and other symbol sharing has yet to be achieved.

One possible thesis, then, that a certain type of history-of-religion observation might perhaps proffer, is the following. The subsequent ramifications in world history of the message of Zarathushtra and the religious orientations of ancient Iran are to be traced outside as well as within the tradition that is explicitly called Zoroastrian or Parsi. Who is to say that the movement stemming from Jesus (and before) is not to be traced as much outside the explicitly Christian Church as within?

The other way 'round, also. Western historians tend to hold that Islam as a religion began in the seventh century A.D. in Arabia. Muslims affirm that Islam started on the day of creation, if not before; that Abraham was a Muslim, Jesus was a Muslim. Not to understand (and even: not to accept?) these affirmations is not to understand Islam.

And in some sense, not to understand them is not to understand either Abraham or Jesus.

At the very least, not to understand and to accept them is not to understand Arabic. (And some historians would say: to suppose that Islam began in the seventh century is not to understand the fifth and the sixth centuries, in the Near East.)

Traditional Muslim theologians perhaps were inclined, like traditional Christian ones, to exclude outsiders; but a modern liberal Islamic thinker would doubtless agree, as the Sufis have classically done, that Christians, at their best, have been *muslims* in the true meaning of the term, devoting themselves to God in faith.

It would seem to me perhaps rewarding if those of us who are concerned—whether historically or theologically or in any other serious fashion—with these matters (or indeed with religious interrelations generally) would think out what our position would be, confronted with a thesis such as the following. For such a thesis could, not implausibly, be championed.

"Christianity and Islam"

Christians throughout their history have been *muslim* (in the literal meaning of that term; they have consecrated themselves to God's will and truth) as best they have been able to discern how to be so; in the highest sense to which in the best light of their intellect and conscience they could rise. Muslims throughout theirs have been *Christian* (in the literal meaning of that; they have been followers and reverers of Christ) as best they have been able to discern how to be so; in the highest sense to which in the best light of *their* intellect and conscience they could rise. And if it be retorted that Muslims have not been Christian in the *true* sense of that word, or that Christians have not been *muslim* in the true sense of that, then a possible riposte might in turn be that also relatively few Christians have been Christian in the true sense, or Muslim muslim.

Less pointedly, the argument might be developed in terms of accepted goals, thus; and is in this form perhaps worth pondering. In the modern world many are not so sure, any longer, that the true meaning of following Christ actually or optimally or transcendently is explicitly known, nor the true meaning of committing oneself to God's will, yet both meanings are well worth our striving to find out; both are well worth our remaining or becoming involved in the process of loyally pursuing. In such process we must expect in part to differ, both from other members of our own group and from members of other groups. Yet we may and should respect their striving, their discerning, their process; and expect them to respect ours. This applies both to individuals and to groups. In the modern world, we are jointly involved in the quest for truth and righteousness; and in our groping response to all divine initiatives to illumine these.

This much, at least, in conclusion, is perhaps manifest: that a modern historiography, and even a modern theology, if either is to be at all sophisticated, must approach the question of Muslim-Christian relations in terms of a single complex of which the two parts are different, but not discrete; they are to be understood as elements of a dynamic whole.

The history of what have been called Muslim-Christian relations has never been written, nor so far even conceived, except by those who consciously or unconsciously have thought of themselves as outside one or other of these groups, or outside both of them; and this thinking has coloured their perception of what has gone on. A different—and I would submit, a truer—perception and formulation of that history will be the work of someone who sees him- or herself as within the total complex, and can present it therefore so. For every participant in that history has in fact been within the total complex; and his or her history has been what it has been in substantial part because of this transcending fact.

A history of Catholic-Protestant relations can be written by a thinker who is primarily a Catholic or a Protestant less adequately than by one who is first of all a Christian and who sees the interrelations of these two groups as a development with the total history of the Christian Church (or even, some might contend, by an outsider who sees them not as absolutely two but as two divergent yet inter-connected facets of that one Church, evolving in a society of which one is oneself a member?). Just so, the historiography of the Islamic-Christian encounter will be moved to a new level when we have learned to see it as the intertwining destiny of human beings whose relation to God has for now fourteen centuries taken these two classes of forms.

The religious history of the world is the history of *us*. Some of us have been Muslims, some Christians. Our common history has been what it has been, in significant part because of this fact. Yet it is a common history for all that; and cannot be properly understood otherwise.

And if that be true of the past fourteen centuries, how much more so of the coming fourteen.

"Christianity and Islam"

14

II

Islamic-Christian Dialogue:
Approaches to the Obstacles

BY JACQUES LANFRY

Introduction

Why limit to Christians and Muslims the research that justifies this article? To be more precise, why not also take into account Jewish believers? As is known, their faith is chronologically located at the source of the religious current from which issue the three great religions that recognize Abraham as Father. Let me explain.

Even if the Qur'an acknowledges as divinely inspired the Torah of Moses, the Psalms of David, and the Gospels, these books do not appear to be known directly in the Qur'an, nor are they even cited textually, as, for example,

Translated in part by Denise Pappiani and Raymond Cormier, Temple University

Revised from the author's Report presented to the Seminar on Islamic-Christian Dialogue at Tripoli, Libya, February 1-5, 1976.

Jacques Lanfry studied theology at the Seminary of St. Sulpice, Paris, and Arabic literature at both the Institut des Belles-Lettres Arabes in Tunis and the Faculté des Lettres in Algiers. He was ordained a priest as a member of the Society of the White Fathers, serving as assistant general from 1957 to 1967. He is a consultor on the Secretariat for Relations with Non-Christians in Rome. His books include Ghadames, étude linguistique et ethnographique *(Algiers, 1968), and* Ghadames, Glossaire (parler des Ayt Waziten) *(Algiers, 1973). This essay is taken from The Journal of Ecumenical Studies, 14.3, S77, pp. 484-500, and is reprinted by permission of the publisher.*

when the Gospels quote Isaiah or the Psalms; rather, they are simply named and that is all. The Qur'an retains a certain number of Judeo-Christian traditions, biblical and non-biblical, which comprise some noteworthy and shared values in the three religions. These religious traditions derive from Jewish or Christian spheres contemporary with the beginnings of Islam. Their primary source is not always the Bible. Certain episodes about the Patriarchs recorded by the Qur'an are not of direct biblical origin; one Qur'anic tradition on Jesus is found only in an apocryphal gospel (see Qur'an 3:49). Hence we can see what kind of information the Qur'an conveys to the Muslims about the Jewish and Christian faiths. Strictly speaking, no common scriptural basis exists between Muslims and Jews or between Muslims and Christians. The Qur'an is separate, apart.

Moreover, a widespread conviction among Muslims, based on this or that verse of the Qur'an (and not without underscoring its objective importance), affirms that the very text of our Bible, with its two great divisions, does not conform to the authentic text—a text that has undergone certain manipulations (*tahrif*) at the hands of Jews and Christians alike, or by Jews and Christians of false faith or no faith. Muslims view this Scripture with suspicion; except for the educated, enlightened few, Muslims do not read the Bible (not, in fact, unlike Christians, who are similarly ignorant of the Qur'an). Thus, Holy Scripture cannot serve as a common point of reference, a serious obstacle on the path of understanding. Christians and Jews of course possess the Old Testament in common, and it constitutes a privileged basis with mutual appeal—an interesting but useless fact in the Muslim dialogue as long as this deep-rooted prejudice remains.

The Qur'an retains traces of the serious difficulties raised by Arabic Jews opposed to Nascent Islam. It is very hard on the Jews. The Qur'an acknowledges Jesus as God's chosen prophet-"messenger." It manifests, at least in certain verses, confidence and consideration for Christians, such as in this verse: "Of all men thou wilt certainly find the Jews, and those who join other Gods, to be the most intense in hatred of those who believe; and thou shalt certainly find those to be nearest in affection to them who say, 'we are Christians' " (5:85). There is nothing like this regarding the Jews. But in spite of such positive attitudes toward Christians, the Qur'an opposes certain essential articles of the Christian faith. It overwhelms some Christians with reproach for their unfaithfulness to divine Revelation and, above all, for their infidelity to monotheism, as revealed by God to Abraham and to those who followed the Father of the Believers.

The history of Islamic-Jewish relations is quite different from that of Christian-Islamic relations. We should think not only of the current struggle of the Arabs against the Israeli state, but let us recall also from the past the long period of coexistence in Spain, for example, when Jewish communities were in contact with the Muslim towns of Andalusia. Between Christians and Muslims, however, there were the struggles of the Christians against the conquests by Caliphate powers on the one hand, and on the other, conquest and domination of Muslim countries by Western powers (usually considered Christian by the Muslims)—all this complex past is at the root of the deep wounds, grievances, and prejudices. They have only compounded the difficulties at the doctrinal level and the disagreements over scriptural traditions.

One is doubtless inclined to hope that the time will come when Christians, Jews and Muslims will be able to study together, objectively and in tranquillity, the obstacles to mutual understanding. But the experience of problems and delays encountered in ecumenical efforts among separated Christians invites our caution in these delicate diverse, and heterogenous areas which are only now becoming accessible. It seems much more prudent at present to define the interlocutors, with the firm hope of uniting them one day. Moving too rapidly or aimlessly risks burking or bungling the real issues.

The following text draws essentially from a report to the Seminar on Islamic-Christian Dialogue in Tripoli, Libya, in February, 1976. The Seminar's organizer, Colonel Kaddafi, extended invitations to Christians and even to the Vatican itself in order to initiate this dialogue with Muslims. He himself expressed the sincere hope of one day seeing a tripartite meeting of Jews, Christians and Muslims on the religious questions, but, in fact, Tripoli was only a two-party meeting.

The author of this report is informed on Islamic-Christian problems, but much less so on Jewish problems. This is why that subject is absent, for these remarks are limited to a communication presented at Tripoli as part of a contribution to the development of relations between Muslim and Christian believers.

Can the thirteen centuries of history which Christians and Muslims have in common serve as a lesson for today's believers? The two groups have inherited a sum of prejudices and an ensemble of behavior patterns which have left their mark on the level of conscience and in the inner recesses of the mind. A Lebanese Muslim recently said: "Christianity and Islam are two sister religions. Both are monotheistic. Rarely have two religions had such close relations down through the centuries as have Christianity and Islam. Yet these relations have been those of hostility rather than friendship. Their belief in God has separated them far more than it has united them. Why is it that hostility rather than friendship has governed these relations? What are its causes? Are they essential or accidental causes? Can we rediscover the authentic sources common to the two religions, and from them draw new understanding that will contribute to the moral regeneration of people today? Now, more than ever, Christianity and Islam must subordinate their relations to their spirit of charity and mercy rather than to any other consideration."[1]

In order to suppress the prejudices and reduce the misunderstandings which today are still the cause of so much havoc, especially where Christian or Muslim communities happen to be a small minority (in the Middle East, Sudan, the Philippines, or Ethiopia, for instance), believers—and, it would seem, Christians first of all—are invited to contemplate and to repent of past

17

faults, to weigh and evaluate actual prejudices and misunderstandings, to examine and make known the already prodigious efforts that have been made to reduce and suppress them, and to give expression to hopes and regrets in the interests of keeping one another better informed.

I. Admitting Past Errors and Injustices

"Muslim-Christian relations are as old as Islam. They have appeared in the most contradictory forms. There were hard and painful periods on both sides," admits a former Christian member of the Vatican Secretariat for relations with Non-Christians,[2] periods of Muslim conquests and of crusades, recent periods of colonization and, still more recently, those of struggles for independence. A semi-official document frankly states that "... Past events as well as those of recent years have left a deep feeling of bitterness towards the West in certain regions of the world. In the course of history there have been short but happy periods of collaboration, at Damascus, Baghdad, and Toledo. But such items on the credit side of the balance go little way towards correcting in the minds of the Muslims the firm impression that Christians have always blocked the development of their civilization. According to their reading of history, the Crusades first of all helped to bring to an end the most brilliant period of their existence. Then they complain that colonialism rendered less fruitful than had been hoped the renaissance (*nahda*) which began in the 19th century."[3]

This bitterness, the same document goes on to admit, "has suddenly flared up again in recent years in connection with their struggle for liberty. Every one of their reviews and newspapers, all their political and ... religious leaders, have stressed the link between the distant past and what is happening at the present moment, and they have all found this comparison to be one of the most effective arguments to sway the emotions of the East against the peoples of the West. Even the political and economic maneuvering of the West, carried out by men who are well-known as being without faith in any religion, is seen and explained to their own people as a continuation of the Crusades in but another way,"[4] or of colonialism. Imperialism today is very quickly accused of being Christian-inspired, even if Christians themselves deny any such collusion or confusion. And the responsibilities of traditionally Christian countries in the dramatic difficulties surrounding the Palestinian affair have only added to the misunderstandings of history.[5] If Christians today are earnestly invited to renounce the political methods of the Crusades, and of colonial and imperialist enterprises, they must also examine themselves with regard to other errors and injustices if their dialogue with Islam is to be an honest one.

In fact, beyond political and economic confrontations, a vast cultural and religious misunderstanding between Christians and Jews has developed in the course of history. Each has dramatically ignored the other and each has disregarded the proper value of the other.

In the Middle Ages, the scientific and philosophical contribution of the

18

Approaches to the Obstacles

Arabs (Muslims) was clearly paramount, a fact recognized in the West only by a well-informed elite. With a few notable exceptions (Ramon Lull and Thomas Aquinas), it was rare for Christian theologians to ponder the religious abundance of Islam. Professor Norman Daniel has recently outlined for us the essentials in the false representation of Islam by Western Christians.[6] This is what made Prof. Abd al-Rahmân Badaoui respond: "What monstrous slanders and what frightful lies have been heaped upon our Prophet and upon Islam! I myself have seen the disastrous effects, still rooted in the opinions of both simple people and the educated alike . . . All sorts of circumstances have contributed to the formation and growth of this misunderstanding: circumstances in the religious, political and even economic sectors . . . with its origins dating as far back as St. John Damascus."[7]

However, let us not accept too readily Christian ignorance and misjudgement about Islam as normally deliberate or intentional. We must not forget that for centuries the Christian Greco-Latin West was wrapped in deep ignorance of Muslim reality because of a lack of knowledge of the language and of Arabic culture. Eastern Christians, aware from birth of this very culture, have not been quite so terribly locked into their prejudices as the Christians of the West. And the Eastern churches of Antioch, Damascus, and Baghdad have been attentive to Muslim reality, so to promote, under present social and political conditions, mutual understanding.

One cannot therefore overemphasize the work of linguists and of Western orientalists who have granted Westerners an understanding of Islam and also some access, through Eastern culture, to knowledge of the truths and religious values conveyed in the Qur'an and Muslim traditions.

Christians could no doubt complain as well of having been misunderstood by their Muslim brothers and sisters, even though the exigencies of the Muslim-Christian controversy during the Middle Ages led quite a number of Muslim scholars to take a close interest in Christian dogma. The fact is that all too often the other's religion has been judged on the basis of the "practice" and everyday behavior of its followers, and not according to the ideal proposed or to the precepts revealed. Each one knows that there is a fundamental injustice here, even as it is unjust to appraise the other's religion solely on the basis of personal criteria. If, indeed, sincere efforts were made in the West at various times to comprehend the Muslim religious experience "from the inside," they enjoyed but a fleeting existence and hardly disturbed the accumulated mass of prejudices. It is of these prejudices, therefore, that the Christian of today is asked to become aware. The Second Vatican Ecumenical Council was pleased to repeat that "although in the course of the centuries many quarrels and hostilities have arisen between Christians and Muslims, this most sacred Synod urges all to forget the past and to strive sincerely for mutual understanding."[8] To forget the past does not mean that one ought to ignore the present consequences of it—on the contrary; pardon for past errors cannot be exchanged between Christians and Muslims unless they are of a firm mind to "convert" their mentalities and attitudes. As Professor Abd

"Christianity and Islam"

al-Rahmân Badaoui has said: "We must do our best to see to it that every false concept and all the lies attributed to the one or the other religion disappear. By this joint effort at profound and sincere understanding, we could dispel all misunderstanding growing out of religious differences."[9]

There is an issue that disturbs the Muslims more than any other in their approach to Christians: it is the silence and reserve of Christians regarding Mohammed. He is, for Muslims, of course, the last and the greatest of the Prophets. Our reticence on this subject surprises and scandalizes them. They do not understand why we refuse to grant Mohammed the respect they themselves grant to the person of Jesus.

The question is difficult and deserves to be treated by competent and discerning experts who know the exigencies of both the Christian and the Muslim faiths—experts who know as well the dimensions of heartfelt respect (and not just out of courtesy or politeness) that we owe to each other. The fact is that for many years among us Christians there has been a tradition or an ingrained tendency to disparage and judge severely Islam's Prophet. We Christians ought to become fully aware of what we have said and written in the past (and even recently) about Mohammed. There has been inexcusable subjectivity in our harsh judgments, not to mention the written errors regarding Mohammed, the respected Prophet of Islam. As we are well-informed about these unfortunate attitudes, let us express at the opening of a dialogue with Muslims our sincere and deep regret for these erroneous judgments and abusive expressions, such fruitless and inappropriate utterances for a Christian. This small step is a prerequisite to any endeavor toward friendly and confident relations with the Muslim believer.

II. Weighing the Importance of the Prejudices to be Combatted

In an interview given to the Lebanese daily, L'Orient, Father Joseph Cuoq said: "The past was the past. Let us file it away in the archives and together, now, write a new history in which brotherhood will replace opposition, and mutual love, indifference. Come and see: we have rebuilt our house."[10]

Though, it must be added, the great mass of Christians have yet to learn from those responsible what is this renovated outlook with regard to the Muslims which the Second Vatican Council bids them develop in the spirit of the Gospel. Owing to historical analyses and to the efforts of conversion realized in recent years, the Christian authorities are quite aware for the future of the various prejudices to be combatted. Thus the Guidelines of the Secretariat for Non-Christians acknowledges that "we have to make a thorough re-evaluation of our way of looking at things. We are referring in particular to certain 'ready-made' judgments often preferred to the detriment of Islam. A fundamental point would seem to be to avoid harboring in our innermost hearts hasty or rash judgments which would appear ludicrous to any sincere Muslim." It would not be a waste of time, therefore, to list some of these "ready-made" ideas on Islam "so that we may have the matter straight in our own minds before engaging in dialogue."[11]

20

Approaches to the Obstacles

The same directory applies itself to a rapid enumeration of those prejudices which, on the level of language, behavior, and written judgments, are constant in the way they present themselves. Its interest in doing this is not merely to denounce them, but to provide immediate proof that they do not correspond in reality and truth to authentic Islam, even thoug they have been encouraged at times by certain failings or decadent aspects which Muslims are the first to denounce in their own history. It is a fact that many Christians with little education too often imagine Islam to be the religion of fatalism, legalism, and fear, of laxism, fanaticism, and opposition to progress. These are false accusations which continue to be directed toward Islam by numerous Christians.

But people of knowledge and experience know very well that "if Muslims believe in the Divine Decree and accept without questioning the inscrutable Will of God," developing in its regard perfect obedience and admirable patience, the individual is aware too of the need to make a personal effort of reflection (*ijtihâd*) since one also creates or invents one's own acts and is denied all passive resignation and fruitless abandonment by the present Reformists. Likewise, if Muslims love the Law, the perfect expression of the will of God, they know that "actions are only worth the intentions behind them," and that "piety" is also reverential fear and confident expectation before the mystery of divine mercy. One cannot therefore accuse them of legalism, just as it would be unjust to assert that Islam is the religion of fear. "There is no question of a 'religion of fear'; it is a matter of obeying God because one trusts in his Mercy and one loves his Commandments." Furthermore, "in 1965 one of the principles daily papers of Cairo published an article by the *shaykh* of al-Azhar, entitled *al-Islâm, dîn almahabba* (Islam, religion of love). It was mainly a question of the love of one's neighbor, but based on faith in God."[12]

To correct more decidedly the "false notions" prevailing with regard to laxism in Islam, the same directory stresses that "there is a moral code in Islam based on the Qur'anic *akhlâq* (customs) and it is very strict ... It would be quite wrong to say that there is no family morality in Islam. It does exist and it has many fine points... [And] an act of disobedience-... deserves punishment..." It goes on to explain that it is Muslim zeal for the diffusion of their religion and the impatient manifestations of that zeal which may have led many to see there a fanaticism too easily sustained by fairy tales and ridiculous formulas. As for opposition to progress, this is a social defect which some Christian societies have also suffered; it is to confuse particular historic situations with the religious message which attempts to give them life and meaning. "It is really very difficult to see anything in Islam itself that is opposed to the findings of modern science-... [though] it is quite true that there are communities in certain parts of the Islamic world whose social structures, dating from the Middle Ages, give the impression of being completely static ... The Christian must be on the alert to discover the sincere efforts at renewal being made in contemporary Islamic thought."[13]

21

Other prejudices are still expressed or implied in certain socio-political attitudes. Too often, Christians have the idea, rightly or wrongly, that the distinction between religion and the State does not exist in Islamic countries. Basing themselves on particular situations or dramatic events in which religious factors alone are taken into consideration, they conclude that there is no room in Islamic society for anyone who is not a Muslim, just as it is impossible to guarantee freedom of religious choice or to maintain there the free exercise of their religious worship. Certain competitive methods of presenting the religious challenge to non-believers, in Asia and Africa, sometimes encourage such prejudices, as does the rejection by some predominantly Muslim countries of a certain cultural or religious pluralism. The Secretariat for Non-Christians gives particular attention then to this question, showing that Islam also recognizes a distinction between religion and the State, though the two sides may approach it from different angles,[14] and that many modern States now have a different understanding of it.

There is yet another domain in which incomprehension is almost total, though it involves the highest forms of charity and of mutual aid. Christians and Muslims throughout the world are far from respecting one another when they dedicate themselves to the aid of disinherited populations; work to educate new generations in the schools, colleges, and universities; or serve the sick and dying in hospitals and dispensaries. Very quickly, the most violent accusations of treacherous proselytism are exchanged and amplified instead of concentrating on a healthy religious "competition" in the realm of respect of persons and societies. The duty of the apostolate as conceived by one or the other religion is often expressed by strife and the expending of energy in which the glory of God is no longer assured.[15]

III. Efforts Made by the Christians

What is important for the subject here treated is not the more or less exhaustive enumeration of the prejudices and misunderstandings that still exist, but rather the presentation of the efforts made by both sides to suppress and diminish them. In what concerns Christians, they can here affirm that their efforts in the last quarter century have been sincere as well as immense and varied. It is not possible to give a full account of what has been done, though the highlights will be recalled, since such a survey necessarily encompasses the areas of thought and action, at the level of both persons and societies, in secular as well as religious domains. And it should be stressed here that if the texts of the Second Vatican Council represent the happy outcome of the courageous research of a few brave pioneers, since 1962-1965 they constitute for Christians the essential charter for renewal of relations with Muslims.[16]

Encouraged by the Council, the various local churches inaugurated a new mode of behavior; for this they attempted to secure the collaboration of some special "secretaries." At the Vatican level, Paul VI established, on Pentecost of 1964, the Secretariat for Non-Christians, which had as successive president and animators Cardinals Marella and Pignedoli. On March 1, 1965, an Undersecretriat for Islam was added to it, with the essential task of promoting a Muslim-Christian dialogue in all its dimensions, directly, while working at the same time to bring about a change in the mentalities of the Christian populations. A diligent reading of the *Bulletin* of the Secretariat[17] gives one an idea of its undertakings and initiatives, just as the introduction to its *Guidelines* provides some notion of the spirit of its interventions. "The aim of such dialogue is not to 'convert' the other party, nor to make them doubt their own faith. It should quite simply stimulate those taking part not to remain inert in the positions they have adopted, but to help all concerned to find a way to become better people in themselves and to improve their relations with one another, so as to make the world as a whole a better place in which to live."[18]

Numerous have been the Christian theologians, historians, exegetes, and legal scholars who have tried in the last half century to update the knowledge of the Christian world with regard to Muslim religious experience. There has been no lack of books and reviews on the subject, in which such men as Massignon, Montgomery Watt, Asin y Palacios, Gardet, Anawati, Jomier, Hayek, Moubarac, and many others have placed their learning and skill at the service of better dialogue. Is it not first necessary, after all, to provide Christians with a scientifically exact and religiously sympathetic acquaintance with Islam and Muslims? Several Catholic theological faculties, especially in Rome at the present, include instruction at university level on "the religious reality" throughout the world, with a more or less important place given to Islam. The professors strive to present the Islamic religion to Christians in a way recognizable to Muslims by having recourse to the Qur'an and to the classical works of the Muslims themselves.[19]

If scientific publications have multiplied in number, studies more specifically consecrated to Muslim-Christian dialogue have also appeared on the scene to attack head-on the prejudices mentioned earlier and to propose new ways of acting. Thus *The Guidelines for a Dialogue between Christians and Muslims* has gone into successive editions in many languages.[20] It is a small booklet in which the authors do not try "to fix definite formulae for such a dialogue, but rather to define the spirit in which it should take place. We should be animated," the authors go on to say, "by a deep respect and a disinterested love for those who are taking part in this dialogue with us. This does not mean that we must agree with our partners all along the line, but what it does exclude is merely expressing disapproval or indulging in polemics" (p. 9).

The diffusion of documents such as this has made possible an increase in the number of new initiatives to remedy former attitudes; for instance, the revision of certain catechetical manuals and textbooks for young Christians in which the faith of their Muslim friends is presented with respect and understanding;[21] regional meetings between those in charge of local churches—Catholics and Protestants—to put into practice the "new spirit," share experiences of dialogue, and resolve problems and conflicts in which the religious factor appears basic; where local situations permit, Muslim-Christian conferences or seminars,[22] temporary loan or permanent transfer of places of worship from one community to the other,[23] participation in the formal opening of new mosques and churches (whether in the Middle East or in Africa);[24] exchange of messages on the occasion of special celebrations, in particular at the end of the month of Ramadan;[25] and reciprocal visits of delegations from Cairo or Riyad and the Vatican for the purpose of improving mutual understanding.

It was the desire of Pope Paul VI that there be in Rome itself an institute staffed by specialists in Islamics where the Arab language could be studied and scientific research could be carried out into Islam and the culture arising from it. This investigation is pursued with the regular collaboration of Muslim scholars, and on the basis of texts and books which Muslim religious tradition has developed from early centuries down to our own times.

Meanwhile, a renewed Christian theology of non-Christian religions, already given expression in the texts of the Council, enabled each of them, and Islam in particular, to be more clearly situated in the history of salvation. The "religious value of the Muslim faith" no longer needs to be proved; it "bears ... on great religious truths—strict monotheism, God's Word spoken to men by the prophets, the origin and end of the world, the resurrection and the Judgment..." Even though *"on the level of doctrine,* the two faiths [Christian and Muslim] are formally different, despite many common elements, ... *on the level of religious attitudes* determined by the motive of faith, the essential characteristics of the Muslim faith give it a high religious value in itself and can even open it up to the economy of salvation which God has willed" because it is a "theocentric, personal, supernatural faith."[26] One may better understand, then, the declaration of the Second Vatican Council in its Dogmatic Constitution on the Church: "The plan of salvation also includes those who acknowledge the Creator. In the first place among these there are the Muslims, who, professing to hold the faith of Abraham, along with us adore the one and merciful God, who on the last day will judge mankind."[27]

Always in the same spirit of clarification sought by Pope John XXIII, the Second Vatican Council wished to affirm at the same time the requisites of religious freedom and to condemn all forms of religious proselytism. And we know that very strict instructions on this matter were conveyed everywhere. Thus, with regard to the misssionary activity of the Catholic Church it is stated that "Christian charity truly extends to all, without distinction of race, social condition, or religion. It looks for neither gain nor gratitude. For as God has loved us with a spontaneous love, so also the faithful should in their charity care for the human person himself ... [by] taking part in the strivings of those peoples who are waging war on famine, ignorance, and disease, and thereby struggling to better their way of life and to secure peace in the world."[28] And as the Vatican Council "declares that the human person has a right to religious freedom,'' it also asserts that "religious bodies have the right not to be hindered in their public teaching and witness to their faith, whether by the spoken or by the written word. However, in spreading religious faith and in introducing religious practices, everyone ought *at all times* to refrain from any manner of action which might seem to carry a hint of coercion or of a kind of persuasion that would be dishonorable or unworthy, especially when dealing with poor or uneducated people.''[29] Absolute condemnation of all proselytism and a reminder of the duty of the apostolate, that is "to present one's faith,'' such are the two pillars of an exacting "religious freedom."

It is clearer than ever before, to the whole world, that Christianity should not be confused solely with the fate of the traditionally Christian countries of the West. In every corner of the world, Christians consider themselves full-fledged citizens of the city in which they live and of the country they love, without any discrimination, adopting as their own the words of Gamal 'abd an-Nâsir (then President of the Arab Republic of Egypt), spoken at the laying of the cornerstone for the new Coptic-Orthodox cathedral in Cairo: "The equality of opportunities is one of the first principles proclaimed by revealed religions, because by brotherhood, and equality between citizens and their opportunities, we can build the type of healthy community that religions aim at... Over the centuries, Christians and Muslims have always been brothers... God has never called us to fanaticism but to love... [so] no distinction is made between citizens [though] we may encounter difficulties... We must invite the fanatics to wisdom, whether they be Muslims or Christians... This is a problem that concerns the whole nation.''[30]

IV. Hopes and Regrets

Let me confide to the reader certain mute sufferings. Both sides want so much to be recognized for what they are and above all for what they wish to become in the fullness of their faith. Christians experience deep suffering whenever their friends cast doubt on their belief in the One God. On this point, did not Professor Mahmûd Abû Rayah himself have to fight his co-religionists who regard Christians as unbelievers, having no God, and "Associationists" — in brief, creatures automatically condemned to the fires of hell?[31] Christians run the risk at times of being deeply offended by this doubt hurled at their monotheistic belief, a monotheism which is just as unbending as that of their Muslim brothers and sisters. The Christian mysteries do not run counter to the unity and uniqueness of the divine *nature*. This will have to be demonstrated to them continually in the manner of Cardinal Koenig when he presented his theological conference on March 31, 1965, at the University of al-Azhar on the subject of Christian monotheism and the Christian struggle against every form of atheism, ancient and modern.

We are just as sensitive, if not more so, to the constant refutation of our Sacred Scriptures. The wish is often expressed that we Christians might produce an "authentic Gospel" (*injil sahih*), which, we are perfectly well aware, signifies that the Gospel we are presently using is unauthentic (*ghayr*

"Christianity and Islam"

saḥīḥ). An assertion of this sort does not so much offend our intelligence, which is inclined to be humble before historical science and the requirements of textual criticism (which is highly developed and carefully defined); rather, it is in our hearts as believers that such a repetition of unsubstantiated legends, injurious to our faith, leaves its wound.

Furthermore, Christians too often hear talk of a Holy Alliance against the growing forces of materialism or of communism, and they fear then—are they right or wrong in this?—that Muslim-Christian collaboration has only negative aims. Cardinal Duval of Algiers has said that "one must not seek in this dialogue a closing of the ranks aimed at uniting Christians and Muslims against a common enemy. The basis of dialogue between Christians and Muslims is the action of God in the lives of both. It is not for me to say whether Muslims can profit from the example of Christians; but many Christians—and this involves a requirement of their faith—are aware of having received help from sincere Muslims to affirm, in all areas of their life, the transcendence of God, by prayer, the sense of his presence, and the thought of his judgments, and a human conception of the duties of almsgiving and of hospitality."[33] A dialogue of action, composed of a convergence of interests or values, would not satisfy the Christian who expects a fraternal sharing of religious experiences in which each may speak of God to others. It is faith in God that must reunite us and urge us to serve our brothers and sisters. It is because we believe in the living God, who is just, who gives love freely and is merciful, that our "common commitment" to the service of humankind has as its aim to promote and defend life, justice, freedom, and mutual love.

For this reason, Christians would like to be better understood in their current efforts. Let us make a distinction between their efforts and witness, and the deeds of the nations—lay-States, and sometimes atheist—whose free citizens they are. Faith in God is first and foremost an intimate and personal reality. It is submission to God alone and to no one else. This is the basis of its strength to resist all the modern new idols and its weakness as well since it refuses to use the means of "human force." Today's Christians have rediscovered the significance of prophetic behavior through a conversion whose dimensions are ill-appreciated by their friends. They are often accused of collusion or political intent when what they are really trying to do is to hold to the level of a strictly religious affirmation, in pure faith and without relying on any material support. Was this not the case, in fact, with the conciliar declaration on Judaism? Hassan Saab, a Lebanese Muslim, could write: "It is regrettable that fear of zionist exploitation of the Declaration has prevented the Arabs from closely examining it in its totality. The Catholic Church, focused on its own truth, turns for the first time to look at the reflections of truth in other religions. Islam is presented as a sister religion. The Christian is exhorted to cease all discrimination, not only against Jews but against all non-Christians. In this new attitude, the Church deserves to be imitated rather than criticized."[34]

Thus, has the time not come for both sides, whenever they have a choice between various theological schools on a point of doctrine or practice, to prefer that school which more clearly favors encounter with the other party and mutual existence in peace and friendship? Though Christians and Muslims envisage differently the difficult distinction between "religion" and "state," is it so hard to imagine them opting for doctrines which protect pluralism and reject every sort of privilege hidden behind denominationalism, feudalism, and provincialism? In the modern world there are many countries whose citizens belong to different religions. Over and above simple peaceful co-existence, must not believers seek together criteria for work and culture based exclusively on the personal worth of individuals, without any privilege being attached to their confessional adherence? This would solve many conflicts and would help to avoid others in many African and Asian countries.[35]

Conclusion

It is difficult, of course, after centuries of polemical combat or in the horror of certain present-day dramas, to trust in the complete disinterestedness of the interlocutor. Christians are well aware of this difficulty, and, yet, they would like to hope that their friends will believe them more after this conference in which they have presented the sum of their efforts, endeavoring to do so in truth and humility. The mistakes of the past and of the present have been and are at once acknowledged and denounced in what remains of them today: prejudices and misunderstandings which can only be suppressed little by little through a long effort of clarification, conversion, and sensitization. The hope of Christians is their certitude that some of their Muslim brothers and sisters are bent on doing as much from their side to make themselves better known in the fullness of their faith and the totality of their tradition, including their Sacred Books. The discussion to follow should throw further light on our common road, uncover yet a thousand more obstacles along the way, and give us the courage to help one another as brothers and sisters to overcome them one by one. For their part, Christians know they must persevere by means of protracted patience, comforted by these words of Pope Paul VI: "May your work make the light of God's glory . . . shine ever more brightly in the world. And may Christians learn in their turn to know and properly esteem 'what treasures a bountiful God has distributed among the nations of the earth' (*Ad Gentes*, 11). Thus do you lend your personal collaboration to the plan of God in history, conscientiously and humbly, even though you do not yet see its fruits or success here below. We must give witness of patience, faith, and detachment . . ."[36]

"Christianity and Islam"

1) *Resumé of an article entitled "Relations between Christianity and Islam," by Hassan Saab, published in Arabic in* Travaux et Jours, *Beirut, no. 14-15 (32 pp).*

2) *In "For an Islamo-Christian Dialogue," by Joseph Cuoq, in* Bulletin *of the Secretariat for Non-Christians, English ed., no. 1 (May, 1966), pp. 23-27.*

3) Guidelines for a Dialogue between Muslims and Christians *(Rome: Edizioni Ancora, 1969), p. 83—hereafter cited as* Guidelines. *The text continues: "In point of fact the reality was a great deal more complex than one might gather from these reactions, but we have no desire here to indulge in detailed historical analyses. What we are trying to do is to understand how our partner in dialogue feels about these things." Father Robert Caspar provides a keen appreciation of this "Islamo-Christian encounter . . . begun in misunderstanding . . . carried on over the centuries with open hostility, the clash of arms, and apologetical controversies, . . . armed conflicts giving rise to a body of ideological literature aimed at providing them with a doctrinal foundation and fanning the ardor of the combatants . . . On both sides, detraction and apologetical rhetoric flourished" ("La Religion Musulmane," in* Les relations de l'Eglise avec les religions non chrétiennes *[Paris: LeCerf, 1966], pp. 201-236).*

4) Guidelines, *pp. 83-84.*

5) *Ibid., p. 84, where the document adds: " . . . Whatever judgment we express should be based on charity, justice, and honor . . . [and] at least we should show our sympathy for those who suffer most . . ." This is not the place to give a full review of the attitude of the Holy See on the one hand and of Christians on the other regarding a just solution of the Palestinian question. An objective investigation of their positions will suffice to exonerate them of all accusation.*

6) *See his two books,* Islam and the West *(Edinburgh, 1960), and* Islam, Europe and Empire *(Edinburgh, 1965).*

7) *Interview in the Cairo review,* Images, *March 13, 1965.*

8) *Declaration of the Relationship of the Church to Non-Christian Religions,* Nostra Aetate *(October 28, 1965), no. 3. English translations of Council texts are taken from Walter M. Abbott, SJ, ed.,* The Documents of Vatican II *(New York: Guild Press, 1966).*

9) *Interview, March 13, 1965 (see above, note 7).*

10) *Reprinted in* Informations Catholiques Internationales *(I.C.I.), November 15, 1965.*

11) Guidelines, *pp. 86-87.*

12) *Ibid., pp. 91, 92.*

13) *Ibid., pp. 92-100.*

14) *In this it bases itself on theoretico-historical studies, such as that of Shaykh Alî Abd ar-Râziq,* L'Islam et les bases du pouvoir *(Cairo, 1925; French translation in* Revue des Etudes Islamiques, *1933, III, pp. 353-391, and 1934, II, pp. 163-222), as much as on socio-political positions of religious leaders such as Shaykh al-Bashir al-Ibrahîm of Algeria, in his editorials in al-Basā'ir (reprinted in his book,* 'Uyun al-Basā'ir: Fasl ad-dîn ' an ad-dawla.

15) *Another misunderstanding arises constantly and unconsciously from that deep-seated conviction that the West (Europe and America) represents the "perfect model" of human culture, parliamentary democracy, economic development, and the successful balance between faith and reason. The rest*

28

Approaches to the Obstacles

of the world, and thus the other religions, are then automatically judged on the basis of such criteria, which make one form of the historical realization of Christianity (successful or not, from the point of view of faith, God only knows!) the necessary model for all modern evolution! From there it is but a short step to the exclusion of others from the benefits of culture, if not of salvation. There was a time when the principle, "Outside the church there is no salvation," was applied literally, producing in its wake a certain scorn, or at least profound indifference, toward all other forms of religious experience.

16) *The first text, very brief, is to be found in the Dogmatic Constitution on the Church,* Lumen Gentium, *no. 16. The second constitutes all of no. 3 of the Declaration on the Relationship of the Church to Non-Christian Religions,* Nostra Aetate *(cf. the second of the four conferences of this seminar: "The doctrinal bases common to the two religions, and different areas of convergence").*

17) *The* Bulletin *began to appear in May 1966, with editions in English and French, at the rate of four issues a year, with supplementary "booklets" and other publications included from time to time. Since 1974 (with issue no. 25), this has been reduced to a single bilingual edition. For a survey of the Secretariat's activities, see Michael L. Fitzgerald, "The Secretariat for Non-Christians Is Ten Years Old," in* Islamochristiana, review of the Pontifical Institute of Arabic Studies (I.P.E.A.) of Rome, no. 1 (1975), pp. 87-96.

18) Guidelines, *pp. 9-10.*

19) *Space is lacking here to provide an exhaustive bibliography in all the principal languages. We shall simply cite, as a model of its genre, Louis Gardet,* L'Islam, religion et communauté *(Paris: Desclée de Brouwer, 1970), which sets forth the "first principle" of all true dialogue: "Each one must be concerned to get to know the other as he is and* as he wishes to be" *(P. 420). This principle was the first of the main themes of the Islamo-Christian encounter at Cordoba in September, 1974 (see the report on this meeting, Maurice Borrmans, "Le Congrès islamo-chrétien de Cordoue-9-15 Septembre 1974," in the* Bulletin *of the Secretariat for Non-Christians, Rome, 1975/X-1, no. 28-29, pp. 199-205). Let is suffice to mention that for the city of Rome alone, courses in Islamology are offered by the Gregorian, Lateran, Urban, Antonian, and Regina Mundi Universities, while a more specialized training is given at the Pontifical Institute of Arabic Studies.*

20) *The* Guidelines *are in their 2nd English edition (Rome: Edizioni Ancora, 1971);* Les Orientations pour un dialogue entre chrétiens et musulmans, *3rd French edition (Rome; Ancora, 1970);* Christiani e Musulmani: Orientamenti per il dialogo fra cristiani e musulmani, 1st Italian edition *(Roma; Ancora, 1971);* Musulmanes y Cristianos: Orientaciones para un dialogo entre Cristianos y Musulmanes, 1st Spanish edition *(Madrid, 1971).*

21) *For instance by the* Catechetical Center of Paris, *and* Recherches fraternelles *in Mali.*

22) *See Michael L. Fitzgerald, "The Secretariat for Non-Christians Is Ten Years Old,"* Islamo-christiana (I.P.E.A., Roma, no. 1, 1975), pp. 87-96; *John B. Taylor, "The Involvement of the World Council of Churches in International and Regional Christian-Muslim Dialogues," pp. 103-114; Abdelmajid Charfi, "Quelques réflexion sur la encontre islamo-chrétienne de Tunis (11-17 Novembre 1974)." Also see the rubric "Dialogue in the World," a regular feature of the* Bulletin *of the Secretariat for Non-Christians.*

"Christianity and Islam"

23)   At Cologne, and later at Lille.

24)   Muslims were present at Kampala, Uganda, in 1969, when Pope Paul VI blessed the cornerstone of the Basilica of the Martyrs of Uganda. And President Gamal 'Abd an-Nasir participated in 1965 at the blessing of the cornerstone of the new Coptic-Orthodox cathedral of Cairo (Abbassiyeh). In Kampala, the Pope told the leaders of the Muslim communities: "How can we express our deep satisfaction in meeting you, and our gratitude to you for granting our lively desire to greet, in your persons, the great Muslim communities spread throughout Africa? You thus enable us to manifest here our high respect for the faith you profess, and our hope that what we hold in common may serve to unite Christians and Muslims ever more closely, in true brotherhood ... In our prayers we always remember the peoples of Africa, for the common belief in the Almighty professed by millions of them must call down upon this continent the graces of His Providence and Love, most of all, peace and unity among all its sons. We feel sure that, as representatives of Islam, you join in our prayer to the Almighty, that He grant all African believers that desire for pardon and reconciliation so often commended in the Gospel and in the Qur'an." And he added: "May the shining sun of peace and brotherly love rise over this land, bathed with the blood of generous sons of the Catholic, Christian, and Muslim communities of Uganda, to illuminate all of Africa! And may our meeting with you, respected representatives of Islam, be the symbol of, and the first step toward, that unity for which God calls us all to strive for His greater glory, for the happiness of this blessed continent!" (Bulletin of the Secretariat, English ed., no. 12 [December, 1969], 4th year/3, pp. 156-157).

25)   See "Christians and the Fast of Ramadan" (Bulletin of the Secretariat, English ed., no. 7 [March, 1968], 3rd year/1, pp. 41-44), in which are given the texts of two radio messages composed by Father Joseph Cuoq, then under-secretary of the Secretariat for Non-Christians, and read by him over Vatican Radio on the occasion of the close of the fast of Ramadan, 1967. In the first, entitled "Introducing the Fast of Ramadan to the Christians," Father Cuoq said: "The spirit of drawing close to God and of submission to His Will, expressed by the fast of Ramadan, is a genuine religious value. Christians can only rejoice to find it expressed by others ... So let us rejoice at seeing God so honored by millions of men and women, adults and adolescents, sometimes at very great sacrifice ... Therefore we invite you who are Christians and have tried to understand Islam from inside rather than outside to show your Muslim neighbors your appreciation of this religious act ..." The second message, "To the Moslem Communities: Greetings for Ramadan, 1967 (30 December 1967)," began a practice which has been continued ever since, and to which the late King Faysal once referred in the course of a speech welcoming delegations of pilgrims to Mecca (January, 1968).

26)   R. Caspar, "The Religious Value of the Moslem Faith," in Bulletin of the Secretariat, English ed., no. 13 (March, 1970), 5th year/1, pp. 25-37.

27)   Lumen Gentium, no. 16. Professor Louis Gardet gives a good resumé of the various positions of Christian theology with regard to non-Christian religions in a chapter of his book, L'Islam, religion et communauté (Chap. II, additum on "L'Islam du point de vue chrétien," pp. 407-418, especially p. 417). Father J. Moubarac delineates very well the new perspectives of this Christian theology in Book 3 of his Pentalogie islamo-chrétienne, especially

30

Approaches to the Obstacles

pp. 93-130.

28) *Decree on the Missionary Activity of the Church,* Ad Gentes, *no. 12.*

29) *Declaration on Religious Freedom,* Dignitatis Humanae, *nos. 2 and 4, which goes on to add: "Such a manner of action would have to be considered an abuse of one's own right and a violation of the right of others." In this same vein, the "Hong Kong memorandum" (1975) stated: "Of special concern for our religious communities in some situations is the matter of proselytism. We are moved to call upon all religious bodies and individuals to refrain from proselytism, which we define as the compulsive, conscious, deliberate, and tactical effort to draw people from one community of faith to another" (in John B. Taylor, "The Involvement of the World Council of Churches in International and Regional Christian-Muslim Dialogues," in* Islamochristiana, *no. 1 [1975], p. 101).*

30) *The President went on to say: "Where there are Muslim fanatics altogether too extreme, Christians must show moderation; where there are extreme Christian fanatics, let Muslims in their turn show proof of moderation. [For] the country does not know nor does it recognize any sectarianism" (discourse of July 24, 1965, in* Proche-Orient Chrétien, *tome 15 [1965], pp. 384-387).*

31) *See his book,* Dīn Allāh wāhid *(The Religion of God is One) (Cairo: 'Alam al-Kutub, 1970), 2nd ed., in which he refutes his co-religionists by means of Qur'anic texts, and proves that Christians are and remain "People of the Book."*

32) *"In Cairo we were told of the happy surprise of many listeners, professors and students of the Great Mosque when they heard the Cardinal of Vienna proclaim, without reservation, absolute faith in the One God" (Louis Gardet,* L'Islam, *p. 424). For the integral text of the Cardinal's conference, in its French version, see* Mélanges de l'I.D.E.O. *of Cairo (Dominicans), no. 8.*

33) *Interview accorded by Cardinal Léon Duval to* Révolution Africaine *(December 25, 1965), weekly of the F.L.N.*

34) *In the Lebanese daily,* L'Orient *(December 6, 1964), Mr. Saab added: "The Church comes very close to the Qur'ânic concept of the unity of the family of God, as well as the Qur'ânic idea of the unity of the people of the Book, this people comprising Jews, Christians, and Muslims who adore God, the Father of Abraham, the Father of all monotheists. Christianity and Islam cannot but agree on the Declaration and rejoice at its spirit. This agreement is hampered by their differences over zionism, and not by Judaism."*

35) *Should not the experiment of Lebanon–"a common homeland of religious communities united by the same faith in God, the same attachment to the primacy of the spiritual, and the same will to live in peace and brotherhood," as Lebanese President Hèlou said in his address to Pope Paul VI on the occasion of the latter's visit to Beirut in 1964–be carried through, by means of a process of laicization, carefully understood, and free of all religious discrimination? (For the text of the President's speech, see* La Croix, *French Catholic daily, December 4, 1964; also in* Documentation Catholique, *January 3, 1965; English text in* L'Osservatore Romano, *December 4, 1964.) It was in this same country of Lebanon, in the setting of the "Cénacle Libanais," that Christians and Muslims were able to join together (May-June 1964) in saying: "[The speakers affirm] the meeting point of the*

"Christianity and Islam"

two religions in their faith in the one God, and in their desire to unite in fostering spiritual values and common moral principles which safeguard the dignity of man, proclaim his right to the highest kind of human life, and lift up the world in a breath of charity, peace, and concord. They are convinced that Lebanon is the chosen land for such a Muslim-Christian dialogue, and that on the day it becomes more vitally aware of the content of these two messages, it will have contributed to the renewal and the safeguard of the spiritual energy of man." The manifesto continues: *"They commit themselves before God to bring about a permanent fraternal encounter which permits all to draw upon the intimate riches of the two universal religions, each of the partners acting in full conformity with the teachings of his religion, while seeking to understand what the other religion contains of lessons, exhortations, and norms aimed at bringing man closer to his fellowmen and brothers"* (see Ephémétides islamo-chrétiennes, *bulletin no. 2* [September 1, 1964-April 30, 1965], pp. 143-144).

36) Allocution delivered during an audience for members of the Secretariat for Non-Christians, September 25, 1968. See Bulletin of the Secretariat, English ed., no. 9 (December, 1968), 3rd year/3, pp. 115/116.

32

III

The Doctrinal Basis Common To Christians And Muslims And Different Areas Of Convergence In Action

BY MAURICE BORRMANS

Precis

The common spiritual heritage of Christians and Muslims includes: the ways of knowing God; belief in the existence of one God, who is Creator of heaven and earth, who loves humankind, who pardons and is merciful, and who is worthy of being praised and glorified; a belief in a God who has sent prophets and who raises the dead and fulfils human desires; belief in a life of faithful adherence to God's will, notably by concern for the neighbor.

Christians and Muslims, as common believers in the same God and common human family, face a common challenge from an unbelieving modern world. This should prompt cooperative efforts to protect life wherever threatened, and to promote freedom, peace, justice and equality in the spirit outlined in Vatican II's *Constitution on the Church in the Modern World.*

Christians and Muslims have had, fundamentally and from the very beginning, a common spiritual heritage. For they all, with one voice, say: God exists and God is one. By this they bear witness that matter, life, and spirit do not owe their origin to necessity or pure chance, but to the Creator who is spirit and life.

This lecture was written first for the Muslims who were attending the Congress of Tripoli, Libya, February, 1976, and, second, for the Christians who were present there. For the Muslims, it was meant to show the insights we already have in common concerning the Mystery of God. For the Christians, it attempted to explain how the Christian vision of the One God can try to meet the unyielding monotheism of Islam. It wan an opporunity to meditate together on what is common to both sides, and to reflect on the religious motives which impel believers of both religions to serve their fellow humans in this present time.

33

"Christianity and Islam"

I. A Common Heritage

A. The Ways of Knowing God

They know, by experience, that this world is not self-made and that humanity has not fashioned its history on its own. They recognize that the wonders and greatness of the cosmos and of history, as well as the gigantic progress made by modern science, imply, and indeed postulate, a "master builder." They affirm that the human mind is capable—and this is already a gift from God—of knowing that God exists and that God is endowed with all the attributes of perfection.

Christian and Muslim theologians have established, in ways which differ but are analogous, proofs for the existence of God, in the same way that the sacred scriptures of each of the two religions invite meditation upon the "signs" of God and the "pointers" to God in the worlds which are open to human investigation: that which has its beginning it time requires the existence of an "eternal" being. Contingent being supposes a necessary being. The harmony in the universe supposes someone who directs this harmony. Human nature itself makes people desire to discover the One who made them, who guides them and who awaits them. So it is that for Christians the First Vatican Council wished to recall once more this fundamental dignity of human intelligence, made in such a way that it can arrive at a knowledge of the Creator by means of the manifold created signs with which is has been provided.[1]

Muslims and Christians know by experience that humanity is, in fact, not able to carry out this magnificent program. Throughout history we see that it has often preferred, and still prefers today, falsehood to truth, injustice to justice, death to life. It refuses to acknowledge truth; it murders and enslaves; and it fashions for itself idols to its own likeness! That Christians should call

One will not find here an essay in comparative theology; it should have included a mention of the basic differences in doctrine which keep Muslims and Christians apart, i.e., God's revelation in Jesus Christ, the Word incarnate, and the historical expression of God's great love through the Cross and the Resurection. The present lecture thus had a very precise aim, and its limitations come from the concrete requirements of the Congress of Tripoli. It could not deal with all the possible attitudes a Christian can take, but could be only "the view-point of a Catholic concerned with unity," unity among Christians and unity among all who seek God.

Maurice Borrmans (Roman Catholic) was ordained into the priesthood in 1949. He received his Docteur ès lettres from the Sorbonne in 1971, specializing in research on the Fiqh, Hadith, and Muslim spirituality. He has taught for more than twenty years at the Pontifical Institute of Arabic Studies in Rome, and is editor of Islamochristiana, *which was founded in 1975 to give a scientific approach to Christian-Muslim dialogue. He has also published numerous articles in several French and Italian journals. This essay appeared in the* Journal of Ecumenical Studies. 14.1. w 77. pp. 32-50 *and is reprinted here by permission of the publishers.*

34

this "original sin" and Muslims see in it the action of the "soul which incites to evil" does not change the basic fact which can be stated as follows: humanity cannot alone achieve perfection. It bears a deep wound which leads it to turn in on itself and to refuse God's signs and commands. This is the sin which is seen by believers to be an act of disobedience and a betrayal, and the principal source of depravity, both social and personal.

Christians often meditate on a text of St. Paul: "For what can be known about God is perfectly plain to humans since God has made it plain. Ever since the creation of the world God's everlasting power and deity—however invisible—have been there for the mind to see in the things God has made. That is why such people are without excuse: they knew God and yet refused to honour God or to thank God; instead, they made nonsense out of logic and their empty minds were darkened . . . . They have given up divine truth for a lie and have worshipped and served creatures instead of the creator, who is blessed for ever" (Rom. 1:19-25).

Christians thought down the centuries has always affirmed that there are two sources of knowledge: creation on the one hand and revelation on the other. The First Vatican Council restated this in very clear terms: "The Catholic Church . . . holds that there are two orders of knowledge, distinct not only in origin but also in object. They are distinct in origin, because in one we know by means of natural reason; in the other, by means of divine faith. And they are distinct in object, because in addition to what natural reason can attain, we have proposed to us as objects of belief mysteries that are hidden in God and which, unless divinely revealed, can never be known."[2] This is why Christians and Muslims are at one and the same time people of reason and people of faith. They are believers and it is quite legitimate for them to think that they have a doctrinal basis in common.

B. The Heritage Common to Christians and Muslims

What are the aspects of this common doctrinal basis which make it possible for Christians and Muslims to consider themselves as sharing in one and the same religious heritage? Both are united by faith in God, in God's angels, and in eternal destiny which is to follow death and resurrection. They both have the certitude also that God has sent prophets and has communicated the divinely-revealed word in sacred books, though they may differ in regard to the identity of the former and the character of the latter. This is why they are both equally believers, and it is in the mystery of these beliefs that they find the ultimate reasons for their manner of behaving here on earth and for their commitment as human beings. Of course, there is divergence between the beliefs of Muslims and Christians on many substantial points, but there is convergence also with regard to essential realities.

Let them, in a spirit of fellowship, give consideration to the divine realities which unite them, even if the terms they use are different and the way they designate them arises from an outlook and a religious sentiment which sometimes diverge more than they converge.[3] We quote here the text which rallied the unanimous agreement of Christians during the Second Vatican Council (1962-1965), found in the *Declaration on the Relationship of the Church to Non-Christian Religions*. The members of the Council declared, in the introduction, that: "All peoples comprise a single community, and have a single origin, since God made the whole human race to dwell over the entire face of the earth. One also is their final goal: God. His providence, His manifestations of goodness, and His saving designs extend to all people against the day when the elect will be united in that Holy City ablaze with the splendour of God, where the nations will walk in His light" (par. 1).[4]

In the same way it is recognized that: "People look to the various religions for answers to those profound mysteries of the human condition which, today even as in olden times, deeply stir the human heart: What is a human being? What is the meaning and the purpose of our life? What is goodness and what is sin? What gives rise to our sorrows and to what intent? Where lies the path to true happiness? What is the truth about death, judgment, and retribution beyond the grave? What, finally, is that ultimate and unutterable mystery which engulfs our being, and whence we take our rise, and whither our journey leads us?" (par. 1). Now to these questions Islam gives replies which are very similar to those of Christianity. This makes it possible for the *Declaration* to affirm: "Upon the Muslims, too, the Church looks. with esteem. They adore one God, living and enduring, merciful and all-powerful, Maker of heaven and earth and Speaker to humanity" (par. 3).

C. God—One, Living, and Subsisting

Christians, and those who have preceded them, have always believed in God, living and subsisting. Their books, on every page, bear witness to God's oneness. The Jew loves to repeat: "Listen Israel: Yahweh our God is the one Yahweh" (Deut. 6:4), and the Christian affirms: "I believe in one God, the Father almighty, creator of heaven and earth, of all things visible and invisible," because of Jesus' reminder that the first and greatest of the commandments is: "You must love the Lord your God with all your heart, with all your soul, with all your strength, and with all your mind" (Lk. 10:27; Deut. 6:5). St. Paul also makes this explicit: "There is one Lord, one faith, one baptism, and one God who is Father of all, over all, through all and within all" (Eph. 4:5-6). So when they say, with the Psalmist, "Who else is God but Yahweh, who else is a rock save our God?" (Ps. 17:32), Christians are bound to Muslims who also proclaim that "there is no divinity except God."

Throughout the centuries each Council has recalled with insistence that there is only one God. Definitive expression to this was given in the Second Vatican Council: "The Church believes and professes that there is one true and living God, the creator and lord of heaven and earth. He is all-powerful, eternal, immeasurable, incomprehensible, and limitless in intellect and will and in every perfection. Since He is one unique spiritual substance, entirely simple and unchangeable, He must be declared really and essentially distinct from the world, perfectly happy in Himself and by His very nature, and inexpressibly exalted over all things that exist or can be conceived other than Himself."[5]

For Christians and Muslims "Yahweh is God indeed; there is no other" (Deut. 4:35); "We for our part acknowledge no other God than Him" (Judith 8:20). God is the only God: "He is God, one, God alone" (Qur'ân 112:1-2) says the Qur'ân, as also the Psalms (Ps. 17:32). Question and statement are parallel: "Who is like Yahweh our God?" (Ps. 112:5); "Like Him there is none" (Qur'ân 112:4). God is "the first and the last" (Is. 41:4), the One "who does not change" (Mal. 3:6), because God is the one who subsists for ever, the Ever-Sure, who "does not grow tired or weary" (Is. 40:28), the Eternal One (Is. 40:28) whose face abides, true being, the All-sufficient. "Yahweh lives" (Jer. 4:2; cf. Qur'ân 2:255). God lives "for ever and ever" (Ap. 1:18), the "Living God, the Undying" as the Qur'ân says (Qur'ân 25:60). Therefore God remains the sole inheritor of all things since with the Psalmist we can say: "Before the mountains were born, before the earth or the world came to birth, you were God from all eternity and forever" (Ps. 89:2).

D. God—Creator of the Heavens and the Earth

God, the Living One, is made manifest to us as the Creator who "in the beginning created the heavens and the earth" (Gen. 1:1), the "Creator of the heavens and the earth" (Qur'ân 2:117). God is the All-Creator, the fairest of creators, the Maker, the Shaper. God does what God wills without being subject to any necessity.[6] "Yahweh, my maker, my preserver" (Ps. 118:73), exclaims the Psalmist, and adds: "All creatures depend on you to feed them throughout the years . . . . You turn your face away, they suffer, you stop their breath, they die . . . . You give breath, fresh life begins, you keep renewing the face of the world" (Ps. 103:27-30). God is the Guardian, the All-benign, the Giver and the All-provider. God is not "heedless of creation" (Qur'ân 23:17) and "it is in Him that we live, and move, and exist" (Acts 17:28). Christians and Muslims are at one in saying this.

The believer will never finish admiring the works and deeds of God in creation and in history. Does not the Psalmist say: "I look up to your heavens made by your fingers, at the moon and the stars you set in place—ah, what is man that you should spare a thought for him, the son of man that you should care for him? Yet you have made him little less than a god, you have crowned him with glory and splendour, made him lord over the work of your hands, set all things under his feet . . . . Yahweh, our Lord, how great your name throughout the earth" (Ps. 8:47, 10)? It is with reason that, faced with the wonders of creation and the wonder of wonders which is humanity, the Psalmist should exclaim again: "How many wonders you have done for us; you have no equal. I want to proclaim them again and again, but they are more than I can count" (Ps. 39:6). "It is good to give thanks to Yahweh, to play in honour of your name, Most High, to proclaim your love at daybreak and your faithfulness all through the night" (Ps. 91:2-3). This is why true believers are ever ready to give thanks.

37

"Christianity and Islam"

E. God Who Loves Humankind

God is the All-knowing, the All-wise. God knows the whole of creation, as the Psalmist recognizes: "Yahweh, you examine me and know me, you know if I am standing or sitting, you read my thoughts from far away, whether I walk or lie down you are watching, you know every detail of my conduct. The word is not even on my tongue, Yahweh, before you know all about it; close behind and close in front you fence me round, shielding me with your hand" (Ps. 138:1-5). God is indeed the most Generous, the Benevolent, the one who has knowledge of everything, the All-preserver, the Lord. "He sees the whole human race; from where He sits He watches all who live on the earth, He who moulds every heart and takes note of all people do" (Ps. 32:13-15). That is why Christians, together with Muslims, call God the "All-seeing," the one who is "watchful over everything, the All-knowing, the one who keeps a watchful count over everything" (Qur'ân 4:86) and who has "numbered everything in numbers" (Qur'ân 72:28).

Humankind, therefore, must confess that its destiny is dependent on God's decree. God is the Arbiter and Judge whose justice and equity Muslims proclaim and of whom the Psalmist affirms: "He loves virtue and justice" (Ps. 32:5). Believers then have nothing to fear from their Creator. St. Paul reminds them: "We know that by turning everything to their good God co-operates with all those who love Him. . . . With God on our side who can be against us?" (Rom. 8:28-31). So the believer accepts the fact that God grasps and outspreads, for God puts in our way what can profit us and what is harmful to us, and brings forward or postpones the appointed times. The Christian is pleased to meditate on the following text: "Yahweh gives death and life, brings down to Sheol and draws up: Yahweh makes poor and rich, He humbles and also exalts. He raises the poor from the dust, He lifts the needy from the dunghill. . . . He safeguards the steps of His faithful but the wicked vanish in darkness" (1 Sam. 2:6-9). Thus the Psalmist can proclaim: "I will celebrate your love for ever, Yahweh, age after age my words shall proclaim your faithfulness" (Ps. 89:2).

F. God Who Pardons and Is Merciful

For all believers God is vengeful, but is above all witness over everything. "God of revenge, appear," says the Psalmist, "Rise; judge the world; give the proud their deserts; how much longer are the wicked to triumph? Yahweh knows exactly how people think, how their thoughts are a puff of wind" (Ps. 93:1-3, 11). God will never disappoint the creature. God suffices as guardian, as guide, as helper. Truly God gives security for God, as the Muslims say, is "the Merciful, the Compassionate," "the most merciful of all." God, as Christians and those who have preceded them have learned, is "a God of tenderness and compassion, slow to anger, rich in kindness and faithfulness; for thousands He maintains his kindness, forgives faults, transgression, sin; yet He lets nothing go unchecked" (Ex. 34:6-7).

This is why believers are not afraid to acknowledge their sin, exclaiming

38

The Common Doctrinal Basis

with the Psalmist: "From the depths I call to you, Yahweh, Lord, listen to my cry for help! If you never overlooked our sins, Yahweh, Lord, would anyone survive?" (Ps. 129:1-3). "Have mercy on me, O God, in your goodness, in your great tenderness wipe away my faults; wash me clean of my guilt, purify me from my sin.... Against none other than you have I sinned, having done what you regard as wrong.... Create a clean heart in me, put into me a new and constant spirit, do not deprive me of your holy spirit" (Ps. 50:3-6, 12-13). Muslims know that "humanity has been created fretful" (Qur'ân 70:19), "sinful, unthankful" (Qur'ân 14:34), and even "very foolish" (Qur'ân 33:72). But all believers are equally aware that they can say to God: "Turn to me and pity me" (Ps. 85:16), for God is the first to turn to people in order to pardon their sins, since God is the All-forgiving, the All-pardoning, who pardons often because God is very patient, All-clement, All-compassionate, All-loving. Does the Qur'ân not say: "Ask forgiveness of your Lord, then repent to Him; surely my Lord is all-compassionate, all-loving" (Qur'ân 11:90)? For God has claimed to be merciful (Qur'ân 6:12) and a hadîth echoes this: "My mercy precedes my anger."

G. God-Worthy To Be Praised and Glorified

Who, then, is this generous Creator and merciful Judge who is "the light of the heavens and the earth...light upon light" (Qur'ân 24:35)? As the Psalmist says: "Yahweh is king, robed in majesty, Yahweh is robed in power, He wears it like a belt.... Yahweh reigns transcendent in the heights. Your decrees will never altar: holiness will distinguish your house, Yahweh, for ever and ever" (Ps. 92:1-5). Majesty and generosity are God's, whose "will is sovereign" (Ps. 113:11). Christians and Muslims call God the Holy One, the Most High and Inaccessible, the Great and All-embracing, with whom are "the keys of the Unseen; none knows them but He" (Qur'ân 6:59), as the Qur'ân says. God is transcendent, the one who is to be praised and glorified. How could God the All-high, the All-great, powerful over everything, possibly be unworthy of these Beautiful Names? God is "the King, the All-holy, the All-peaceable, the All-faithful, the All-preserver, the All-mighty, the All-compellor, the All-sublime...the All-mighty, the All-wise" (Qur'ân 59:23-24). God it is who "gives the victory."

This can only lead humans to a better knowledge of this Being who is both near and distant and whom Christians call "the one who comes." They can easily adopt the Muslims' prayer which closes the litany of the Beautiful Names of God, asking God to be able to approach the Mystery "by every Name of yours which You have called Yourself or which You have revealed in Your book or which You have taught to one of your creatures or whose use You have reserved according to the knowledge that You have of your own Mystery." For the Messiah, Jesus, son of Mary, has said: "Eternal life is this: to know you, the only true God" (Jn. 17:3) and they believe, as Christians, that they have learned from the very Messiah some of these names which "until then had been hidden" (Col. 1:25).

39

"Christianity and Islam"

H. God Who Sends Prophets

Such is the substance of the religious heritage which Christians and Muslims have in common. Flowing from this there are many other things that can be considered common or analogous. Muslims and Christians believe that God has spoken in history "at various times in the past and in various different ways, through the prophets" (Heb. 1:1), "by revelation or from behind a veil, or by sending a messenger to reveal whatsoever He will, by his leave" (Qur'ān 42:50-51). Both Muslims and Christians call Abraham "God's friend," and Moses "God's interlocutor," and we find in their lives models of faith and obedience. The Second Vatican Council has twice recognized this fact. The first time is in its meditation on the history of salvation which "includes those who acknowledge the Creator. In the first place among these are the Muslims who, professing to hold the faith of Abraham, along with us adore the one and merciful God, who on the last day will judge humankind" (*Lumen Gentium* par. 16). Secondly there is the passage of the *Declaration on the Relationship of the Church to Non-Christian Religions* which recognizes that Muslims "strive to submit wholeheartedly even to God's inscrutable decrees, just as did Abraham, with whom the Islamic faith is pleased to associate itself" (*Nostra Aetate*, par. 3).

It is true that Christians and Muslims differ with regard to the criteria for recognizing that prophecy which is definitive. Christians consider that "the fulness of prophecy" has been realized in Jesus, but they recognize that the spirit of prophecy continues to be made manifest from generation to generation. Muslims, on the other hand, see in Muhammad "the seal of the prophets," recognizing at the same time that there is a "mystery of Jesus" of exceptional dimensions. Authentic dialogue requires that each side should respect totally the viewpoint of the other and show extreme patience, leaving it to God to purify this viewpoint, illuminate it, and perfect it. In the same way that the Christian must not ask a Muslim to recognize in the Messiah all the qualities which Christianity attributes to the Messiah, so also Muslims are invited not to require that a Christian should recognize as belonging to Muhammad all the qualities which Islam attributes to Muhammad. The same thing can be said with regard to sacred books, bearing in mind nevertheless that both Christians and Muslims recognize that the divine words entrusted to the prophets have been recorded in books which they must read, meditate upon and comment upon in order to understand their "apparent and hidden" meaning.[7]

I. God Who Raises the Dead to Life and Fulfills Human Desires

There are still more things common to all believers. All know that there are other beings, angels and demons, whose missions have been assigned to them by God and who are, as it were, witnesses of human history. All are aware especially that the world will come to an end in time just as it began in time. The face of the Creator alone will abide. All things will return to God by means of a recapitulation spoken of, with an abundance of imagery, in all the

40

sacred books. Thus the Psalmist can ask: "Tell me, Yahweh, when my end will be, how many days are allowed me, show me how frail I am. Look, you have given me an inch or two of life, my life-span is nothing to you" (Ps. 38:5-6).

The Second Vatican Council recognizes the fact that Muslims, like Christians, "await the day of judgement when God will give all their due after raising them up" (*Nostra Aetate*, par. 3). The hour will come. Its precise moment remains hidden, but some of its signs are known, particularly Jesus' second coming. Christians, in their creed, affirm that: "He will come again in glory to judge the living and the dead," and a hadîth even states that "there is no other mahdî except Jesus." This day will be the Resurrection Day, the Last Day, the Day of Retribution, the Day of Judgment, though Christians and Muslims base themselves on different proofs in affirming the resurrection. It will be the Day of Muster when "all the nations will be assembled before God" (Mt. 25:32). "Upon that day people will issue in scatterings to see their works and whoso has done an atom's weight of good shall see it, and whoso has done an atom's weight of evil shall see it" (Qur'ân 99:6-7). "All the truth about us will be brought out in the law court of Christ, and each of us will get what is deserved for the things done in the body, good or bad" (2 Cor. 5:10), in the hope of hearing God's words: "Well done, good and faithful servant; you have shown you can be faithful in small things, I will trust you with greater; come and join in your master's happiness" (Mt. 25:21).

Christians and Muslims affirm that there exists an Abode of Reward, Paradise, and an Abode of Punishment, Hell, though they differ widely in the description they give of these places and in their understanding of what constitutes their essential elements. Does not Jesus announce in the Gospel that "those who did good will rise again to life; and those who did evil to condemnation" (Jn. 5:28-29)? Whereas Islamic tradition recognizes the existence of "pleasures of the mind and the senses," often interpreted metaphorically, and would seem to confine the "vision of God" to a few rare moments and to the "nearest amongst the elect," since "the eyes attain Him not" (Qur'ân 6:103), yet "upon that day faces shall be radiant, gazing upon their Lord" (Qur'ân 75:22-23), Christian tradition has always affirmed that "when it is revealed we shall be like him because we shall see him as he really is" (1 Jn. 3:2). The First Vatican Council restated this in the following terms: "God, in His infinite goodness, has destined the human being to a supernatural end, namely to share in divine realities which completely transcend human understanding" (*De fide*, cap. 2). In any case, Muslims and Christians are united in affirming that at this moment each soul will be "at peace," "well pleased, well pleasing" (Qur'ân 89:28) and that the "Mystery of God" awaits us—as would seem to be indicated by a hadîth which echoes Isaiah and St. Paul—a mystery "which no eye has seen, no ear heard, no heart imagined" (Ghazâlî, *Ihyâ', k. al-mah abba*). Thus history has its finale and creation its fulfillment: to meet the Lord of All-Being.[8]

"Christianity and Islam"

J. Humankind and Worship

It is out of fidelity to this idea of God, humankind, and history, that Christians and Muslims alike, yet in their own ways, seek to submit to the mysterious will of God. They thus accomplish true "islâm" as did Abraham and his son, Moses and al-Khidr, Mary, her son and his Apostles, all of whom were among "those who submitted." Christians say, and here they are in agreement with a Muslim view which is completely justified, that it is by faith that a person is saved. They repeat the words of the author of the Epistle to the Hebrews: "Anyone who comes to God must believe that He exists and rewards those who try to find Him" (Heb. 6:11). Hence the whole of human conduct must consist in obedience to God. Christians and Muslims can echo the Psalmist: "Here I am! I am coming. In the scroll of the book am I not commanded to obey your will? My God, I have always loved your law from the depths of my being" (Ps. 39:8-9). Is not the ideal of the perfect believer to be acting always in conformity with God's law? "Expound to me the way of your statutes, Yahweh, and I will always respect them. Explain to me how to respect your law and how to observe it wholeheartedly" (Ps. 118:33-34); such is the prayer the Psalmist suggests.[9]

The Second Vatican Council states that Muslims "prize the moral life, and give worship to God, especially through prayer, almsgiving and fasting" (*Nostra Aetate*, par. 3). Though the rites and forms of prayer, fasting, and almsgiving may be different, the reality remains the same: we are all trying to adore God in truth, "confessing with your tongues, attesting to the truth in our hearts and showing our sincerity by our acts." For we refuse any kind of hypocrisy, since Jesus told Christians: "And when you pray, do not imitate the hypocrites" (Mt. 6:5), and the Qur'ân states: "The hypocrites seek to trick God, but God is tricking them" (Qur'ân 4:141). Prayer, invocation, litanies, meditation, intercession, and retreat are all old customs which are common to Christians and Muslims. In these, and in these alone, can they find the continuous renewal of their spiritual energy and their moral resolution. Numerous are the expression of worship and faith which Christians and Muslims hold analogically in common. On the basis of a fundamentally religious personalism we hold that each person is responsible before God alone for his or her personal development and faith. Yet at the same time we require that each should belong to a particular community, the *Umma* for Muslims, the church for Christians, providing a living milieu which teaches the content of the faith and keeps a check on its authenticity, while at the same time it brings about an appreciation for religious and moral values in rites and in human relations. Does not each community have its own rites for incorporating new members, its special places of worship (mosques and churches), a body of religious leaders (the "men of religion" in Islam; priests, ministers, and religious in Christianity)?

K. Humankind and Recognition of the Rights of God

Since Christians and Muslims desire in this way to recognize the rights of

42

The Common Doctrinal Basis

God and to submit to God's commands, they try to follow a pattern of human behavior which corresponds to what God has ordained for human happiness. The "commandments" which were handed down to Moses also form a moral and religious heritage common to us. "Honor your father and your mother.... You shall not kill. You shall not commit adultery. You shall not steal. You shall not bear false witness against your neighbor. You shall not covet your neighbor's house. You shall not covet your neighbor's wife, or servant, man or woman, or ox, or donkey, or anything that is your neighbor's" (Ex. 20:12-17). Respect for persons and for their freedom which puts us under an obligation to state together that "there can be no constraint in adhering to a religion,"[10] the fundamental equality of men and women (having due regard for the diversity of their functions and missions), the glorification of almsgiving, hospitality, fidelity to one's promises, concern for the common good at the price of subordinating private interests to it—all this has for a long time been the habit of believers in both Islam and Christianity.

They have learned, as is to be found repeated in certain hadîths which may extend to cover the whole of humanity, that "believers are but brothers" and that "no one is a true believer until he loves for his brother that which he loves for himself" (Ghazâlî, *Ihyâ*, k.*al-mahabba*). The Gospel is constanly reminding us that the second commandment is like the first: "You must love your neighbor as yourself," and that it is on the works of faith that we shall be judged on the last day. Happy those who will then hear said to them: "I was hungry and you gave me food; I was thirsty and you gave me drink; I was a stranger and you made me welcome; naked and you clothed me, sick and you visited me, in prison and you came to see me . . .[for] in so far as you did this to one of the least of these my brothers or sisters, you did it to me" (Mt. 25:35-40). Is it not said in a hadîth that "whoever gives relief to a believer for one of the afflictions of this world, will be relieved by God from one of the afflictions of the Day of Resurrection"?[11]

II. Areas of Convergence

A. *The Challenge of the Modern World*

Such are the aspects of the doctrinal basis common to the two religions. These provide meeting-points for reflection and research. But can believers be content to enumerate their points of convergence and to respect the points of divergence while their contemporaries look on, silent and cynical spectators of theoretical and academic dialogues? The modern world presents thousands of challenges to faith in God, with regard to the manner in which it is to be justified, as well as the ways in which it is expressed and influences daily life. Should not Christians and Muslims renew their methods and exchange experiences so that together they may face up to the challenges of modern thought and give positive answers to the questions set by an atheistic culture? Believers have not finished exploring the dimensions of faith, particularly those corresponding to the expectations of the scientific culture of our age. Is there not here a first area of convergence for our religious investigations today?

If one states with Jesus the Messiah that "no servant can be the slave of two masters" (Lk. 16:13), one is bound to acknowledge that paganism is forever springing up again and that the new idols are more powerful than ever, these idols which oppress God's creatures in the name of the state, of sex, or of money, in the name of technical achievements, productivity, or the consumer society, or in the name of empty fame, false freedom, and illusory happiness. People today are waiting for a new freedom which will allow them to recognize their God and, by this very fact, to recognize their own essential natures. Cannot this struggle to free their brothers and sisters from all forms of oppression unite Christians and Muslims, in accordance with the invitation issued by the Second Vatican Council in its *Declaration on the Relationship of the Church to Non-Christian Religions?*" "Although in the course of centuries many quarrels and hostilities have arisen between Christians and Muslims, this most sacred Synod urges all to forget the past and to strive sincerely for mutual understanding. On behalf of all humankind let them make common cause of safeguarding and fostering social justice, moral values, peace and freedom" (*Nostra Aetate*, par. 3). Will the Psalmist's vision be fulfilled, thanks to the efforts of all? "Love and loyalty now meet. Righteousness and Peace now embrace; Loyalty reaches up from the earth and Righteousness leans down from heaven" (Ps. 84:11-12).

B. The Believer's Commitment

Faith in God is the very basis of such a commitment to the service of our sisters and brothers, for there lies in each of them that person which "God has created to his image," as is stated in both the Bible (Gen. 1:26) and the hadîth.[12] Jesus told Christians: "Love your enemies and pray for those who persecute you; in this way you will be the children of your Father in heaven, for he causes his sun to rise on bad as well as good, and his rain to fall on honest and dishonest alike . . . . You must therefore be perfect just as your heavenly Father is perfect" (Mt. 5:44-48). Muslims know that, according to Ghazâlî, believers of old said: "Put on the habits of God . . . . Perfection for the believer consists in approaching the Lord by following the way of His attributes which are most praise-worthy: knowledge, justice, goodness, kindness, bounty, mercy, good counsel, encouragement to do good and preservation from harm."[13] Is it not this way, leading to an "exchange of attributes," that is referred to in this other hadîth *qudsî* quoted by Ghazâlî: "The closer my servant comes to me through supererogatory practices the more I love him, says God, and when I love him I am the ear by which he hears, the eye by which he sees and the tongue by which he speaks"?

It is because one believes in the living God who loves life and wishes to see it produce all its fruit that one strives to protect life wherever it is threatened—helping the sick and the dying in hospitals, developing medical research and methods of medical treatment in laboratories, condemning abortion and euthanasia in permissive societies, disapproving methods of birth control which are over-simple, refusing war and homicidal experiments on a planetary scale. It is because life is a gift from God that humankind cannot dispose of it as it wills. Councils and popes have never ceased reminding Christians of this fact, whatever might be the difficulties of the present time.[14]

It is because one believes in a just God who created the good things of this world for all its inhabitants that one fights against all forms of discrimination, whether their motivation be sexual, racial, cultural, religious, or national. One combats the selfish accumulation of wealth in different forms of capitalism, whether these are practiced by individuals or by governments, in the East or in the West. One struggles against the unjust division of natural resources and the selfishness of some rich countries that forget to give assistance to poorer countries through the channel of international organizations. This, at least, is what the best Christians are trying to do untiringly, taking part wherever they can in the fight against underdevelopment and for the progress of nations "without expecting any reward other than that of doing God's will," with complete respect for persons, cultures, and civilizations. Their work and suffering is offered in the service of life and of humanity, in a spirit of equality with all, and with respect for all forms of freedom.[15]

It is because one believes in a God who is free to create and to initiate things that one defends everywhere freedom values: freedom of movement and freedom of expression, freedom of thought and freedom of religion. For freedom alone allows the flowering of the human spirit in each person and each community; freedom alone gives humanity the opportunity to be responsible for its own acts and to achieve integrated personalities; freedom alone gives the believer the joy of adoring God without constraint and of offering a service worthy of God. "Human dignity demands that one act according to a knowing and free choice. Such a choice is personally motivated and prompted from within. It does not result from blind internal impulse" (*Gaudium et spes*, par. 17), declared the Second Vatican Council.

Finally it is because one believes in God who is Peace and who gathers that one strives to create a human family on an international scale, while at the same time respecting national cultures. This too is why one encourages dialogue as the sole means for resolving conflicts and why one combats all forms of nationalism that are closed and inward-looking. It is because one believes in a God of mercy and pardon that one rejects the spirit of vengeance and any justice that might in fact be unjust. For pardon alone can revive in the prisoner, the condemned person, or the sinner, that strength of soul which enables the start of a new life, and only human mercy can bear witness here below to the limitless and endless mercy of God.

C. *Believers and Our World of Today*

Life for all, justice for all, freedom for all, the unity of the human family—these are human values which, since they are at one and the same time values of faith, undoubtedly constitute possible common ground for the commitment of believers amidst the contemporary problems of civilization. Despite some fundamental divergences in matters of doctrine, particularly with respect to the approach to the divine mystery and to the role of prophets in history, all have a common doctrinal basis sufficient to justify, in the name of faith itself, their commitment on behalf of humanity, through a "dialogue of values" where we ourselves must be ready to pay the price. These various areas of convergence have been brought to the consideration of Christians by the Second Vatican Council in a long document entitled *The Church in the Modern World*. This document aims at defending the absolute dignity of humankind which lives under the eye of God and in submission to divine laws, fully respecting life, justice, equality, and freedom which are among the fundamental contemporary rights.

This document first reminds believers of the "human condition" today: its hopes and fears, the psychological, moral, and religious transformations that are taking place; new imbalances; more universal aspirations; a deeper questioning. Three broad areas are given priority: human dignity, the unity of the human community, and the promotion of human action in the universe. Believers, conscious of *human dignity* but also of the manifold contradictions within people, have the duty of reminding all of the dignity of the mind destined for truth and wisdom, of the dignity of conscience destined for freedom and uprightness, yet accepting at the same time dialogue with all representatives of contemporary atheism. Believers concerned for the *human community* have the duty of insisting on the community aspect of the human vocation: the interdependence of person and society, the primacy of the common good, respect for persons, respect and love for adversaries, the essential equality of all people, the need to go beyond a purely individualistic ethic. Believers, convinced of the *value of human action*, have the duty of respecting the autonomy of earthly realities while at the same time helping to bring about the fulfillment according to God's plan for creation. Are they not awaiting "a new heaven and a new earth" (Apoc. 21:1)?

D. The Dignity of Earthly Values

Some urgent problems are then put forward for the attention of Christians. These can constitute further common ground for the commitment of believers. The first of these is the *dignity of marriage and of the family:* the holiness of marriage and the family, the fundamental value of conjugal love, the fruitfulness of marriage, respect for human life from birth and even before birth, the eminent dignity of woman and the promotion of her interests. The second area of concern is that of *cultural development:* the relationlship between faith and culture, the harmony of different values within cultures, the recognition that all have a right to culture, efforts to achieve an integral human culture. A third series of questions concerns the *socio-economic order:* economic development for human benefit, removal of socio-economic inequalities, social justice in industrial disputes, participation in management and in the running of the economy, private property and concern for the common good, the use of the world's resources for the benefit of the whole of humankind. In fourth place is *politics:* the cooperation of all citizens in the life of the nation through democratic systems which respect the liberties referred to above. Finally, there are the *maintenance of peace and the building up of a community of nations:* proscription of war, or at least its "humanization" when sin forces us to tolerate it; the struggle for a growing and general disarmament; work for international cooperation in all fields (economic, social, cultural); and the development of international bodies.[16]

III. Conclusion

It is perhaps through such action on behalf of life, justice, freedom, and fellowship that believers can today prove the human effectiveness and the real credibility of their faith in God. They cannot invoke God as Creator and Saviour of all if they refuse to believe in a familial spirit toward all. Christians say: "Anyone who says, 'I love God,' and hates her or his brother, is a liar, since whoever does not love a brother that is seen cannot love God, who is not seen (1 Jn. 4:20); "our love is not to be just words or mere talk, but something real and active" (1 Jn. 3:18). Muslims are well aware that they are required to act in conformity with their faith: "Work, and God will surely see your work, and his Messenger, and the believers" (Qur'án 9:105). Christians and Muslims seem, therefore, to have a certain common ground, as regards both belief and commitment. For this reason it is important to define to what extent religion constitutes, for each side, an "ideology for life," and to what extent faith in God encourages believers to dedicate themselves wholly to the achievement of social justice. In the very fight against prejudices and in attempting to lessen misunderstandings they will discover how much unites them already. For this to come about it is desirable that believers should listen to the inspirations God gives them today, and that they should extend their activity on behalf of their fellow humans for the glory of God and the joy of humankind. Then they will hear the Psalmist saying to them: "Happy those who find their strength in you, Lord; they will set out on the road" (Ps. 83:6).

1) *"The same holy Mother Church holds and teaches that God, the origin and end of all things, can be known with certainty by the natural light of human reason from the things of creation; 'for since the creation of the world his invisible attributes are clearly seen, being understood through the things that are made' (Rom. 1:20); and she teaches that it was nevertheless the good pleasure of His wisdom and goodness to reveal Himself and the eternal decrees of His will to the human race in another and supernatural way, as the Apostle says: 'God, who at sundry times and in divers manners spoke in times past to the fathers by the prophets, last of all in these days has spoken to us by His Son' (Heb. 1:1-2)"* (Const. de fide catholica, cap. 2; TCT 58).
The original texts of the decrees and canons of the Councils have recently been republished by the Institute of Religious Sciences in Bologna, Italy. The

"Christianity and Islam"

volume is entitled: Conciliorum Oecumenicorum Decreta *(Bologna: Istituto per le Secienze religiose, 1973). An English translation of the most important documents is to be found in* The Church Teaches *(St. Louis: Herder, 1955), abbreviated* TCT.

2) Const. de fide catholica, *cap. 4; TCT 75. The same Constitution, in chapter 3, declares: "Because man depends entirely on God as his creator and lord and because created reason is wholly subordinate to uncreated Truth, we are obliged to render by faith a full submission of intellect and will to God when He makes a revelation" (TCT 63).*

3) *These difficult problems of Christian-Muslim dialogue have been considered by Professors Ali Merad and Roger Arnaldez in the journal* Islamo-christiana *(Rome: Ponificio Istituto di Studi Arabi) 1 (1975). Many passages of these articles, "Langage commun et dialogue" (pp. 1-10), "Dialogue islamochrétien et sensibilités religieuses" (pp. 11-24), would be relevant here.*

4) *The* original Latin text *of the Constitutions, Decrees, and Declarations of the Second Vatican Council can be found in the volume* Conciliorum Oecumenicorum Decreta *(see note 1). There is a handy English translation, with notes and comments: Walter M. Abbott, ed.,* The Documents of Vatican II *(London: Geoffrey Chapman, 1966). For a French translation, with the Latin original side by side. see du Centurion, ed.,* Concile oecumémique Vatican II (constitutions, décrets, déclarations, messages) *(Paris, 1967). An Arabic translation has been published by Dar al-'âlam al-'arabî, Cairo, separate fascicles, n.d. Numerous studies have appeared on Vatican II, for example in the French series* Unam Sanctam. *Of particular interest is the volume in this series edited by A. M. Henry and entitled* Relations de l'Eglise avec les religions non chrétiennes *(Paris: Cerf, 1966).*

5) Const. de fide catholica, *cap. 1; TCT 355. The Apostles' Creed states: "I believe in God the Father almighty, creator of heaven and earth" (TCT 1);* The Nicene Creed *(325): "We believe in one God, the Father almighty, creator of all things both visible and invisible" (TCT 2); the* First Council of Constantinople *(381): "We believe in one God, the Father alimighty, creator of heaven and earth, of all things both visible and invisible" (TCT 3); the* Council of Florence *(1442): "The Church firmly believes, professes and preaches that the one true God, Father, Son and Holy Spirit, is the creator of all things visible and invisible. When God willed, in His goodness He created all creatures both spiritual and corporeal. These creatures are good because they were made by the Supreme Good, but they are changeable because they were made from nothing. The Church asserts that there is no such thing as a nature of evil, because every nature insofar as it is a nature is good" (TCT 94).*

6) *This was also stated by the First Vatican Council in the following terms: "In order to manifest His perfection through the benefits which He bestows on creatures—not to intensify His happiness nor to acquire any perfection—this one and only true God, by His goodness and alimighty power and by a completely free decision, from the very beginning of time has created both orders of creatures in the same way out of nothing, the spiritual or angelic world and the corporeal or visible universe. And afterwords He formed the creature, who in a way belongs to both orders, being composed of spirit and body"* (Const. de fide catholica, *cap. 1; TCT 356).*

48

The Common Doctrinal Basis

7)   *True dialogue is, in fact, based on complete respect for the beliefs and behavior of the partner in dialogue. It aims at improving mutual awareness and understanding, while seeking to penetrate God's inscrutable decrees. It flourishes in an atmosphere of friendship, frankness, gentleness, mutual confidence, and patience in the face of the various stages that have to be covered.*

For some general information on Christian attitudes toward dialogue see the directives given by Pope Paul VI in his encyclical letter Ecclesiam suam [*August, 1964; Latin and Italian texts in the* Osservatore Romano, *10-11.8. 1964; English translation:* The Church in the Modern World *(London: Catholic Truth Society, 1965); French translation in the* Documentation catholique, *Paris, 6.9. 1964, pp. 1058-1093*] See also Guidelines for a Dialogue between Muslims and Christians *(Rome, Ancora: Secretariat for Non-Christians, 1971), 2nd impression, with editions also in French, Italian and Spanish.*

A first preliminary survey of efforts dedicated to Christian-Muslim dialogue has been published in Islamochristiana *I (1975), including: Michael Fitzgerald, "The Secretariat for Non-Christians Is Ten Years Old," pp. 87-96; John B. Taylor, "The Involvement of the World Council of Churches (W.C.C.) in International and Regional Christian-Muslim Dialogue," pp. 97-102; Emilio Galindo Aguilar, "Cordove, capitale califale du Dialogue islamo-chretien," pp. 103-114; and Abdelmajid Charfi, "Quelques réflexions sur la recontre is islamo-chrétien de Tunis, " pp. 115-124.*

8)   *It would be interesting, within the framework of dialogue on religious experience, to study together what God's "good pleasure" means for Muslims and Christians. For Catholic Christians it is considered to be a process of justification which transforms the creature's very being. Thus the Council of Trent (1545-1563) states: "Justification is not only the remission of sins, but sanctification and renovation of the interior man through the voluntary reception of grace and gifts, whereby a man becomes just instead of unjust and a friend instead of an enemy, that he may be an heir in the hope of life everlasting . . . . The only formal cause is the justice of God, not the justice by which He is Himself just, but the justice by which He makes us just, namely, the justice which we have as a gift from Him and by which we are renewed in the spirit of our mind"* (Decretum de justificatione, cap. 7; TCT 563). *But the same Council declared that one cooperates freely and efficaciously: "If anyone says that the free will of man, moved and awakened by God, in no way co-operates with the awakening call of God by an assent by which man disposes and prepares himself to get the grace of justification; and that man cannot dissent, if he wishes, but, like an object without life, he does nothing at all and is merely passive: let him be anathema"* (Canones de iustificatione, can. 4; TCT 578).

9)   *The whole of Psalm 118 could be quoted here. It presents a meditation on "love of the Law," a religious attitude common to all believers, whether Christians or Muslims. All seek true wisdom and could adopt the prayer of the Sage: "God of our ancestors, Lord of mercy, who by your word have made all things, and in your wisdom have fitted man to rule the creatures that have come from you, to govern the world in holiness and justice and in honesty of soul to wield authority, grant me Wisdom, consort of your throne, and do not reject me from the number of your children"* (Wisdom 9:1-4).

49

"Christianity and Islam"

10) *The Second Vatican Council judged it useful and necessary to dedicate a complete document to this important question.* The Declaration on Religious Freedom *states among other things: "This Vatican Synod declares that the human person has a right to religious freedom . . . . In matters religious no one is to be forced to act in a manner contrary to his own beliefs. Nor is anyone to be restrained from acting in accordance with his own beliefs, whether privately or publicly, whether alone or in association with others, within due limits. The Synod further declares that the right to religious freedom has its foundation in the very dignity of the human person, as this dignity is known through the revealed word of God and by reason itself. The right of the human person to religious freedom is to be recognized in the constitutional law whereby society is governed. Thus it is to become a civil right . . .provided with an effective constitutional guarantee"* (Dignitatis Humane, *par. 2, par. 15*).

11) *The hadīth continues: "Whoever makes life easier for someone who is in difficulties, God will make everything easier for him in this world and in the next. Whoever 'covers' a Muslim, God will 'cover' him in this world and in the next. God comes to the help of each of His servants as long as each comes to the help of his brothers"* (Ghazâlî, Ihyâ', k.al-mahabba). *These hadīths are to be found in Ghazâlî's work as an introduction to a section on "the exchange of attributes."*

12) *Of course, many experts interpret this hadīth in the following way: God created Adam to "his" image, that is in conformity with the image which God had of Adam, an image existing from pre-eternity in the mind of God. It would seem that Ghazâlî interprets the hadīth rather differently, given the context in which he uses it. He declares in fact: "The special proximity pertaining to man is alluded to by God's word: 'They will question thee concerning the Spirit. Say: The Spirit is of the bidding of my Lord,' for God explains that it is something divine, beyond the range of created intelligences. Even clearer is His word: 'When I have formed (Adam) harmoniously, and breathed into him of My Spirit;' that is why God made the angels bow down before Adam. This is what is shown also by his word: 'We have made you a viceroy on the earth,' for Adam merited to be God's viceroy only by reason of this resemblance. This is referred to by the Prophet's saying: 'God created Adam to His image', to the point that certain narrow-minded people have come to believe that the only image is an external image, that which is perceived by the senses . . ."* (Ghazâlî, Ihyâ', k.al-mahabba).

13) *Ghazâlî, Ihyâ', k.al' mahabba. It would be fitting here to consider the entire "fifth cause of love (of God)" as expounded by Ghazâlî: "resemblance and likeness, for like is attracted to like, and a form has a greater inclination to a (similar) form."*

14) *Reference could be made, among other documents, to the encyclical letter of Pope Paul VI,* Humanae vitae, *of 25.7. 1968; on "birth control" and responsible parenthood with complete respect for the nature and ends of the conjugal act and in fidelity to God's purpose with regard to the "transmission of life." See the Italian text in the* Osservatore Romano, *1.8. 1968; English translation,* On the Regulation of Birth *(Tipografia poliglotta vaticana, 1968); French translation in the* Documentation catholique *(Paris; 1.9. 1968), pp. 1442-1458.*

The Common Doctrinal Basis

15)   Is it necessary to recall here that Christian charity is shown to all, without distinction of race or creed, without proselytism and without any type of pressure being exerted? This is the constant attitude of Catholics, shared by many Protestants. See the Hong Kong Memorandum of 1975, quoted in John B. Taylor, "The Involvement of the World Council of Churches (W.C.C.) in International and Regional Christian-Muslim Dialogue," Islamochristiana 1 (1975): 97-102.

On social matters and questions concerning "development" reference can be made to recent papal documents, such as Matter et Magistra of Pope John XXIII, of 15.5 1961, on "recent developments concerning the social question in the light of Christian doctrine" [Italian text in Osservatore Romano, 15.7. 1961; French text in the Documentation catholique, Paris, 6.8. 1961, pp. 946-990; English translation: New Light on Social Problems (London: Catholic Truth Society, 1961)], and the letter of Pope Paul VI, Populorum Progressio, of 26.3. 1967, on the complete and harmonious "development of peoples" [Italian text in the Osservatore Romano, 28-29.3. 1967; English translation: The Great Social Problem (London: Catholic Truth Society, 1967); French translation in the Documentation catholique, Paris, 16.4. 1967, pp. 674-704; Arabic translation, privately edited by the Secretariat for Non-Christians, Risâla jâmi'a liQadâsat al-Bâbâ Bûlus al-sâdis fî Taqaddum al-shu'ûb wa-ritqâ`i-hâ (Jounieh, Lebanon: Paulist Publishers)].

16)   To make efforts and declarations for the establishment of peace has been the constant concern of leaders of the Catholic Church. Reference could be made here to the encyclical letter of Pope John XXIII, Pacem in Terris, of 11.4. 1963, on "peace between nations founded on truth, justice, charity, and freedom" [Italian text in the Osservatore Romano, 11.4. 1963; English translation: Peace on Earth (London: Catholic Truth Society, 1963); French translation in the Documentation catholique, Paris, 21.4. 1963, pp. 513-546]; to Pope Paul's speech to the General Assembly of the United Nations in New York, on 4.10. 1965 [French text in the Osservatore Romano, 6.10. 1965; and in the Documentation catholique, Paris, 17.10. 1965, pp. 1729-1738; English translation: The Pope's Appeal for Peace (London: Catholic Truth Society, 1965); and to the institution, by Pope Paul IV, of a Day of Peace to be celebrated annually on January 1st. "No more war, no more war," he had said to the delegates assembled at the United Nations, "it is peace, peace, which must direct the destiny of peoples and of the whole of humanity."

IV

Islam and Dialogue
Some Reflections On a Current Topic

BY MOHAMED TALBI

A Current Topic

Our century has seen the splitting of the atom, and it has also witnessed the disintegration of all forms of monolithic ideologies. Pluralism of cultures would appear to be undeniable, a movement that cannot be reversed. This fact, however, makes it indispensable that various intellectual disciplines should encounter one another, and that there should be a constant dialogue between different systems. In this line of thought, the last Council inaugu-

The author of this paper, as he himself reminds his readers in his concluding remarks, is a historian. In fact he is the head of the department of history of the University of Tunis.

His main work has been on the Aghlabid dynasty, on which he produced his doctoral dissertation: L'Emirat aghlabide: histoire politique, *Paris, Maisonneuve, 1966, 768p. He has also made a number of contributions to the Encyclopedia of Islam, 2nd edition, including the article on Ibn Khaldun.*

In November 1971 Professor Talbi was invited to give a series of lectures at the Pontifical Institute of Arabic Studies, Rome. On this occasion, on November 25th, he gave a public lecture in which he delivered the substance of the present paper. He repeated the same lecture later in Tunis and edited it as a booklet: Islam et Dialogue: réflexions sur un théme d'actualité, *Tunis, Maison Tunisienne de l'Edition, 1972, 55p. It is this final version which has served as the basis for the translation presented here.*

This essay is taken from Encounter· Documents for Muslim-Christian Understanding. Nos. 11 & 12, January, February 1975, and is reprinted by permission of the publisher.

"Christianity and Islam"

rated in September 1962 opened up encouraging perspectives for reconciliation and for exchange of ideas, not only between Christians, but also between all the human families, whatever their spiritual and ideological attachment. Islam, no more than any other system of thought, cannot afford to remain a mere spectator of this movement without risking a condemnation, which this time could be final and without appeal. Indeed what is at stake today is far more important (and attractive) than any issue which arose in the dark ages of Muslim civilization, a period of decadence whose after effects, in spite of a laborious *Nahda* (Renaissance), are still very much with us.

Revelation and Dialogue

Thus dialogue for Islam is first and foremost a necessary and vital re-establishment of contact with the world at large. This is still more urgent and beneficial for Islam than for other religions, such as Christianity, which have never really lost such contact, something which puts Christianity in a relatively privileged position today. It is also, in a certain sense, a revival of an old tradition. In fact the whole of Revelation invites us to do just this, and there is no sign of opposition to it. To be convinced of this point, one has only to meditate upon the following verses:

"Call thou to the way of thy Lord with wisdom *(bi-l-hikma)* and good admonition *(wa-l-mawʿizat al-hasana)*, and dispute with them in the better way *(wa jâdilhum bi-l-latî hiya ahsan)*. Surely the Lord knows very well those who have gone astray from his way *(inna rabbaka huwa aʿlamu biman dalla ʿan sabîlihi)*, and He knows very well those who are guided *(wa huwa aʿlamu bi-l-muhtadîn)*" Q.16, 125.

"Dispute not with the People of the Book save in the fairer manner *(wa lâ tujâdilû ahl al-kitâb illa bi-l-latî hiya ashan)*, except for those of them that do wrong *(zalamû):* and say, 'We believe in what has been sent down to us, and what has been sent down to you *(âmannâ bi-l-ladhî unzila ilaynâ wa unzila ilaykum);* our God and your God is one *(wa ilâhunâ wa ilâhukum wâhidun)*, and to Him we have surrendered *(muslimûn)'* " Q.29, 46.

Thus the Revelation invites the Prophet and the Muslim to discuss and to enter into dialogue with men in general, and especially with the faithful of the biblical religions. We notice also that the duty of apostolate, which is implicity referred to here and which is something which we must not try to avoid but which we shall have to discuss further, harmonises well with respect for other people and other beliefs, for it belongs to God and to God alone in the final instance to acknowledge His own: "Surely thy Lord knows very well those who have gone astray from His way, and He knows very well those who are guided."

The Handicap of Past History

Why then, someone may say, did things happen in the way they did? Why

Islam and Dialogue

are we so badly handicapped by our past? Why has there been so much opposition, such misrepresentation, so many insults and so much abuse? Why in fact has force prevailed over courtesy?

The answer is that nothing is simple in the lives of men, and we have to examine carefully the sad past we have inherited so as to avoid making the same mistakes in the future. It is a fact that today people think of Islam as a religion of violence, not as one of dialogue. So we need to explain this point briefly. In the first place, let me emphasise that although certain countries were opened (fath) by force, it is practically unheard of that Islam was anywhere imposed on people. It is also right that we should examine the world situation at the time of Islam's entry on the stage. The two super powers of the time, the empires of Byzantium and Ctesiphon, were striving to impose their supremacy over the other existing nations. Nobody thought it wrong to expand the empire by force. You either had to persecute the others or suffer persecution yourself. We have since learned too that all wars are just or can be justified. The martial spirit was — and alas perhaps still is — the noblest road to glory. And what are we to think of modern revolutionary movements which are supposed to win happiness for various races, and to sweep aside anything that might hinder progress? Islam then, having been revealed at a given time and in a specific country, enters into history, is lived by men and becomes subject to the law of contingency. Whether it liked it or not, Islam could not help but fit into its own period. The train was already moving; Islam had only to catch it.

And so it is a fact that more than one verse of the Qur'ân incites to combat and promises the palm of martyrdom and paradise to whoever falls while striving in God's way. Such combat, however, is always put forward as second best, a last resort, which must conform to all sorts of material and moral restrictions in order to be acceptable. It is above all important to bring out clearly that the verses which incite to war have an essentially circumstantial application, connected with specific contingencies which today, we would hope, are definitely something of the past. They do not present us with the deep, permanent spirit of the Message, which is that of a hand respectfully and courteously held out to our neighbour, as we have already emphasised. It is this deep and permanent spirit that we must rediscover today in order to clear the path to dialogue of all misunderstandings which have blocked it in the past and which are in danger of blocking it again today in combination with other difficulties of the present time.

Present-Day Difficulties

Even when the mortgage of the past has been paid off, there still remain problems to be solved. Other difficulties continue to exist even after good will can be counted on.

Disparity between those taking part in dialogue

We must begin by emphasising the major difficulty: the enormous differ-

55

ence between those taking part in dialogue as well as the different level of studies within the respective traditions. There can be no doubt that this obstacle is the hardest to overcome in the immediate future as, even with the finest dispositions and the best will in the world, one cannot just instantaneously produce, as if by enchantment, people fully qualified and capable of taking part in dialogue. How, it goes almost without saying that most of modern Islam belongs to the disinherited zone of under-development, an under-development which is not only material but perhaps above all intellectual. The fact that one can call to mind the names of one or two eminent thinkers does not affect the situation as a whole: the exception only goes to prove the rule. So we can say (with apologies to Corneille) that there is not only a risk of dialogue coming to an end, but of it never really beginning for lack of 'dialoguers.' It is this fact, far more than any difficulties over principles or methods of approach, which explains the hesitation, the reticence, the lack of trust even, and generally speaking the present sterility, despite several efforts made, as only to be expected, on the initiative of Christians.[1]

Unequal theological development

There is also the fact of unequal theological development. Christian theology has been able to profit by its confrontation with other intellectual systems. The most dangerous of these have finally been the most salutary for its development, by subjecting it, under the pressure of contestation and criticism, to a fruitful tension. It has thus been able to understand its own values, work out answers, undertake at times agonising revisions, in the course of which it has also, and perhaps most importantly, been enriched by elements which have proved to be compatible with its own internal dynamism. Christian thought has thus been constantly vitalised and, while safeguarding and even reinforcing its attachment to what is purest and most authentic in its Tradition, it has adapted itself to each age and continues daily to progress in this direction. This effort, noticeable from the 19th Century onwards, resulted in the break-through of the recent Council. This of course did not take place without a certain amount of drama, of heartbreak and even of crisis.[2] But after it all the Church feels more committed, better armed and more ready for dialogue.

In every domain and in every scientific discipline the Church can produce people qualified to enter into dialogue, many of them real experts. Quite recently, for example, the book by Jacques Monod, *Le hasard et la nécessité,* was almost immediately answered by that of Marc Oraison, the title of whose book, *Le hasard et la vie,* shows an evident desire for dialogue, such as really did take place between the two authors, and to which the television assured the widest possible audience. Within the special framework which interests us, that of Islamology, there is a tremendous choice amongst clerics who are eminent specialists, such as G.C. Anawati, L. Gardet, Fr. Hayek, Fr. Jomier, Canon Ledit, Kenneth Morgan, Y. Moubarac, Fr. Pareja, Dr. Hermann Stieglecker, Wilfred Cantwell Smith, W. Montgomery Watt, and many

56

others, without mentioning the numerous lay Islamologists, to one of whom I owe a special mention, my eminent master Louis Massignon whose whole life was a living dialogue. Some younger men, such as M. Allard and Fr. Caspar, are beginning to make a name for themselves and there are many others still who are preparing to take the place of the older men.

And what is Islam doing in face of such an unprecedented effort by the Church? It offers us a theology whose evolution practically came to an end in the 12th Century. Muslim theology thus progressively lost contact with the world. For centuries, no new problems arose to challenge it and force it to investigate more closely the mystery of the world and of God. It is thus seen as something congealed, something often merely of historical interest. It is true that there was the *nahda*, the renaissance of the 19th Century, but this, while far from being something negative, has not yet succeeded in reinstating Islam in the movement of history. The distance covered may well seem slight in comparison with the journey which still lies ahead. Islam is far from possessing experts in all domains. In particular as far as I know, we cannot mention one real Muslim Christologist to set beside the numerous Christian lay people and clerics who are Islamologists. One can understand how Muhamed Arkoun could ask in disillusionment: "How can we possible get people to enter into useful dialogue, when their very conscience is divorced from its true tradition, and when they struggle on in economic and political misery, while the other side is fully conscious of its past as well as of its present condition?"[3] In other words, how is an earthenware pot to argue with an iron one? If we wish to overcome this difficulty, which gives birth to mental reservations and distrust, we must expose it in public in all frankness and serenity. As long as one side suffers from a superiority complex and the other from an inferiority complex, no useful purpose can be served in trying to open dialogue.

Islam must overcome its difficulties

In order to avoid any misunderstanding let us say first of all that if at the present moment Christians and Muslims are unequally prepared for dialogue, as we have just stressed forcefully, Islam in itself has no need to maintain any sort of complex with regard to Christianity.

It still remains that at every level there is an unequal development of the followers of the two beliefs. And so we turn towards the Muslims who are liable, in such circumstances, to give way to the temptation to isolate themselves in a spirit of self-preservation, to become more rigid and to retire within their own camp and proudly reply with a resounding "No"! We would like to ask them whether this is the right solution. There is no doubt that in this way they can preserve the things they value and they will survive. But for how long? Frontiers today are full of gaps: they fail to stop human contacts, the seductive attraction of example, books, films, and still less radio transmissions, to be followed soon by television broadcasts. Isolation becomes more and more a pipe dream in a world in tumult and plunged in contestation.

"Christianity and Islam"

It is just as if humanity today is going through a new crisis of adolescence. There is no way of escaping the upheaval. The democratisation of teaching, the possibility of going to school and even to the university, the raising of the standard of life and thought, with all the demands this creates, all these changes which take place sometimes without any transition, could prove fatal to Muslims who have never been exposed to such infection nor vaccinated against it. Religions are becoming less and less a social factor and more and more a personal and conscious commitment. So then if present-day Islam does not succeed, through dialogue with all systems of thought without exception or exclusion, in renewing the spirituality of its followers and in assimilating, as in the past, all values which are not opposed to its Witness, it will certainly be on the way to failing in its mission on earth. Such de-Islamisation can already be detected in the universities, among the youth in general and among the members of the more developed classes who often, at best, keep a certain vague affection for Islam as a venerable cultural heirloom. Finally, then, the adventure of dialogue with both believers and unbelievers, whatever the differences and the inequalities of formation at the present moment and taking all things into consideration, is less perilous than becoming more rigid in one's attitudes and fighting to defend frontiers in a world where frontiers are becoming more and more an anachronism. Unless one is to suppose that the Muslims, by some sort of despair or avowal of impotence, are to finish up by discharging on others — if such a thing were possible — the deposit *(amâna)* which Heaven has confided to their care.[4] For how else can one explain, other than by despair which torments some of our most lucid thinkers, the solution proposed by M. Arkoun in his *Supplique d'Un Musulman aux Chrétiens* where he is reduced to saying: "Under these conditions Christians could take over and assure the religious future of Islam, with the same determination, total commitment and the same depth of conviction with which they serve Christianity. It seems to us that this is the best way of preparing for future dialogue, since when one strives to set others free one frees oneself at the same time".[5] May I be allowed to be less pessimistic? Thank God, things are not as bad as all that! In spite of all sorts of inequalities which we have not in any way tried to hide, we think that dialogue, with certain precautions, is still possible between partners who make no secret of their own convictions. One should never await passively to be liberated by others, but one should set about freeing oneself.

Preliminary Conditions for Dialogue

Of course it is evident that however possible dialogue may be it is not easy to realise. So we must establish clearly the conditions required in order to allow it the maximum possibility to succeed and to be equally fruitful for all taking part. The hidden obstacles are indeed numerous, and so we must discover them in some way in advance, so as to avoid them more surely and to make sure also that once we do begin we are not stopped in our tracks. For this purpose we must avoid two attitudes both of which could prove to be

Islam and Dialogue

fertile sources of misunderstanding, disappointments and bitterness. These are the spirit of controversy and that of compromise and complacency.

We must avoid controversy

A polemical spirit caused untold harm in the Middle Ages, not only in the material, but also in the moral and intellectual spheres, by giving rise to caricatures and falsifications and by spreading lies in the name of truth. It is rare, in fact, that disputes do not lead to a set-back and an abdication of the mind. In spite of the evolution of mentalities — which in any case is perhaps only relative — the temptation remains strong for all religions to find themselves, little by little, forced into a blind alley. Let us say clearly to anyone who is tempted by a spirit of adventure that the clashes between the great universal religions of today have no more chance of producing conclusive victories than they had in the past. W. Montgomery Watt is absolutely right when he says: "If a Christian and a Muslim are merely seeking arguments against one another, they will easily find many, but this will not lead to dialogue."[6]

We must be very careful then to exterminate the hydra of polemics. The surest means of making it impossible for it ever to renew the immense damage done in the past and the sins committed against reason, is to renounce any idea of using dialogue, either openly or in one's own mind, as a means of converting the person we are talking to. If, in fact, dialogue is conceived as a new form of proselytism, a means of undermining convictions and bringing about defeat or surrender, sooner or later we shall find ourselves back in the same old situation as in the Middle Ages. It will merely have been a change in tactics. To address Muslims as, for example, Henri Nusslé does in his *Dialogue avec l'Islam* with such words as: "The West can offer you not only its culture, not only its genius for invention, but still more it can offer you the Kingdom of Christ,"[7] is to use unsuitable language in spite of the sincerity of the author and the undoubted nobility of his sentiments.

Frontiers have changed

To take that tone does not even offer the advantage of a tactical success. It just puts the backs up of people who are more inclined to connect Western technical superiority with the fact of its emancipation from the religious yoke and its cult of material progress. The only really important mass conversions taking place today are from faith to atheism or agnosticism, considered as the new religions of efficiency and progress. All believers then, abstraction made of any sectarian divisions, must grasp the fact that the world has greatly changed since the Middle Ages. The dividing lines between different faiths no longer run in the same direction as before. The opposition today is not so much between different concepts of God and of the way in which to serve him. A far deeper division has taken place between those who are striving to attain to man's destiny without God, and those who can only conceive of man's future in God and through God; between those who consign indis-

59

criminately to the rag-bag of myths all forms of religion, and those who continue to believe in their fathomless infinite truth. Thus Gennie Luccioni remarks with evident satisfaction in a review, which was in fact of Christian inspiration to begin with, and in a recent issue entitled *Le Mythe aujourd'hui,* that there is "a strange lack of anyone who remarks on, if only to deny it, the collapse of our religious myths. No doubt silence under the circumstances is more eloquent than speech; so that we have been tempted to underline this by leaving an empty page. If the Christian myths are passing away one may suppose that they are disappearing just as others have done before them and in the way indicated by Levi-strauss in the same series. It should therefore be possible to rediscover traces of them in literature or in political, historical or philosophical writings. However the vault of heaven is disintegrating and the celestial map no longer means anything except to 'mythomaniacs.' "[8] Surely there is no question of calling on those who believe to pledge themselves to some anachronistic and sterile Holy Alliance to engage in some queer new crusade. But they should understand all the same that polemics used to forward some doubtful sort of proselytism only falsifies and obscures the truth instead of illuminating it. It can only confuse sincere souls, cause them to lose their faith, and so add to the number of those to whom "the celestial map no longer means anything."

Conversions are no longer brought about by argument

Besides, in the case of the great religions which have evolved to an equal degree, conversions are no longer obtained through proselytism and polemics. Neither that of Carlo Coccioli, the author of *Tourment de Dieu,* who went from Christianity to Judaism, nor that of Edith Stein who took the opposite road but was nevertheless sent to the furnaces at Auschwitz for being fundamentally a Jewess, nor that of Isabelle Eberhardt who took refuge in *L'Ombre chaude de l'Islam,* were brought about in this way. They were the final destination of a more demanding and more complex spiritual odyssey, the fruit of an intense individual psychological drama, whereby they acquired a higher value and a greater depth.

The duty of the Apostolate

But then, for a religion to renounce as one of its objectives the conversion of those who have not yet come under its sway, is that not equivalent to abandoning its universalist vocation, deny its past, and failing to carry out its duty of the Apostolate?

This is precisely the moment when we must get rid of any equivocation and point out, in order to be completely sincere and totally successful, the second peril to be avoided, that of excessive complacency and compromise. Nobody, whether believer or atheist, should ever compromise with his convictions or his ideas. This is the unquestionable law of progress and of the asymptomatic progress towards Truth. Besides, true convictions that have become part of one's life are not negotiable. And so it is not a question of going from one extreme to the other and seeking at all cost, in a pure spirit of conciliation and without a real change of heart, accommodating solutions which only result in syncretism and confusion of thought. The sort of dialogue in which we are interested is not a question of policy, an exercise of the art of compromise. It is something much more important. It supposes total sincerity and, to be fruitful, it requires everyone to be completely himself, without aggressiveness or compromise.

Thus we get back to the full requirements of the apostolate, but this time purified from the slag of polemics and of a proselytism which leads to blindness. Seen from this point of view the apostolate becomes essentially an attentive openness towards our neighbour, an incessant seeking for truth through a continuous deepening and assimilation of the values of faith, and, in the final analysis, pure witness. This sort of apostolate is called, in Arabic, *jihâd*. This statement may well surprise all those for whom this word recalls the clash of holy wars past and present. Let me explain to them that *jihâd* both etymologically and fundamentally has nothing to do with war. Arabic has no lack of words to describe all kinds of warfare. If the Qur'ân had really wanted to talk of war there would have been an embarrassing choice of words to be found in the rich and colourful vocabulary of pre-islamic poetry, which is entirely given over to exalting the 'great days' of the Arab race *(ayyâm al-ʿArab)* when this people engaged in their favourite pasttime of disembowelling one another. *Jihâd* must therefore be something different. Essentially and radically it is an extreme, total effort in the Way of God *(fi sabîl Allâh)*. Tradition makes it clear that the purest, most dramatic and most fruitful form of it is *al-jihâd al-akbar*, the combat which takes place in the secrecy of one's conscience. This means that the finest form of apostolate is the witness of a life in which the struggle for moral perfection has succeeded. This form of apostolate through witness is the only one which gives results and is, moreover, in agreement with modern thought. It has no need of proselytism. Did not the Qur'ân itself remind the Prophet personally that he could not guide men towards God just as he liked, but that it is really God who guides toward Himself those whom He chooses? *(Innaka lâ tahdî man aḥbabta wa lâkinna Allâha yahdî man yashâ u wa huwa aʿlamu bi-l-muhtadîn* — "Thou guidest not whom thou likest, but God guides whom He will, and knows very well those that are guided." Q.28, 56) In fact, as far as the apostolate is concerned, our duty is to give witness, and it is for God to convert people. "Thus we appointed you a midmost nation that you might be witness to the people, and that the Messenger might be a witness to you." *(wa kadhâlika jaʿalnâkum ummatan wasatan li-takûnû shuhadâ'a ʿalâ al-nâs wa yakûna al-rasûlu ʿalaykum shahîdan, Q. 2, 143)*. So it is quite possible to develop a Muslim theology of the apostolate which scrupulously respects the rights of others. It is evident of course that this is just as possible for Christianity — a religion of witness through martydom — as well as for all other religions. Consequently co-existence, or better still co operation, without any denial of self or renunciation of one's own convictions, is not only possible but very fruitful. So when both extremes of polemical proselytism and complaisant compromise have been avoided the duty of the apostolate is not done away with. Rather it takes on its most noble and most difficult form, that of an interior *jihâd*, and opens the way to a healthy spirit of emulation in the pursuit of Good. However this interior *jihâd* should not deteriorate into a selfish mystical, or rather static, concentration on self, or into an all too easy form of self-satisfaction, or even tranquil indifference. It must remain at the same time witness, and bear evidence of a questing spirit marked by openness and a sense of disquiet. It is at this level that dialogue can be decisive. By creating a healthy climate of mutual exchange and of intellectual and spiritual tension, it can help towards a continuous and reciprocally deeper understanding of the values of faith. Movement will replace inertia.

Plurality of ways of salvation

This attitude implies, however, if ambiguity is to be avoided, that we admit that there are several ways to salvation. Now this problem is not the easiest one to resolve. The influence of the past makes itself felt here more than anywhere else.

With very few exceptions the theological systems of all religious confessions have been based on the axiom, expressed in different ways, that "outside the Church there is no salvation." Within each faith the group of faithful to benefit by salvation has been still more restricted by the rejection of various heresies whose followers have been consigned to eternal damnation. This leads to the conclusion that apart from certain chosen ones, the vast majority of human beings are destined for perdition. And yet all faiths proclaim that God is Justice, Mercy and Love! It is precisely in this area that we need a real theological renewal and a radical change of mentality. For what chance is there of an open-minded dialogue free of distrust if, from the very beginning, we lay down the absolute principle that those of the other side will inevitably be condemned to hell solely on account of their convictions?

On the part of the Church there has been a very evident evolution since Vatican II, which in particular addressed Muslims in these terms:

"Upon the Muslims too the Church looks with esteem. They adore one God, living and enduring, merciful and all-powerful. Maker of heaven and earth . . .whose decrees are sometimes hidden, but to which one must submit wholeheartedly, just as Abraham submitted to God, Abraham with whom the Islamic faith is pleased to associate itself. Though they do not acknowledge Jesus as God, they revere him as a prophet. They also honour Mary, his virgin mother; at times they call upon her too with devotion . . .Consequently they give worship to God especially through prayer, alms giving and fasting. They strive to live a moral life in obedience to God at the individual, family and social level.

Although in the course of centuries many quarrels and hostilities have arisen between Christians and Muslims, the council urges all to forget the past and to strive sincerely for mutual understanding. On behalf of all mankind, let them make common cause of safeguarding and fostering social justice, moral values, peace and freedom."[9]

In the same spirit G.C. Anawati states that where salvation is concerned "it has long been admitted that the two requisites for faith laid down by St. Paul exist in Islam." And he adds: "This means that when I wish to engage in dialogue with a Muslim, I do not have to begin by automatically placing him in hell merely because he is a Muslim. On the contrary I can assure him that under certain conditions, which are quite realisable, he can find salvation while still remaining a convinced Muslim. Can one think of any better way of beginning a fruitful dialogue?"[10]

On the Islamic side, contrary to what one might think, the same attitude of mind already existed in the Middle Ages. One finds it expressed by a completely orthodox theologian whom all Sunnites without exception consider to be the authentic spokesman for Islam *(Hujjat al-islâm),* namely Ghazâli (1058-1111) who in his book *faysal al-tafriqa* admits that under certain conditions, particularly those of sincerity and an honest life, non-Muslims can be saved.[11] Nearer to our times a theologian of the *nahda,* Muhammed ʿAbduh (1849-1905) expresses a similar opinion in his commentary on the following verse of the Qurʾân:

"Surely they that believe (in Islam), and those of Jewry, and the Christians, and those Sabaeans, who so believes in God and the Last Day, and works righteousness — their wage awaits them with their Lord, and no fear shall be upon them, neither shall they sorrow" (Q.2,62). Confirmation of this verse is found, with some slight variation, a little further on (cf.Q.5,69; see also 2,111-112).[12]

It is not impossible therefore, neither for Islam nor for Christianity, nor indeed for the other main religions, on the basis of their texts and with the support even of a certain ancient theological tradition, to elaborate a theology which would allow for a certain degree of plurality in the ways of salvation, were it only because one cannot forbid Divine Goodness from overflowing, in a gesture of justice, of mercy and of love, beyond the strict limits of any given Church in order to embrace all men of good will who live exemplary lives. In the end God remains entirely and freely the one who judges, and we must abandon ourselves confidently to His Wisdom. In any case we must abstain from passing judgement in His place.

This does not necessarily lead to a comfortable quietism or to a fading away of Truth seen as something vague and interchangeable. The danger which all religions face from this pluralistic outlook on the ways of salvation is that of becoming something relative. I trust that my readers will have understood that in my way of seeing things such a danger exists only for one who is not a true believer. For the true believer continues to be the epicentre of the Absolute of the faith he professes and to which he gives witness. Within the precise limits of the question with which we are concerned we must in fact stress, in order to keep our perspectives as clear as possible, that the Qurân, by a multiplicity of arguments and warnings, forcefully and insistently calls people to Islam as to the final message from God which confirms and completes all the Scriptures which preceded it. It makes it crystal clear that if anyone, while being naturally convinced in his heart of the veracity of the Qur'anic message, wants to practise another religion for opportunist or other reasons, this will not be accepted from him: "in the next world he shall be among the losers" (Q.3,85).

In a word, there is only one truth: it is our powers of understanding that vary. And what complicates the matter still more is that such powers are given to us by another. For if in fact we are not entirely passive and exclusively receptive, if we are indeed responsible for what we do and if we must work to fulfil our own destiny, tragically seeking our way through the shoals, it is also true that finally it is God who pilots our boat and keeps it from shipwreck. Our situation as men is an ambiguous one. Is it surprising then that we follow divergent paths to salvation? Under these circumstances complete good faith and sincerity are the only absolute requisites and the imperatives which allow for no exception. And so we set sail, trusting in God's grace. The fact, then, of admitting a variety of roads leading to salvation does not imply that we abdicate our faith, nor that we give up holding as true what we believe to be exact. Quite the contrary, the need to adhere to our faith becomes more imperative as it becomes more lucid. Then our faith ceases to be simply membership of a sociological group and a form of subordination. It becomes a real communion and a binding commitment. And so we'come back to the duty of the apostolate through witness, which is as much a question of self-respect as of respect for others. For nobody has the right to water down his own convictions or to lose all consistency through bending over backwards trying to understand others and thus, in fact, refusing to face up to his own reality.

Object and Purpose of Dialogue

Object of Dialogue

Perhaps someone will formulate the following objection: once the difficulties mentioned have been overcome, and the conditions postulated have been realised, does dialogue still make sense or have any object?

Of course it does! Basically it becomes a disinterested and unqualified collaboration in the service of God, that is to say in the service of Goodness and Truth. In such a straightforward, relaxed and serene atmosphere, everyone without exception can profitably engage in dialogue. For let us have no illusion on this point: if dialogue is not equally fruitful at all, it will either not take place at all or it will get nowhere. Any community which feels itself in danger will raise customs barriers and will take refuge in a sort of intellectual protectionism, which, though it has no more chance of success than its economic counterpart, will nevertheless become firmly established. This is because, when in grave peril, people do not consider what they stand to lose by isolating themselves. In such cases the primitive instinct of self-preservation takes over.

Islam and Dialogue

On the contrary, in an atmosphere of confidence ideas circulate more freely, and if they are capitalised on and invested in they pay dividends to all. So the primary objective we must fix for ourselves in any dialogue is to remove barriers and to increase the amount of Good in the world by a free exchange of ideas. On all the great problems which confront us and which sometimes challenge the very meaning of our existence, all human families, whether their outlook is materialistic or spiritual, have something to gain from comparing their own solutions and coordinating their solutions wherever this is possible. Across the heights that divide us it is not all that difficult to hold out our hands to one another, even when we draw our inspiration from divergent or even discordant sources. Growing cultural unification, which is perhaps the most striking phenomenon of our time, is daily drawing men closer to one another and placing them on the same level. Concerning the crucial problems of our time, believers and unbelievers, whatever their opinions, often hold useful discussions together which bring enrichment through the confrontation of different points of view.

It should therefore be still easier for all believers, united in a unanimous service of God, to discuss matters between them and to discover, when the right atmosphere has been created in the manner indicated, a common language. For example, there is absolutely no reason at all why we should not consider together what answers should be given to the questions asked in the conciliar document *Nostra Aetate*. It may be useful to recall to mind these questions: "What is man? What is the meaning and purpose of life? What is goodness and what is sin? What gives rise to our sorrows and to what intent? Where lies the path to true happiness? What is the truth about death, judgement and retribution beyond the grave? What finally is that ultimate and unutterable mystery which engulfs our being, and whence we take our rise, and whither our journey leads us?"

Each one of these questions could serve as the theme for one or more meetings. Why not organise these meetings and invite representatives from all religions, whether they have their Scriptures or not? In order to avoid any apperance of confrontation it is very useful indeed that such meetings include people with outlooks as diversified as possible. Already historians, philosophers and doctors from all over the world, meet in their regular congresses. Why should not the same thing happen with believers of all shades of opinion who could thus bring their various sources of light to bear on the problems which face us all? Such meetings would be extremely useful, if only because they would accustom, not merely the odd intellectual, but the officials in charge of different churches to meeting one another. Thus they would get to know one another and learn to communicate. In the world of contestation in which we live for any religion to close in on itself would be like taking an overdose of morphia in order to die peacefully.

Naturally one must be careful not to tread on any banana skins, and one must be on the watch for wolf traps in the forest! For example, one should be very careful to avoid inserting in the programme of such meetings the sort of questions put by Y. Moubarac to his correspondents. This is a form of interrogation, not dialogue. Besides the replies given to these questions prove beyond doubt that the whole area is mined and to wander about without taking due precautions is always likely to produce unfortunate explosions. The "dialogue" in writing organised by Moubarac has thus at least served the useful purpose of showing us how not to go about it. [13]

So we must be very careful and prudent in choosing, with the agreement of both sides and unilaterally, subjects which are capable of giving rise to fruitful communications from all sides. Thank God, there are sufficient such projects to provide matter for research and deliberation now and for a long time to come. Gradually the way will be prepared for greater progress and more ambitious plans. One must not be in too much of a hurry.

For example, one could study together in greater depth the legacy of spiritual values which belong to all religions that follow a Biblical tradition. On 31st March 1965 Cardinal Franz Koenig of Vienna spoke about monotheism to two thousand students and professors in the most representative Muslim university of theology, that of Al-Azhar in Cairo. There can be no doubt that his talk helped to foster better feelings and dissipate various misunderstandings. And in fact his conference met with a really enthusiastic reception which was very revealing. [14] Shaykh Hasan Ma'mûn, in concluding his vote of thanks, could not refrain from quoting the following passage from the Qur'ân: "And thou wilt surely find that the nearest of them in love to the believers are those who say 'We are Christians'; that because some of them are priests and monks, and they wax not proud." (Q.5,82)

So there are real possibilities of communicating and exchanging ideas. The chief thing is to discover them and make the most of them. The elaboration of a theology of religions, which has still to be done, of a moral theology as well as a social theology directly concerned with the problems of today, can only gain from the collaboration of those who are convinced that man's destiny is a part of God's plan, in reply to those who would make man the ephemeral yardstick of everything in a world closed-in on itself and without anything to follow, someone produced not by a conscious creative act of God, but someone evolved by sheer necessity and pure chance. If then we purge dialogue of anything which might lead it astray into useless argument, we shall find that it is far from being an empty and useless exercise. It is more likely to become more profound and more meaningful. In our drifting world of today, which is seeking new social structures and a new scale of values, the vast domain of ethics would supply alone a safe and practically unlimited basis for dialogue. What has the Message of God to offer to all the dispossessed people of the world, to all those without distinction who are alienated, to those who either cringe, beg and supplicate or who revolt and fight back and blaspheme? Here lies the most urgent need for dialogue because, in all religions, on the answer to these questions will depend the presence of God in men's hearts. For:

Islam and Dialogue

"If heaven (leaves) us alone like a still-born world,
The just man will oppose disdain to absence,
And his only response will be a loveless silence
in answer to the eternal silence of the divinity.

One can see from this that Vigny had already experienced this crisis, and well before his time one could mention the case of Maᶜarrî.

Does this mean that one must always remain on the heights? Is it indispensible to lay down as an absolute and strict law that one should never tackle some precise point of doctrine concerning one or other religion in particular? Of course not. But here vigilance will be all the more necessary, and one should not try to go ahead too quickly. In the case of Islam and Christianity the general lines of a compared theology have already been traced out, which should make it all the easier for both sides to travel more freely along this road. Certain questions should be relatively easy to discuss together, such as the general economy of salvation that we have already referred to in these pages. But would it not be possible to work out something on these lines by making use of the Qur'anic ideas of *hidâye* (guidance), *lutf* (protection-help), *tawfîq* (assistance-direction), *dalâl* (the trial of going astray), etc. And if Islam and Christianity were to study together these respectively similar values, would it not lead to a better understanding of them, and a deepening of our appreciation which would benefit all concerned? There are plenty of other examples one could mention. For instance there is the extremely difficult problem of how to reconcile human liberty with the existence of a transcendent and almighty God. Would not the Christian and Muslim solutions stand to gain by being confronted, and would it not be possible to go beyond them both in the light of recent advances in human science, from genetics to metaphysics through the various discoveries and theories of social psychology? An immense field of investigation in common is available to us, and with a little imagination one should be able to find several points of contact. The only real limits to such an investigation come not from the objective but the subjective point of view, namely whether or not those taking part are properly prepared for dialogue. This brings us back to the difficulties we have already mentioned.

At the same time we must not expect too much. However prepared both sides may be for dialogue there are certain subjects which, for a long time yet, will be difficult to discuss together. It is far better not to touch them at all so as not to get bogged down in discussions in which neither side listens to the other and where the only results are bitter polemics. The Qur'ân does indeed speak with respect and veneration about Jesus, the son of the Virgin Mary, and the Word of God. The same veneration is found in works about Jesus by al-ᶜAqqâd, Kâmil Husayn, Khâlid Muhammed Khâlid, ᶜAbd al-Hamîd Jûda al-Sahhâr, Fathî ᶜUthmân, and ᶜAbd al-Karîm al Khaṭîb.[15] However, in spite of all the good will that inspired these writings, a Christian would not recognise in them the Christ God of the mystery of the incarnation and of the

67

redemption. In the same way it is difficult for a Muslim to find in the numerous lives of Muhammad written in the West, often with the best intentions, the Seal of the Prophets who brought to mankind the perfection of the Ultimate Message from God. And how is it possible to carry on a useful dialogue with a Christian or a Jew on the nature of the Qur'ân? To the mystery of the incarnation of Christ and of the redemption corresponds, in Islam, the no less difficult mystery of the taking of a concrete form by the Word of God, consubtantial with Being, and therefore eternal, which yet descended *(tanzîl)* into this world of contingent phenomena. So perhaps it may not be by pure chance that in the Middle Ages there were such heated arguments among Christians, on the one hand, concerning the nature of Christ, and among Muslims on the other, concerning the nature of the Qur'ân. The Mu^{c}stazilites, who were particularly sensitive to the human aspect of the Qur'ân and who consequently considered it to be something purely created — thus doing away with the mystery of its double nature — were in a way the Arians of Islam. It was the Sunnites who prevailed and their understanding of the mystery was accepted by the majority, just as the doctrine of the dual nature of Christ prevailed among Christians. This is what makes it so difficult to subject the Qur'ân to a type of textual criticism based on historicism and methods which are applicable to texts unquestionably written by human beings. Islam and Christianity have not the same concept of revelation. So, for certain questions it is better to accept the situation as it is, at least for the time being, rather than bang one's head against a brick wall. G.C. Anawati is quite right when he remarks: "the more one is firm about the classical points that divide us the better we know where we stand, and our discussion becomes surprisingly open and fruitful."[16]

Purpose of Dialogue

Now although the usefulness and scope of dialogue are limited, there is no limit to its purpose. This is to shake people up and to make them get a move on, and to prevent them from remaining bogged down by their own convictions. Naturally everyone has the right to refuse to adopt any given point of view, but he has no excuse at all for not finding out first exactly what that point of view is and getting to know more about it. Before pontificating on someone, even if there are points on which it would serve no useful purpose to dialogue with him, one should at least listen to what he has to say. For Muslims in particular let me say that sometimes ideas which are considered very dangerous can turn out to be very salutary, if only as a scouring agent. Naturally this only takes place when they act as a type of revulsive on a well-formed and attentive conscience. Otherwise the sole result could be to hasten the collapse and complete disintegration of worm-eaten structures. Such a danger is so real, in the present state of Islam, that attention has to be called to it.

However neither Islam nor any other belief in God has any choice today other than to accept the challenge. Science is advancing daily, and more deeply, into areas of the universe which were formerly shrouded in mystery, and asking questions which no philosophy and theology dare ignore if they wish to respect the fundamental nature of man. Science obliges us all to think more, and it constrains believers to re-read their Revelation in the light of new problems. Is it necessary to stress that our answer cannot be some simple yet vague form of concordism, such as has often been proposed by Muslims since the *nahda?* Hence the need to explore every avenue and to tune into every transmission.

A new exegesis, which does not have to turn its back on past wealth and positive advances, will have to be worked out in a climate of adventure, of exchange of ideas, and of urgency to keep up to date and to settle all the doubts of our day. By creating such a fertile climate of tension, which has so dramatically been lacking in Islam for centuries, dialogue could play the role of shaking Muslims out of their false sense of security and could make their hearts and ears once more attentive to the Message of God. For if the Word of God is eternal, as every Muslim believes, it follows necessarily that, though revealed in time and space, it transcends all temporal and spatial characteristics, and remains always and everywhere perceptible, present and forever new. It must therefore be perceived and accepted, not in a static manner, but rather as a set of properties and potentialities which are to be brought into actual existence by means of ceaseless research. This is not necessarily a revolutionary request. Many exegetes in the past have felt the need for just this sort of thing, because they had rightly become fascinated by the depths of meaning in the Qur'anic word whose exuberant vitality sweeps aside all linguistic barriers. Hence the necessity of listening to God with our present day understanding, listening to Him in the here-and-now of the present moment. The re-launching of a modern type of exegesis, inspired by both daring and prudence, and well aware of the anguish, restlessness and questioning of our day, is therefore imperative if God is not to be banished from the world, but is to become present again in human activity. But it can develóp only in a climate of dialogue open to all, both believers and non-believers.

Such an exegesis has a bounden duty to incorporate everything it can absorb, without any sort of fear or complex. Certainly there is a real danger of crises arising, of deviations taking place and of people losing their way, and such dangers should not be minimised. But is it not the natural vocation of a religion to be in a perpetual state of crisis, always striving to develop fully? In his efforts to understand correctly the Message of God the believer cannot afford to ignore the advances, even of a provisional nature, made by modern scholars in every branch of the exact sciences and human disciplines. Besides, the problem today does not concern orthodoxy or heterodoxy. Has there ever been such a thing as Truth pure, limpid and impervious? Is such truth within man's grasp? Is not Truth like the distant star that guides the traveller on his way, rather than a burning torch that is carried with confidence? The Qur'ân tells us: "Hold you fast to God's bond together, and do not scatter" (Q.3,103). Is not this bond both mooring rope and Ariadne's thread? Tradition adds: whoever makes a sincere effort to reflect and reach his destination is doubly rewarded; whoever makes a sincere effort to reflect but fails to reach his destination will nevertheless be rewarded once. In fact only the fearful, who refuse the rope which draws them nearer to God and prefer to remain immobile and to wallow in stagnation, will be refused a reward. The reward will be reserved for those who make an effort, examine their consciences, and practice their faith in all sincerity and with fervour. Now the precise purpose of dialogue, whatever the circumstances, is to reanimate constantly our faith, to save it from tepidity, and to maintain us in a permanent state of *ijtihâd,* that is a state of reflection and research.

Conclusion: The Horizon Before Us

Where will such research, carried on in an open-minded spirit and not in isolation, lead us? Nobody can say precisely. It is an adventure which we must engage in day by day. Will religious unity be found at the end of the maze? "In the long term, of course," writes W. Montgomery Watt, "it is to be expected that there will be one religion for the whole world, though it may contain within itself permitted variations, comparable to the four permitted legal rites *(madhâhib)* in Sunnî Islam."[17] This perspective is not necessarily at variance with Islam. To the verses we have already quoted let us add this one: "The Messenger believes in what has been sent down to him from his Lord. He and the believers (in Islam), all of them believe in God and His angels and in His Books and His Messengers; we make no division between any one of His Messengers. They say 'We have heard and we obey. Our Lord, grant us Thy forgiveness; unto thee is the homecoming." (Q.2,285)

As far as classical Muslim theology is concerned, it has always proclaimed that the Light of God will finally disperse all darkness and will shine equally for all. "They desire to extinguish with their mouths the light of God; but God will perfect His light, though the unbelievers be adverse." (Q.61,8)

Meanwhile divergences continue and show little sign of fading away, at least in the foreseeable future. One must believe that they have their role to play in the economy of salvation and of the world, among other things by giving an impetus to evolution. Let me give some further quotations from the Qurân:

> "To every one of you We have appointed a right way and an open road. If God had willed, He would have made you one Community; but that He might try you in what has come to you. So be you forward in good works; unto God shall you return all together; and He will tell you of that whereon you were at variance." (Q.5,48)
>
> "Mankind were only one community, then they fell into variance. But for a word that proceeded from thy Lord, it had been decided between them already touching their differences.
> They say: 'If only a sign (casting light on this mystery) had been

sent down on him from his Lord.' Say: 'The Mystery *(ghayb)* of
God is inscrutable. Then watch and wait; I shall be with you
watching and waiting.' '' (Q.10,18-19)

''Say: 'O my God, Creator of the Heavens and the Earth, who
knowest all things visible and invisible, Thou wilt judge in the end
between Thy servants touching that whereon they are at variance.' '' (Q.39,46)

Thus when all is said and done, we find ourselves faced with the unfathom-
able mystery of God's Plan and of man's condition. So we must accept our
differences and disagreements, and by competing with one another in good
works, shorten the time in which the trial of our disagreements will come to an
end. We must also forego expecting too much from dialogue if we are to avoid
bitterness and discouragement and be able to make progress, come wind or
wild weather. For we must not have any illusions on this point: whatever the
precautions we take there will be many discordant voices. Nobody has ever
found in the past a magic wand which could eliminate misunderstandings and
radically change the world. We should not expect one to turn up in the future.
Dialogue means unending patience. If it helps us to draw gradually nearer to
one another, to replace indifference or hostile reserve by real friendship, by
true brotherhood even, in spite of our different beliefs and opinions, it will
have already accomplished much. Dialogue does not necessarily mean finding a common solution; still less does it imply an absolute need to come to an
agreement. Its role is rather to clarify and open up the debate still more,
allowing all those engaged to progress, instead of becoming immutably fixed
in their own convictions. The way towards the Kingdom of Light will prove to
be a long one, and God has chosen to enshroud it in mystery.

There is no need to stress, of course, that these ideas come not from a
professional theologian but from an historian who, by specialising in
Medieval History, has come to realise how equally sincere love of God and of
Truth was able to degenerate till it lead to catastrophe. Besides, living as we
do today in a century of re-examination, of contestation, in which the bounds
of the Universe are continually expanding, we can no longer practise *qu'ûd* or
kitmân, that is to say we cannot afford to give ourselves up to an easy going,
lukewarm indifference while we wait for some miracle or other which would
re-instate Islam in History by enchantment, without effort or suffering on our
part.

''Work, and God will surely see you work, and His Messenger,
and the believers.'' (Q.9,105)

translated by L. MARCHANT

"Christianity and Islam"

Footnotes

1)   We should mention two meetings organized by the World Council of Churches, the first at Geneva-Cartigny in March 1969, the second, a year later, at Beirut-Ajaltoun. Buddhists and Hindus assisted at this second meeting. The book Les Musulmans, Paris, Beauchesne, coll. *Verse et Controverse no. 14, 1971, is also a form of dialogue. It clearly brings out the difficulties we have emphasised and on which we shall have to insist further. We should also mention a discussion, reported in the daily paper* Le Monde *(28/6/71), which, on the initiative of the Fédération Protestante de France, brought together some sixty people in a meeting chaired by Professor Fathi Abd El-Moneim of Al-Azhar University, Cairo, and Professor Roger Arnaldez of the Université de Paris IV.*

2)   See for example the review Esprit, *October 1967, which deals with the topic of* "Nouveau monde et Parole de Dieu"; *as well as the issue of November 1971 where the following question is asked:* "Réinventer l'Eglise?"

3)   Review of the book by G.C. ANAWATI and L. GARDET, Les grands problémes de la théologie musulmane, *(i.e.) L. GARDET,* Dieu et la destinée de l'homme) *in* Arabica *16(1969) p. 102.*

4)   cf.Q.33,72 (Ed.)

5)   Les Musulmans, Paris, Beauschene, 1971, p. 125.

6)   Islamic Revelation in the Modern World, Edinburgh, 1969, p. 121.

7)   Neuchatel, 1949, p. 147.

8)   Esprit, new series, April 1971, pp. 610-611.

9)   The text given here by Professor Talbi is closer to the third draft of Nostra Aetate *than to the final document approved by the Council. cf.* Vatican II. Les relations de l'Eglise avec les religions non-chrétiennes, *Paris, Cerf, coll. Unam Sanctam 61, 1966, pp. 206, 303. (Ed.)*

10)   Vers un dialogue islamo-chrétien, in Revue Thomiste *64(1964) p. 627; see also R. CASPAR,* La foi musulmane selon le Coran, *in* Proche Orient Chrétien *19(1969) pp. 167-172 (off-print pp. 67-72).*

11)   Cairo edition, 1319/1901 pp. 75-78; see also R. CASPAR, Le salut des non-musulmans d'aprés Ghazâlî, *in* IBLA *31(1968) pp. 301-313.*

12)   Cf.Tafsîr al-Manâr, 1st edition, 1346/1927-8, vol. 1, pp. 333-5. Rashîd Ridâ (1865-1935), a disciple of Muhammed ʿAbduh, takes up his master's commentary and continues it in the same spirit. In particular he makes clear that: "It is equally evident in this verse that the condition of faith in the prophecy of Muhammad – may the blessing of God be upon him – is not required. In fact the Qurʾanic discourse here concerns the way in which Almighty God will treat all religions (firâq), or all communities (umam), whose members believe in a given prophet and a specific revelation which is addressed to them, and who think that their salvation (fawz) in the future life is more or less assured by the sole fact that they are Muslims, Jews, Christians or Sabaeans. For their benefit God makes it clear that salvation is not the automatic result of belonging sociologically to any given religion (lâ yakûnu bi-l-jinsîyât al-dîniyya). On the contrary it depends both on the sincerity of one's faith (îmân sahîh) and on activity which improves the lot of men. Thus it is denied that the question of salvation can be settled by God in accordance with the vain desires (amânî) *of Muslims or of those who possess the Ancient Scriptures. On the contrary, it is affirmed that it is conditioned just as much by virtuous activity as by sincere faith." (Vol. I, p. 336).*

(Professor Talbi points out in the continuation of this note that the majority of Muslims give a less liberal interpretation to this verse, considering it to be abrogated by Q.3, 85: "Whose desires to profess a religion other than Islam, it shall not be accepted of him; in the next world he shall be among the losers." For Talbi this verse, taken in its context, means "that one cannot, at the same time, be intimately persuaded that the Message handed on by Muhammad is true and yet refuse to listen to it for all sorts of social reasons, through pride or self-esteem, etc., or change sides whenever one's material interests suggest doing so. Such people, and such people only – whatever their religious persuasion – slam the door of salvation in their own faces ...On the contrary, those who, in all sincerity, and good faith, fail to discover the way of Islam and make use of other roads to salvation, will all the same be rewarded according to the effort they make. So there is no contradiction between Q.2,62 and 3,85 when we see them in their proper context and in the general direction indicated by Qur'anic preaching. In fact only those will lose their way who fail to seek God.")

13)   *Cf.* Les Musulmans *referred to in note 1).*

14)   *Le monothéisme dans le monde contemporain, in MIDEO 8(1964-6) pp. 407-422.*

15)   *AL-ᶜAQQAD, ᶜAbqarîyat al-Masîh, Cairo 1952, re-edited 1958 under the title* Hayât al-Masîh; KAMIL HUSAYN, Qaryatun zalima, Cairo 1954; KHALID M. KHALID, Maᶜan ᶜalâ al-tarîq, Muhammed wa-l-Masîh, Cairo 1958; JUDAH AL6SAHHAR, Al-Masîh ᶜIsâ b. Maryam, Cairo 1959; FATHI ᶜUTHMAN, Maᶜa al-Masîh fî-l-anâjîl al-arbaᶜa, Beirut, 1962; ᶜABD AL-KARIM AL-KHATIB, al-Masîh fî-l-Qurân, wa-l-tawrât, wa-l-injîl, Cairo 1966.*

16)   *Vers un dialogue islamo-chrétien, in* Revue Thomiste 64(1964) p. 627.

17)   Islamic Revelation in the Modern World, *Edinburgh 1969, p. 127.*

V

Christians and Muslims in Britain

D uring the past thirty or so years, the arrival of large numbers of Muslims, Hindus, Sikhs and others in Britain has brought to the attention of Christians their new "multi-faith" situation and their own responsibility toward people of other faiths.

The emphasis here is perhaps mostly on what the World Council of Churches has called "Living in Dialogue."* For the British response to these new citizens has been in the fields of housing, social services, education, health, employment; the religious dimension however is generally well appreciated by secular as well as by religious organisations.

Christian-Muslim relations in Britain, while in some respects resembling those on the Continent of Europe, are distinguished by factors which are significant.

(i) The presence in Britain of numerous members of other faiths apart from

Miss Penelope Johnstone, born in Surrey (U.K.), studied in Oxford where she presented her Ph.D. thesis on Arabic Botany and Pharmacology *with particular reference to the work of al-Zahrawi and Ibn Juljul in Muslim Spain in 1974. After working at the Centre for Study of Islam and Christian-Muslim Relations, Selly Oak Colleges at Birmingham (U.K.), Miss P. Johnstone taught Arabic at Manchester University and is now Research Associate at Cambridge University (Genizah Unit, University Library).*

This essay is taken from Islamochristiana. 7. 81, 167-199, and is reprinted by permission of the publishers.

"Christianity and Islam"

Islam means that the emphasis is upon "interfaith": upon multilateral rather than Christian-Muslim relations.

(ii) While a certain number of the Muslims may be visitors or temporary residents, the majority are intending to stay permanently. Thus the situation of such people is not that of "guest-workers," but of British citizens — by virtue of the former status of their countries of origin — and the British educational and other systems will have to cater for them accordingly.

(iii) In Britain — England, Wales and Scotland — the Catholic Church is still in somewhat of a minority situation, and the main initiative in interfaith matters is taken by the Anglican (Established) Church and by the British Council of Churches (BCC) whose membership is composed of the major Christian churches in Britain, although the Catholic Church is not yet a member.

The absence of any Catholic organisation specifically for "relations with people of other faiths" could be, not a drawback, but an advantage; ecumenical sharing is particularly important in this field of interfaith work. Responsibility does not rest with a commission or committee, but each diocese, parish, group or individual needs to be informed about the local situation, the needs and opportunities, and initiatives undertaken by other churches.

It would be virtually impossible to survey the entire field of Christian-Muslim relations in Britain. Much is done on an informal basis, and local projects and meetings are not necessarily publicised.

The response of the Churches, and of Christians, like that of government organisations, can be documented by reference to the growth and development of official bodies and committees to cover specific areas of concern.

This paper will be divided into the following sections:

I. Muslims in Britain: background
II. British response: Government
III. Muslims in Britain: mosques, organisations
IV. British response: Religious Education
        Christian groups and organisations
V. British Churches: British Council of Churches
        Anglican Church

Every effort has been made to present an overall picture of Christian-Muslim relations in Britain, and to avoid any generalisations. However, some cities, regions or projects have been mentioned in greater detail, as being typical of many others. Selection has had to depend largely on material available, from a variety of sources: visits, interviews, correspondence, study documents, church and government publications; with reference wherever possible to relevant published material. It is hoped that the lists at the end might be useful. My sincere thanks to those who have helped with information and advice; especially the Centre for the Study of Islam and Christian-Muslim Relations, Birmingham, the British Council of Churches, and the Farmington Institute, Oxford.

Christians and Muslims in Britain

Roman Catholic Church
United Reformed Church, Methodists, others
VI. Interfaith Groups: Multi-faith
Jewish-Christian-Muslim
VII. Study Centres and Educational concerns.

I. Muslims in Britain: Background

(1) Generalities[1]

Muslims, with some 1¼ million members in this country at a rough estimate, form easily the largest minority religious group in the United Kingdom.[2] They are probably also in some respects the best-organised, and the most likely to attract attention through their religious and cultural requirements and their wish to present Islam in a favorable light to a supposedly mainly Christian population.

In Britain, there has often been a certain emphasis upon the Arabic nature of Islam; trade and other links with the Middle East, the study of Arabic and classical Islam at universities, have contributed to this. There is also, however, a traditional close relationship with the Indian subcontinent, dating from days of trade and empire. Arabs, although so influential in Islamic affairs, are actually a minority not only world-wide but also in Britain. Most of the Muslims here are from the Indian sub-continent, bringing with them their national culture and customs. There are in addition Turkish Cypriots, and some West Indian Muslims.

Most Christians would probably think of the Muslims in Britian primarily in terms of their nationality, language, and occupation. It is not always realised to what an extent "religious" aspects are inseparable from "cultural." Britian's Muslims could be classified broadly as:

(a) students, undergraduate or postgraduate: Arab, Indian, Iranian, Malaysian; at university, polytechnic, language school; in large towns and cities; single men and women, or men with their wives and families;

(b) diplomatic and business personnel, sometimes with their households; from the Gulf States, Saudi Arabia, etc.; mainly in London and large cities;

(c) professional and business men: often Indian; in large cities;

(d) immigrant workers, at various levels including the highly skilled, but the majority as small shopkeepers or semi-skilled labour; transport, industry, especially textiles; from Pakistan, India or Bangladesh, and some Arabs; industrial areas of cities, inner city areas.

It is the last group which is by far the most numerous, and these are mainly persons intending to stay in Britain permanently.

(2) Patterns of immigration

In the late 19th and early 20th century there were already in Britain some small groups of Muslims, mostly seamen; Arabs from Aden and Yemen, Indians from Bengal, Gujarat, Punjab and Sind. Some married local girls and settled near the dock areas in ports such as Tyneside, London, Cardiff. During this same period, other Muslims, students and professional men, spent varying periods of time in Britain, but on the whole did not form themselves into any organised groups.[3]

During the two World Wars, Muslims were recruited for service with the army or on transport ships; when hostilities were over, some settled in Britain and took up employment.

The post-war period, from 1945 onwards, saw the greatest amount of immigration. The partition of India in 1947, and the subsequent refugee problem, caused a number of Pakistani citizens to migrate to Britain, mainly from rural areas. A little later came Turkish Cypriots, their migration motivated by both the disturbances and the state of the economy in Cyprus. These numbers were added to by the arrival of Asians from East Africa, noticeably those forcibly expelled from Uganda, and smaller numbers from West Africa.[4]

These "ethnic minorities" (the usual official term for non-indigenous national groups) are composed mainly of those who migrated to Britain from the "New Commonwealth" (which includes India, Cyprus and the West Indies) and Pakistan, and of their descendants. Since 1972 Pakistan (formerly West Pakistan) and Bangladesh (formerly East Pakistan) have been separate countries. People from Pakistan, Bangladesh and India, are generally referred to collectively as "Asians," though they differ widely in culture and language. The Asian groups in particular have tended to settle in the industrial Midlands and Northwest, and in large cities such as London, Birmingham and Glasgow.[5]

Immigration patterns have changed over the years. At first, it was usual for adult males of working age to come from Pakistan or India, with the aim of earning sufficient money to acquire property or set up in business on their return to the home country. Some decided to settle: these brought over wives and families, and the whole character of the Asian groups in Britain developed from being essentially a working population, fairly self-contained, to a community with more normal age and sex distribution, and with far more contact with the indigenous community at every level.

This tendency was accelerated by the passing of the 1962 Commonwealth Immigration Act, which limited the numbers coming to Britain, but allowed dependents to join Asians already in employment here.

In a fairly extensive documentation on ethnic minority groups, attention has been directed primarily to their social, economic and cultural adaptation, their solidarity as a community, and their educational needs. It is fully acknowledged that religion plays a vary large part in the lives of Hindus, Sikhs and especially Muslims.[6]

Despite efforts made by the various agencies involved, there are considerable pressures acting against any "assimilation" or "integration" of the Pakistani settlers. One researcher argues that "analysis of the home society, the migration process and the ongoing relationship of both with the overseas settlement is essential to an understanding of an ethnic minority in Britain." For, in the case of so many from overseas, "life in Britain is perceived as an extension of life back home."[7]

Christians and Muslims in Britain

"We are now part of a society which is multi-cultural and multi-religious." Such statements are heard frequently, and underline the fact that Britain is no longer considered a mainly Christian country. But terms such as "multi-faith," "multi-cultural" are often used without any clear definition as to their meaning. Would "multi-ethnic" be a better term? Have we an amalgam, an assimilation, or a simple juxtaposition, of the elements of our mixed society today?

The question of this terminology and its implications has been examined recently by John McIntyre, Professor of Divinity in the University of Edinburgh. "Multi-cultural," he claims, is a very complex term, for culture is "the expression . . . of fundamental ideas and concepts, values and convictions, attitudes and emotions, acknowledged and recognised by, as well as being acceptable to, a community or society."[8] What then do we have in Britain? Are there many cultures existing side by side? Is one dominant, with other subordinate but independent? Is a dominant culture challenged by a counter-culture?

Professor McIntyre queries the assumption that "the arrival of immigrants holding other faiths should in a fairly short passage of time create a multi-cultural and multi-faith society of one which had until then been mono-lithically uni-cultural and uni-faith." In fact Britain was never all that uniform, although the events of recent years have accentuated our "mixed" society; as for Western culture as a whole, even in medieval days, it "was constantly under challenge from Islam."

The whole situation is now, unfortunately, seen against the background of civil disturbances during 1981, which draw more attention than all the peaceful moves and initiatives in every part of the country. To call such troubles "race riots" would be far too simple; causes are complex and deep-rooted, to say nothing of the possibility of outside interference. Many agencies, government and church bodies, have done their best to respond to the situation and to encourage the more positive aspects of "multi-cultural" Britain.

II. British Response: Government

(1) Generalities

The arrival of a large group of overseas people in any area can cause tensions, especially in an inner city with problems of housing and employment. Various authorities have made efforts to encourage mutual understanding and to prevent difficulties or hardships. In 1968 there was established the Community Relations Commission (CRC) to foster and develop understanding and bring about "harmonious community relations" in Britain. Some of its publications highlight specific problems of Asians.[9]

In 1977, under the Race Relations Act, the CRC merged with another body, the Race Relations Board, to become the Commission for Racial Equality (CRE). Its duties were envisaged as:

(a) working towards the elimination of discrimination;

(b) promoting equality of opportunity and good relations between persons of different racial groups generally; and

(c) keeping under review the working of the Act, and, when required by the Secretary of State or when it otherwise thinks it necessary, to draw up and submit to the Secretary of State proposals for amending it.

Its duties are thus informative, supervisory and advisory. The CRE has produced various booklets of information with statistical details on immigration, distribution of national and ethnic groups, educational priorities etc.[10]

At a local level, there are regional and urban Community Relations Commissions, who can more easily perceive local needs and help to integrate ethnic minority groups into the community.

(2) *Education*

Education is seen by authorities throughout the country as an area of particular concern. Teaching clearly has to meet the needs of immigrant children and of their families, and also of children living here who have to adapt to the presence of many non-British children in schools. Teachers themselves need help in understanding the background, beliefs and customs of their pupils. Colleges of Education are increasingly coming to realise the need for information and awareness, and "multi-cultural education" seeks to equip both British and ethnic minority children for life in Britain today.[11]

One of the priorities is language teaching. This has come to mean not only extra help with English for children arriving from overseas, and for the adult members of a family, but teaching of their own language and culture to Asian children growing up in Britain. A recent European Community (EEC) directive calls for mother-tongue teaching for ethnic minority children, and this is a question which has not yet been fully responded to by British education authorities.[12] At present, the ethnic minority language is generally taught outside school hours, the community providing its own teachers. In the case of Muslims, the language will be probably Urdu, sometimes Punjabi, along with Qur'ân classes. Turkish language classes are organised in the evenings, at ten schools in London, by the Cyprus Turkish Association. An estimated 600 or so children attend, aged from 7 to 16, for classes in Turkish language and culture.

The importance of mother-tongue teaching is stressed by the Linguistic Minorities Project, a three-year research project funded by the Department of Education and Science, whose main brief is "to provide an account and analysis of the changing patterns of bilingualism in several regions of England." Their research covers adolescents, adults and children inside and outside school, and will include the collection of all details about the provision of mother-tongue teaching in Britain.

(3) *Health*

In times of sickness or accident, any religious and cultural sensitivities are likely to be accentuated, and communication may become difficult. Health authorities often find a need to inform newly arrived immigrants, especially women, about basic health requirements and preventive measures. In some areas health education leaflets are printed in Urdu, Punjabi, Bengali, etc. as appropriate. Language teaching, especially to immigrant women, often focusses upon such situations as visits to the baby clinic, diet and other related subjects where the climate and customs of the home country are very different from those in Britain.

Hospital regulations can cause difficulty and distress; it is important that hospital staff should be aware of various customs and beliefs connected with diet, birth, death and burial. In an effort to improve understanding at all levels, the Lothian Community Relations Council (Edinburgh) has produced a booklet which gives basic information on religious needs of other faith communities.[13] A leaflet "Health Care of Ethnic minorities in Britain," giving a few guidelines and suggestions, has been produced by the Mission and Other Faiths Committee of the United Reformed Church.[14]

A short section in the BCC's *Guidelines . . .* mentions Hospital Chaplaincies and the Pastoral Care of Sick People of Other Faiths, and quotes from "A Handbook on Hospital Chaplaincy" published by the Church Information Office. The BCC itself, in conjunction with the Hospital Chaplaincies Board of the Church of England, will be publishing *Ministry to Others: A Handbook for Hospital Chaplains Concerned with People of Other Faiths and Cultures*. They point out the need for medical, nursing and administrative staff also to be "involved in dialogue with people of other faiths about wholeness and healing in the search for a better human community."[15]

III. Muslims in Britain

(1) *Mosques*

The acquisition of a place for the ritual prayer is one of the first concerns of a local Muslim community, whether by adapting a house or other building or, later, constructing a purpose-built mosque, where the size and permanence of the community and its funds permit this. The first of such were built in the 1890's, in Woking and Liverpool. The number of mosques today is hard to estimate, since a *masjid* varies from a converted terrace house, or a rebuilt warehouse, to a large *jami'* mosque.

These latter, built with considerable financial support from the Muslim community locally and abroad, have existed since the 1960s at Manchester and South Shields; since 1970s at Preston (two, 1970 and 1974), London, Regent's Park, Birmingham; and new in 1981 are those at Glasgow and Bristol. In some places, redundant church property has been acquired by the Muslims for use as a place of worship. In Manchester a former small chapel is now a "Muslim Academy."

(a) *Preston*. Immigration on a large scale began in the 1950s, and the 1975 estimate was of approx. 6,000 Muslims. During the 1960s buildings began to be adapted for use as mosques, and in the 1970s two new mosques were built. Preston has been particularly well documented, in a book *Islam in Preston* for use locally by schools and other institutions, which relates universal Islam to its practice among Muslims in Preston.[16]

(b) *Bristol.* The number of Muslims has been estimated at approx. 5,000, immigration having begun during the late 1950s. In 1973 there were two mosques, one for Sunni Pakistanis in an old church, one for Ahmadiyya in a house. Pakistanis (Christian and Muslim) in Bristol have been documented in a book by P. Jeffery, *Migrants and Refugees.*[17] The new mosque, used as such for several years but only finally completed in 1981, was originally a Free Church chapel, and the design is by an Egyptian architect, who is active in the local community. The pitched roof has been replaced with a flat roof and large fibreglass dome. The building has been given other Islamic external details, and the interior is pleasant. There are offices and a room for social gatherings below the main prayer hall, which has a women's room to the side.[18]

(c) *Glasgow.* The Muslim community may be approx. 8,000, for whom there are seven mosques. A new and very splendid one is being built in a central position near the river; due to be finished during 1981, at an estimated cost of about L. 5 million, of which Saudi Arabia has donated a sizeable amount. The design incorporates in the dome some characteristics of a lantern tower, a traditional Scottish structure. The main *masjid* is approx. 10,000 sq. ft., to hold 1,400 persons; women's gallery on the first floor, approx. 1,400 sq. ft., for 200 persons; there is a community hall and a basement area.

(d) *London:* Regent's Park. Proposals for a mosque in London were put forward in the 1920s, and in 1940 the British Government agreed to purchase a site which was handed over to the Mosque Committee in 1944, at which time the Islamic Cultural Centre was established in Regent's Park. The present Mosque Trust was set up in 1947; in 1973 a design was approved, and work began the following year. The mosque is now virtually complete, with golden dome and tall minaret. The estimated congregation at Eid time is about 15,000. As a centre for Muslims in London and the rest of Britain, the Mosque aims at fostering unity among the Muslims and representing Islamic views and interests. There are a library, several large classrooms, and a residential unit. The Mosque runs an educational programme for Muslim children in London, and arranges classes in Arabic and Islamic studies.[19]

Other new mosques have been projected for London: e.g. at Queensgate, for the Shi'i Muslims.

(e) *Dublin.* A house is used as the Islamic Centre for the local Muslims, of whom there are several hundred, mostly students. The Centre has an upper floor which serves as mosque for men, downstairs a large room which is the office and library, and used by women on Fridays for prayer. The basement kitchen caters for the *Iftar* meal during Ramadan. Arabs are in the majority here, but there are also Muslims from Pakistan and Malaysia, and some have married local women, who have themselves become Muslims.

(f) *Edinburgh.* A Muslim Students' Association has mostly Arab mem-

bers; resident Muslims in the city are mainly Pakistanis, with a few Moroccans and Tunisians. The Muslim population is estimated at about 1,500, with
a congregation of some 250 to 300 for the Friday prayer, which is held in the
"mosque," a room in a flat owned by the Muslim Students' Association.
Some hundred or so children come here for religion instruction from the
Imam. Marriages are solemnised in the mosque, and funerals can be carried
out; the community has a section of one of the city's cemeteries. The mosque
is represented on the local Community Relations Committee, and participates in the Interfaith circle.

Muslim communities in other cities of Britain have been the subject of
study, for instance Bradford in Yorkshire,[20] and Huddersfield (see note 6).

(2) *Muslim organisations*

A number of small, generally local, Muslim advisory groups cared for the
needs of the community in the early stages. As numbers increased, larger,
national organisations were established, concerned with education, welfare,
da'wa and other matters.

In 1962 was established the U.K. Islamic Mission; and in 1966 the Islamic
Foundation in Leicester, which reflects views of the *Jama'at-i-Islam*. The
Islamic Foundation publishes books on Islam, especially on economics and
legal matters; and has recently begun a newsletter called "Focus on Christian-Muslim relations." In 1980 it published *The Muslim Guide:* For teachers,
employers, community workers and social administrators in Britain, giving
clear and detailed accounts of the religious and other requirements of Muslims at work, at home and in hospital; it does tend to assume that all concessions are to be unilateral, however.[21]

The Muslim Educational Trust, founded in 1964, seeks to promote Islam
and to facilitate religious instruction. It is registered as a charity with the
Department of Education and Science. The Trust provides peripatetic
teachers to visit schools where there are large numbers of Muslim children,
and has published First and Second Primers of Islamic teaching, and Primers
in Urdu.[22]

The Union of Muslim Organisations (UMO) was formed in July 1970 with
the aim of "co-ordinating the activities of all Muslim organisations in Britain
and thus evolving a united approach to solve the several problems confront-
ing the Muslim community." An Education Committee was formed in September 1971, to prepare a Syllabus for Muslim education, and also "blue-
prints for the establishment of an Islamic university in Britain."[23]

The call for separate Muslim schools has often been voiced in recent years,
and has met with a mixed reception, not only from the authorities but from
various sections of the Muslim community. It is not clear to what extent
Muslim parents really wish their children to receive instruction outside the
British educational system — a system which, whatever its failings, is likely
to provide the best openings in employment and further studies in Britain.
The Committee, however, saw its responsibility towards the future genera-

tion of Muslims as "to provide an Islamic environment," thus "enabling them to uphold the highest traditions of Islamic morality and ethics."

A National Conference on Islamic Education was held in London in July 1974. Its report, published as *Islamic Education and Single Sex Schools*, concentrated on this point which it considered the main priority. Following the UMO's eighth annual conference, in 1978, a National Muslim Educational Council was formed.[24]

Islamic instruction is generally provided outside school hours, probably in the local mosque, with the imam or a senior member of the Islamic community giving classes in Qur'ân reading. In a large centre there will be several classes each with a volunteer teacher. Such "mosque schools" are often highly organised, and children may attend for two hours or more every evening. Instruction is along traditional lines.

Muslims in Britain face two main problems concerning the religious education of their children: firstly, that Islamic religious instruction follows a pattern which does not harmonise well with the western system; secondly, that there can be difficulty in obtaining suitably qualified teachers. Often an imam will be brought from Pakistan, and until very recently any Islamic qualification could only be gained in India, Pakistan or an Arab country. The latter problem has been partly faced, and gave rise to the idea of founding an Islamic training establishment in Britain.

"Dᾳrul uloom"

In 1974 a section of the Muslim community acquired a large disused hospital near Bury, in the north-west of England. This was extensively renovated and adapted for use as a *madrasa,* and in 1975 "Darul Uloom al Arabiya al Islamiya" (sic) was formally opened. Part of the "Opening Ceremony" speaks for itself:

«Allah ... has sent us far away from the Islamic countries to the greatest dark abode of Europe ... we have not been sent here only for worldly purposes but our greatest purpose is to preach Islam and Islamic education ... We shall have to transform our entire life into an Islamic society which should give an invitation of Islamic way of life to the European civilisation which has itself reached the self-speaking abyss of destruction ... It greatly depends upon this generation of ours which is growing in this country».[25]

Admission at first was to be only for students above the age of 16, but with the hope that eventually secondary education would be provided also. Students were to follow a strict daily time-table, with prayers, Qur'ân study, and classes in orthodox Islamic teachings.

"Darul Uloom" represents a specific rather rigid approach to Islamic education, and would seem to make little concession to western methods and systems. This approach arouses considerable scepticism, alike among British educationalists and representatives of some Islamic organisations.

Active in the field of education and *da'wa* is Minaret House, a small private publishing firm in Croydon. It produces good quality educational works:

books for children and teaching materials. In 1977 it began the publication of *Minaret*, an "Islamic educational review" with articles, book reviews and news. While leaning strongly to the side of piety and orthodoxy, it is more open than are most Islamic publications to a variety of opinions.

The Muslim Institute for Research and Planning, concerned mainly with education, has strong Iranian connections.

The Islamic Council of Europe, established in May 1973 with headquarters in London, seeks to integrate the Muslims of Britain with those on the Continent, where it has constituent organisations. It is recognised by the Islamic Secretariat, Jeddah, as the representative body for Muslims in Europe.

The Muslim Women's Association, based in London, holds meetings for its members, and publishes the *Muslim Woman*: stencilled format, with short articles, news of meetings and activities, recipes, a short section for children with pious injunctions and little stories. The Association supports various charities, including a scheme for a hostel for Muslim girls in London.

In May 1980 an organisation known as Tehrik i Nizam i Quran and Sunnah organised a "1400 years Festival of Islam" - exhibition and seminar, in South London.

Other Muslim Groups

The Isma'ilis have a Research Centre in London, and are building a new Centre in South Kensington, with financial support from the Aga Khan trust funds. A journal *Ilm* is published by "H. H. The Aga Khan Shia Imami Ismailia Association for the U.K." in London.

The Ahmadiyyah are fairly vocal in proportion to their comparatively small numbers, and are active in *da'wah*. Both sections are represented in the UK, the Movement having begun work in London before the split occurred. In 1912, a small mission was established; in 1913, publication of the *Islamic Review* was started, and the mission was transferred to Woking where a mosque already existed. This mission is affiliated to the Ahmadiyyah Anjuman Ishā'at Islam of Lahore, the more moderate branch.

The other branch, the Qādiānis, although they do not make much use of this name, are represented by the London Mosque Gressenhall Road, London. They publish and distribute leaflets on Islam, and publish a small monthly, *Muslim Herald*.[25a]

Students

Most Universities have an Islamic Society, and sometimes more than one, allowing for national groups: Pakistan Islamic Society, Iraqi or Turkish Islamic Society, etc. While some students may become less observant on arrival in Britain, others make a conscious effort to be even more devout than they would be at home, and there can be both national and religious pressure upon a student. Orthodoxy can also be a reaction against what is seen as the decadence of western society: a reason specifically put forward by some Malaysian women students, who have adopted a rigid way of life and wear the long brown robes and white veil.

"Christianity and Islam"

The Students' Islamic Society is responsible for finding a place for Friday prayer for its members. In some cases the Students' Union does not allow religious gatherings on its premises, and prayer may take place in a room loaned by the University chaplaincy. The use of such a room can occasionally lead to an implied sense of proprietorship by the Islamic Society; but on the whole, Christians and Muslims within a university are mutually tolerant. In Birmingham University, for one, the Muslims pray on Fridays in a large room in St. Francis Hall, the ecumenical centre for the University; on this occasion, the Catholics who use this room move downstairs to a smaller one. Discussions and meetings are sometimes arranged, though there is scope for more frequent and informal meeting. An Islamic Society may have a strong sense of its missionary and educational responsibilities.

The Federation of Islamic Students Societies (FOSIS) is the central body to which all individual societies can relate. FOSIS publishes a "Muslim Student Guide to UK and Eire," listing useful information, advice, addresses etc. In the 1977 edition there are 32 constituent societies, 37 associated societies, and 13 other Student Societies in contact with FOSIS.

Muslim organisations: local

The Birmingham area has a particularly large number of Muslims, the majority from Pakistan. The large purpose-built mosque in Balsall Heath caters for these, and is a centre for various activities; it welcomes groups of visitors, and had more than once received a joint Muslim-Christian conference on questions of topical concern. The Sparkbrook Mosque is equally hospitable, though with somewhat smaller premises — in converted terrace houses — and similarly has held conversations and discussions between Christians and Muslims, as well as welcoming visitors for Eid celebrations.

Also in Birmingham, the Muslim Education Consultative Committee runs classes in Arabic, Urdu and Islamic Theology; in July 1980 it held a Day Conference on "Islam and Education in Britain." Under its auspices a Resource Centre had been established, at the Muslim Youth and Cultural Association.

In Birmingham is the Paigham-e-Islam Trust, with a library, *madrasa* and classes. Its small monthly publication, the *Young Muslim,* is inclined towards controversial topics, giving a unilateral view, in its enthusiasm to spread Islamic teachings and encourage young Muslims to religious fervour.

In Bradford, also a centre of Muslim settlement, is a branch of the Islamic Youth Movement UK. Part of its promotion of Islam consists of a small stencilled quarterly *The Movement.*

British Muslims

An Association for British Muslims was founded in 1973; estimates of membership vary from 400 to 5,000. Any accurate number would be difficult to obtain. Converts range from local women who have adopted Islam to a greater or lesser extent of commitment upon marrying a Muslim, to British intellectuals who are highly articulate in expressing their view on a variety of matters.

Christians and Muslims in Britain

In East London is the centre of a circle of about 100 Sufi dervishes, British converts to Islam, some of whom live at the headquarters. A group performed at the "Mind and Body 81 Festival" at Olympia.

There is a limited number of *tariqa* groups, but details are hard to obtain, and there is little evidence that these groups relate very closely to each other.

IV. British Response: Religious Education (RE)

(1) *Government-run Schools*

Regulations in Britain regarding RE stem from the 1944 Education Act, which requires that RE be given in school and that the school day begin with an act of worship ("Assembly"). The "conscience clause" means that no teacher is obliged to teach RE, and that individual pupils can be withdrawn at parents' written request.

This Education Act applied to a system where, broadly speaking, the religious background was assumed to be Christian, even though many pupils might come from homes with little, or no, religious allegiance.

The content of RE teaching is decided by each Local Education Authority (LEA), and forms its "Agreed Syllabus," which reflects a non-denominational, non-controversial form of Christianity. With the arrival of increasing numbers of pupils whose families' strong religious allegiance, and entire cultural life, are of another faith, the existing system was seen to be inadequate. In 1973 Birmingham adopted a new Agreed Syllabus which included the study of other faiths and ideologies; since then, many areas have revised or replaced their Agreed Syllabus, and the situation is constantly changing. In many cases, too, Assembly is no longer "christian worship" but allows other faiths to find their expression or to focus more on moral and ethical values common to all.

Muslims, and others, are often dissatisfied with the approach to religion in a typical modern RE syllabus. Even the "comparative religion" element is for them no better: putting Islam on the same level as other, non-scriptural, religions. Christian parents, too, have often reacted strongly to the multi-faith approach found in schools which no longer have a Christian majority. A typical example is Rochdale, North-West England, must publicised recently. The percentage of Muslim children in the area is very high, and an unexpectedly large number of Muslim parents, presumably with outside encouragement, requested that their children should be withdrawn from RE. The school's response was to attempt to provide a non-specific form of RE; a move quite unacceptable to the Christian parents, who saw it as an undermining of the religion and culture which form part of their children's heritage.

Muslims will almost always demand some kind of specifically Islamic instruction for their children, and will expect it to be given by a Muslim. Such instruction may be provided in the local mosque, or by the visits of peripatetic teachers (see III. 2)

Other "religious" aspects of school life include diet: it is generally possible for a school to provide a vegetarian meal, as this is appreciated also by Hindu and Sikh children. Dress can still be a problem, especially for Physical Education, sport and swimming. Some schools will allow Muslim girls to wear trousers.

(2) *Church schols*

(i) The 1944 Education Act allows for three types of publicly aided church schools, the amount of funding from the Government partly determining the freedom of the school's governing body to decide on syllabus, etc. Most confessional schools are Church of England and Roman Catholic, some are Methodist, some Jewish.

For the Church of England, the RE syllabus is devised by the local Diocesan Education Authorities, with advice from the National Board of Education. In "controlled" schools, RE is according to the Agreed Syllabus of the LEA, with rights for denominational teaching — this being optional, at parents' request. In "aided" school, the school governors are responsible for the RE, which is denominational. RE is becoming more open to other faiths and lifestyles.

Church of England schools are probably those most concerned with non-Christian pupils, since being of the Established Church and in the majority among Christians in this country, they are the more likely to be asked to accept such pupils. Views of persons involved in RE in a Church school vary enormously. Some are facing up seriously to the situation where a Church school, whose trust deeds may commit it to a particular form of religious instruction with the hope of bringing about a real commitment on the part of the children, is now asked to receive large numbers of children who are not Christians at all.

The problems and various lines for a solution, are well highlighted in a discussion paper, shortly to be published by the Manchester Diocesan Council for Education.[26] The paper quotes from two very different viewpoints; the open approach is typified by a headmaster, who says:

«We encourage (Muslim pupils) to be proud of their faith, to talk and write about it, and to teach the rest of us something of the Muslim way of life as we teach them about the Christian faith ... We conceive it our duty to *teach about* religion, not to indoctrinate ... Christianity remains the cornerstone of the religious teaching in the school».

Commitment to Christian belief is here seen as compatible with an openness to Islam.

Another view however they exemplify by quoting a vicar, Chairman of the Governors of a school which also has a high proportion of Muslim children:

"The vocation of the Church is to bear witness to the truth ... The Christian school is, or ought to be, the Church's front line missionary activity amongst the children in the parish ... Christianity ... is the only religion that contains the whole truth ... The Church today has a mission to the Pakistanis."

Each of these views represents a committed position, and would be supported by some incumbents and headmasters; the rigid approach of the second would by some be interpreted as defence of traditional values, and must be taken account of in any overall assessment of attitudes.

The paper lists several standpoints which could be adopted. Some Church schools recognise and exercise a Christian responsibility but without attempting a strictly denominational-based approach. "Thus the Church school seeks to provide a religious education within which it is possible for children and their families of different cultures to share their faith in such ways that all are enriched and nurtured in their spiritual development ..." Reference is made also to a paper by the Co-ordinator of the Schools' Council Project on RE in Primary Schools, a key point being:

"We are concerned with laying the foundations for later understanding and possible acceptance of a particular religious tradition." This is done without persuasion or coercion, but by helping the child to develop all his powers of appreciation and leaving him free.

RE Resource Centres: there is one in Westminster for Catholic RE, and a larger one in Kensington, W. London, for the National Society for Promoting Religious Education (Church of England). This has a reference collection, material and visual aids, runs special in-service and other courses, provides advice and information.

(3) *Interfaith in education*

(i) The first interfaith conference on education was held at Harrogate, Yorkshire, in 1969, organised by the BCC's education department, and was followed by other *ad hoc* conferences. In 1973 the Standing Committee for Interfaith Dialogue in Education (SCIFDE) was established, and now meets three times a year. It functions in collaboration with the World Congress of Faiths. (See VI. 1).

(ii) The SHAP Working Party was set up at a conference in the North of England in 1969, with the intention of identifying problems involved in teaching about world religions, providing and studying relevant syllabus material, generating new ideas and acting as a clearing house for ideas and materials. *World Religions: A Handbook for Teachers* contains information, some short articles, the addresses of groups and organisations, advice on teaching materials, etc.[27] Shap also publishes an annual *Calendar of Religious Festivals*, and a *Shap Mailing* with up-to-date information and articles helpful to teachers of RE.

(4) *Christian organisations*

(i) The Young Women's Christian Association (YWCA) of Great Britain, non-denominational, has traditionally helped young women by providing educational activities and training, recreational facilities, accommodation and residential clubs, in many cities. Over the years the YWCA has become increasingly aware of the needs of young women of other faiths and races, and has taken a particular interest in young Asian girls (including Christians, Muslims, Sikhs and Hindus).

In September 1973 a member of the Indian YWCA undertook a six-month survey in Ealing and Bradford, her report being published as "Girls of Asian Origin in Britain."[28] Arising from this survey and report, the YWCA initiated two projects in Coventry and Loughborough, to discover the immediate needs of Asian girls: summarised in a report, "In Search of Identity."[29]

In various cities the YWCA has been involved in, or has been responsible for starting, schemes to help women of other cultures. In April 1981 a seminar "Working with the Asian Community" gave workers the opportunity to share their experiences and seek a common basis on which to evaluate work and plan for the future. One primary concern of the YWCA is to encourage initiatives and "multi-faith" education programmes, helping all age groups. Their work includes:

Scotland: Glasgow: The centre for Interfaith work is the International Flat, purchased in 1974 and supported by the YWCA, administered jointly by the YWCA and the Joint Churches' Committee. The organiser is Miss Stella Reekie, a Deaconess of the Church of Scotland and formerly a missionary in Pakistan, who lives at the Flat and provides much of the initiative for the various activities, and a warm welcome to all visitors. The "Sharing of Faiths" group includes members of the Christian, Jewish, Sikh, Muslim, Hindu and Baha'i faiths, and holds meetings during the year., Since 1971 an annual event has been the "Presentation" of the Sharing of Faiths, for the whole of Glasgow.

Edinburgh: Here also a "Sharing of Faiths" group, which began about two years ago, meets once a month for informal discussion. The Women's International Centre, where the main priority is teaching of English, holds classes at the Centre and elsewhere. The largest national group is that of the Pakistanis, and other Muslim women include wives of overseas students. The Centre organises a "play scheme" in July for children, mainly so that their knowledge of English will not deteriorate during the summer holidays. Women come for English classes in the afternoons.

Dundee: There is a smaller centre, which concentrates on English teaching. Muslims here are mainly Bangladeshis, connected with the jute trade; there are also Pakistanis.

The YWCA and other organisations are aware that for Asian, and in particular Muslim, girls and young women, there are very strong pressures to conform to the behaviour patterns of the home country, while the girls are also expected to play as full a part as possible in school life. Tensions arise between the generations; there are inevitably conflicts, occasional tragedies, but many girls manage to adapt to their dual role, Asian at home and British at school. Older girls may be sent back to Pakistan to complete their education in a suitably Islamic environment, some may be married off quite young — either here or in Pakistan — and not all arranged marriages stand the strain. Though most difficulties are resolved within the family, this is not always the case. A hostel in a suburb of Manchester, for Asian wives who have been forced to leave home, fulfils a very real need. For older women, the main problems are their inability to communicate in English and often social and

Christians and Muslims in Britain

family pressures which keep them confined to the home.

(ii) *Young Men's Christian Association* (YMCA)

The YMCA offers sport, educational and residential facilities for young men. The organisation realises that as a Christian group it caters for the needs not only of Christians or of the uncommitted, but members of other faiths. The YMCA National Assembly in June 1981 agreed:

"That the National Board instigate a study with a view to issuing guidelines to the movement on the response the movement might reasonably make to the spiritual needs of members and residents of faiths other than the Christian faith. Such a study would review and report on the present pattern of response from within the movement and would seek to reflect upon the use of spiritual leaders from such other faiths."[30]

(iii) *Scouts and Guides*

Though Christian in origin and in general outlook, both the Scout and Guide movements are flexible in allowing members to interpret for themselves the promise "to do my duty to God." Scouts have recently made serious efforts to identify and respond to the needs of ethnic minority youth, sometimes with Government financial support. A local enquiry was undertaken during 1977, on the "Leisure Needs of Asian boys aged 8-14 in Slough, Berkshire."[31] In Birmingham an inner city team of ten full-time adults sees as one of its priorities to develop and expand the participation of minority communities.

(iv) *Other Christian-based groups*

include Christians Against Racism and Fascism (CARAF) inaugurated in January 1978; and All Faiths For One Race (AFFOR) based in Birmingham.

V. Churches' Response to Muslim Presence

The Churches in Britain do not necessarily divide their "religious" from "social" concern, as is reflected in the numerous church agencies which work for development, racial harmony and co-operation.[32] Some of these activities are carried out by each individual church, while for others they combine forces to give more effective witness and service. The British Council of Churches (BCC) is constituted by all the main churches in Britain, with the exception of the Roman Catholic Church which is not yet a member.

(1) *British Council of Churches and Islam*

The Christian churches in Britain have in the past tended to think of other religions, including Islam, as chiefly the concern of missionary societies, even when Muslims were already coming to Britain in large numbers.

World of Islam festival: Probably the first time that some Christians gave much serious thought to the question was in 1976 at the opening of the *World of Islam festival:* a huge programme of exhibitions and cultural events, backed up by some radio and television presentations and with extensive press coverage. This Festival was a purely "cultural" occasion, organised largely by non-Muslims, and as such was not entirely acceptable to Muslims. Under the auspices of the Islamic Council of Europe, an "Interna-

91

tional Islamic Conference" was held in London, with speakers from many different countries, at a date to coincide with the opening of the WIF in April. This combination of events had a considerable impact upon the ordinary Christian, who found himself insufficiently prepared mentally or spiritually.

Largely as preparation for the WIF, and to help Christians to respond positively, the BCC jointly with the Council of the Conference of Missionary Societies of Great Britain and Ireland (CBMS) formed an Advisory Group on the Presence of Islam in Britain, under the Chairmanship of Bishop David Brown: its first meeting was held in December 1974. David Brown wrote a useful handbook, *A New Threshold: Guidelines for the Churches in their relations with Muslim Communities;* intended to "give some basic information about Islam, propose for discussion a Christian approach to Islam, and suggest a code of practice to guide Christians in their contacts with Muslims."[33]

The WIF Trust has continued, in the years following the Festival, to promote the cultural aspects of Islam, through occasional publications, lectures, and exhibitions.

(2) *Committee for Relations with People of Other Faiths* (CRPOF) of the BCC

Publicity given to the World of Islam Festival, the work of the Advisory Group, and subsequent developments, underlined the need for a more formal and regular concern on the part of the Churches with the non-Christian people — not only Muslims — now in Britain. The BCC Assembly in April 1977 agreed the following resolution:

"The Assembly of the British Council of Churches

believes the presence in Britain of significant numbers of people of faiths other than Christian to be within God's gracious purpose;

welcomes the new opportunities this presents to Christians both to learn from those of other faiths and to bear witness to their own faith;

affirms that there is much need and scope for Christians to work together with those of other faiths for the common good of mankind along the lines of the Code of Practice outlined in *A New Threshold;*

instructs the Executive Committee of the BBC, in co-operation with the CBMS, to establish a means of helping the churches and their agencies

(a) to increase awareness of the fact and the implications of the religiously plural character of the world community, and

(b) to promote creative Christian response ..."

A new Committee came into being through the work of the BCC and the CBMS (which is now a part of the BCC); Bishop David Brown agreed to serve as Chairman of CRPOF, and in 1978 the Rev. Kenneth Cracknell, a Methodist minister, took up the work of Executive Secretary. The task of the Committee was seen as:

"To act as an ecumenical instrument of the British Churches and Missionary Societies to help Christian congregations and groups to learn from those of other faiths and to bear witness to their own faith. It aims to do this:

Christians and Muslims in Britain

(a) by acting as a linking-body between denominational committees concerned with relationships between people of different faiths;

(b) by monitoring creative faith-to-faith engagement by the churches;

(c) by helping to clarify Christian convictions and theological reflection on faith-to-faith relationships, our developing plural society in Britain, and in these contexts, the missionary calling of the Church.''

The CRPOF has three Groups, apart from the general Committee, to deal with specific issues:

Religious education in a Multi-faith society;

Theological issues;

Legal and Parliamentary matters

and there are other sub-groups working on the questions of:

Mixed-faith marriages

Interfaith worship

Use of Church premises for other faiths.

In June 1981 the CRPOF published: *Relations with People of Other Faiths: Guidelines on Dialogue in Britain.* In 24 pages it briefly relates the situation in Britain to that elsewhere, to the *Guidelines* of the World Council of Churches and Vatican documents. Practical issues are raised, and there is a good usefull list of addresses and resources.[34] Kenneth Cracknell himself has written two short books, *Why Dialogue?* and *Considering Dialogue.*[35]

(3) *The Anglican Church*

With the largest Christian membership in the United Kingdom (an estimated 27 million in 1977),[36] the Established Church is the first to be approached in any official context. Anglican ministers are at work in hospitals, educational institutions, prisons, and in social work. In some areas, Community Relations Chaplains have been appointed, and in this capacity they are likely to be often involved in interfaith work.

The Anglican Church has overseas commitments, with particularly strong links with countries of the Commonwealth. Missionary societies, among them the United Society for the Propagation of the Gospel (USPG) and the Church Missionary Society (CMS), send pastors, community workers, agriculturalists and others to serve for varying periods of time in developing countries. Those who later return to Britain and continue working for the Church are able to contribute to interfaith understanding, and this is particularly valuable in the case of Church ministry, bringing specialised knowledge and experience of other communities to the British parish or diocese. Probably the best known, through their work and writings, are the Bishops Kenneth Cragg and David Brown.

Missionary training colleges and other establishments often participate in interfaith activities in this country. The CMS, in conjunction with the CBMS, have their own Other Faiths Theological Project, whose representative is the Rev. Christopher Lamb, in Birmingham, formerly a CMS minister in Pakistan. He produces a small quarterly bulletin "Co-ordinate: for Christians who find themselves interfaith" — news items, notices of books and of forthcoming events, comments and ideas and prayers relating to the interfaith nature of modern Britain.

(4) *Local Churches and Interfaith*

In certain areas, churches of different denominations may combine in their response to the presence of people of other faiths, seeking to "build community" for the good of all. In the Bradford area (W. Yorkshire), "Outreach", which began in 1980, has a double aim: "to create greater understanding between the cultures and to build bridges of understanding and friendship..." and at the same time, as part of the churches' Christian committment, "to present positively to people of any culture the Gospel of God, who calls everyone to follow the way of Jesus Christ." In the pursuit of these aims, the emphasis is on a sensitive and caring approach to all, helping members of each culture to understand and appreciate the others. "Outreach" works in co-operation with projects already in progress; and informative leaflets are being prepared about the faiths represented in the area, for educational work amongst Church members.[37]

(5) *Roman Catholic Church* .

(i) The Catholic Church in Britain does not have any organisation specifically for relations with other faiths, although it is in close contact with the BCC, on whose CRPOF it has unofficial "observers."

(ii) Within the Catholic Church, there are groups concerned with matters of relevance to people of other faiths: These include:

(a) *Catholic Commission for Racial Justice* (CCRJ) an advisory body to the Roman Catholic Bishops of England and Wales, set up by the Bishops' Conference in 1971 and supported by the National Catholic Fund. Its brief is to inform and advise Bishops on matters of racial justice in this country and to fulfil a broadly educational role: "to assist the Church ... in developing its ministry within a multiracial multicultural society." CCRJ keeps closely in touch with all legislation concerning minority groups, and its most recent involvement has been with the preliminaries to the Nationality Bill, publishing fact sheets with the background and a brief history of similar legislation.

At intervals CCRJ publishes *Notes and Reports* on matters of concern; these have included "Practical Guidelines for the Church in a Multiracial, Multicultural Society" (1978), with suggestions for priests, parish workers and educationalists; it states that Seminaries and Colleges of Education have a "special responsibility toward the future," and that students in both "must be exposed to a thoroughly multi-cultural education, and their sensitivies must be developed to enable them to play a central role in multi-racial parishes and multi-cultural schools."

(b) *Catholic Institute for International Relations* (CIIR) was first formed in 1940 as "The Sword of the Spirit." It is concerned with conditions and development in many parts of the world; one of its projects is the developing of health schemes in Yemen.

(c) *Catholic Fund for Overseas Development* (CAFOD) the main channel for the Catholic church for funds to developing countries. Not directly linked to mission societies, it has the status of a Bishops' Commission. As with *Oxfam*, emphasis is on self-help schemes and education.

(d) *Justice and Peace Commission*, with groups in most dioceses, has an active concern with issues both in Britain and abroad, seeking to inform and educate Catholics in this country about issues of justice and peace. In some places it encourages and participates in interfaith activities. Currently its groups have been involved in opposing the Nationality Bill.

(iii) In general, there is probably a need for most Catholics to be considerably better informed about the various religions now represented in large numbers in this country. Many missionary societies have long-standing interests in Muslim countries, and a considerable fund of experience and knowledge had been acquired by missionary societies and by individuals; much of this is directed overseas, or towards the training of future mission personnel. Such experience, however, is increasingly relevant to the Church in Britain; missionaries who travel around the country on promotion work have a unique opportunity of seeing at first hand the variety of different situations, and of gaining an overall view which would in turn be of immense use to the bishops and clergy in the dioceses. As suggested by the CCRJ, seminaries and colleges could adopt a more positive and practical approach to the study of other faiths, since this is no longer a concern of theoretical interest for the specialist, or of relevance only to the overseas pastor, but a practical concern for priests and teachers in every part of Britain.

At another level, we are often reminded of the declarations of Vatican II, for instance in *Nostra Aetate*, where Christians and Muslims are encouraged to "forget the past and to strive sincerely for mutual understanding." The establishment of the Secretariat for Non-Christians in 1964, and in 1974 of a Commission for Islam, have affected relations between the Church and Muslims and there has been notable progress.[38] But the practical consequences have not always filtered through to diocesan or parish levels over here.

(iv) The need for better information is underlined in sections of the *Report* of the *National Pastoral Congress*, held in Liverpool in May 1980. This emphasised firstly the changing nature of the Christian's task in England and Wales (and by extension the rest of Britain).

"Our countries are now seen as mission territories. The Church has to commit itself to this mission and the laity should be fully involved in it" (Sector B). On immigrant groups, attention was drawn to "the need for tolerance and understanding," suggesting that "parish clergy need to be sensitive to the difficult work of chaplains concerned" (Sector C). On Evangelisation, the responsibility of all was seen for "this task of witness and of direct proclamation to those outside the Church, the uncommitted, and those of other faiths" ... "This is a task in which ecumenical co-operation is so essential it should be taken for granted." This same Sector shows a positive attitude towards these other faiths: "Christianity is forced to take seriously the witness given by other non-Christian faiths to the power of God's Spirit'' (Sector D).

In *Easter People,* their response to the NPC, the Bishops acknowledged that "Britain has become irreversibly a multi-racial, multi-cultural society," and ask that all should be "sensitive to the particular spiritual and religious needs of ethnic minorities." More specifically they encourage a "spirit of dialogue" in the approach to other faiths, and better knowledge of the "background and beliefs of non-Christian immigrants to our countries," for we can learn from them and at the same time "make known to them our own belief, the Good News of Jesus Christ." They suggest that priests with relevant experience, and returned missionaries, might provide "expert and experienced chaplains to immigrants" (Section 88)[40],

It is to be hoped that all these recommendations, and many others relevant to the life of the Catholic Church in Britain, will be noted and acted upon at all levels.

(v) Whereas missionary societies based in this country previously concentrated their activities at home primarily on recruitment, secondly fund-raising and thirdly informing and educating the general church membership, the order is now reversed, with the greatest emphasis upon "education and awareness." This will also draw attention to the presence of other faiths in this country; and will be likely to attract the alternative type of service: volunteer work with a missionary society. The Volunteer Missionary Movement recruits trained persons who wish to work overseas for a certain number of years and can in this way make a very valuable contribution.

A Bishops' Commission is concerned with missionary work, and an extension of this Commission is the *National Missionary Council* (NMC). This deals with missionary interests in the widest sense, on behalf of all the societies, about two-thirds of which are members together with some other organisations such as CAFOD. The Council holds a meeting every two years, in 1979 choosing the theme "Local Church and Missionary Awareness." The emphasis was on educational priorities, with the aim to inform and involve parish clergy; to widen the scope of school and seminary religious syllabuses; to establish diocesan directors for mission. Another important concern was the pastoral care of immigrants, and for this it is hoped to set up a working party, which will keep closely in touch with the BCC's CRPOF. The 1981 conference theme is to be "Everyone a Missionary."

The NMC has as yet no official links with the other churches. It was suggested by the NPC in 1980 that the NMC should consider applying for full Catholic membership of the Conference for World Mission of the BCC, and for this purpose a working party was set up in November 1980. Two meetings have been held with representatives of the BCC, mainly on the question of what form any membership could take: for the NMC as an institution, or several missionary societies, or for the Missionary Institute.[41]

Until quite recently, missionary training was undertaken separately by each mission society. For various reasons this was realised to be both impractical and unproductive, and since 1967 a dozen or so Missionary Societies have combined for a joint training scheme, at the National Missionary Institute in North London, governed by Provincial Superiors of seven of the societies concerned. Students work for the theology degree of Louvain University, which approves the syllabus.

Teaching about Other Faiths is an integral part of the course, but is rather theoretical It has recently been suggested that more involvement could be undertaken in local parishes with multi-faith populations, as part of practical training. There would seem to be a case also for extending any such schemes to national seminaries, for the benefit of future clergy, who will be working in multi-faith Britain.

(vi) One religious society committed to working with Muslims is that of the Little Sisters of Jesus; their English houses in London and in Aston (Birmingham) are situated among Muslim communities. Living among immigrants and themselves following a simple life-style, they are the more readily accepted by their neighbours, and can act as a valuable link between Muslims and the Christian parish.

Other societies, who specialise in educational and social work, find that they are often able to offer help to Muslims, including Moroccans in London and Pakistanis in Birmingham. This is generally done on an individual basis, for instance where a religious with experience abroad is able to interpret, minister or simply visit.

(6) The *United Reformed Church* (URC) has set up a Mission and Other Faiths Committee as part of its World Church and Mission Department: each member of the Committee undertakes special responsibility as a "consultant" for a particular area, including each of the main religious communities in Britain. The URC sees this as part of its concern for "the local, national and international aspects of the challenge of Christian relationships with people of other faiths." It seeks mainly to gather and provide information, to promote theological discussion, to encourage "pilot projects" and to promote more general study and reflection.

In 1974 the Committee produced a pamphlet "The Local Churches' Approach to Those of Other Faiths," and in 1980, "With People of Other Faiths in Britain: A Study Handbook for Christians." This contains practical questions and ideas, some case studies and personal accounts, and theological perspectives. Particularly useful is its listing of resources and addresses of organisations.[42]

(7) The *Methodist Church's* Working Party on Multi-Faith Society is composed of representatives appointed by other committees within the Church. The Working Party commends the recently produced "Shall we greet only our own family?" described as "a booklet to guide Christians in their relationships with people of other faiths."[43]

(8) The *Church of Scotland*, and other churches in Britain, send ministers to Christian congregations abroad, whether or not as part of a specific missionary outreach. In all cases, the experience gained abroad is of great

value on return home; and it often happens that friendships with Muslims and others, formed overseas, can be continued when these same friends or their families come to Britain for work or study. The links through informal contacts and friendships are far more numerous, varied and long-lasting than could be indicated by any account of official contacts.

(9) *Other groups*

Among some Christian groups can be found what might be best described as less positive approaches to those of other faiths; and these reactions too spring from a genuine Christian commitment. The Evangelical Alliance, the International Bible Reading Association, and others have been criticised for taking a negative and even hostile view of other religions. While all such views can be respected, the Churches in Britain as a whole encourage and exhibit a positive attitude to people of other faiths, through education, information, interfaith projects and meetings between representatives of different faiths.

VI. Interfaith Groups

(1) *World Congress of Faiths.* The first gathering of the Congress was held in London in 1936, largely through the efforts of Sir Francis Younghusband, who had for many years worked as a pioneer of interfaith dialogue. Participants at the Congress included representatives of the great world religions and of smaller religious groups. Other Congresses were held in the following years, and although restricted during the war, have continued since then. Activities include an annual conference on a specific theme, special lectures, and the publication of *World Faiths.* Work of the WCF has been mainly educational, aimed at assisting interfaith understanding. It is also a pioneer of shared worship, a question which has caused some controversy.[44]

(2) *Local Groups* are found in many British cities. In November 1979 the first National Interfaith Conference took place, sponsored by the WCF and BCC, attended by representatives of nearly twenty interfaith groups from around Britain. Short reports were given of work done by groups, among the most active being those in Leeds and Glasgow.

Leeds: Here a branch of the JCM (see VI. 4.) developed in 1977 into the group "CONCORD," since which time the society has been actively engaged in interfaith work and dialogue in Leeds and district. Membership has been extended to Sikhs, Hindus and others, and Concord is a member of the Leeds Community Relations Council; it works locally in co-operation with the CCJ (see VI. 4. iv).

Concord seeks to draw together peoples of different faiths in mutual respect and understanding, reconciliation and co-operation; and is concerned for the promotion of a just and peaceful multi-racial society. Concord has organised or participated in more than a hundred meetings and events of various kinds. An important contribution is made by the regular meeting of small interfaith "house groups." A feature of Concord's activities has been a Three Faiths Conference held annually. Jewish, Christian and Muslim speakers and participants consider a theme: 1980 "The Family," 1981 "The Dignity of Man."[45]

Earlier, meetings were held at Wetherby in Yorkshire between Muslims and Christians, on the themes of "Family" (1974), "Worship and Prayer" (1975); notes on each were published by the Community Relations Chaplaincies of Bradford and Wakefield.

(3) A rather more *ad hoc* is typified by the Standing Conference of Christians and Muslims in the Midlands (SCCMM), which in 1976 organised a day conference in Birmingham, held partly in the Mosque and partly in the United Reformed Church, on the theme "Church and Mosque in Secular Society." In 1977 it held three meetings, on different themes, including a day conference for women, Christian and Muslim, in Aston.

(4) *Jewish-Christian-Muslim* (JCM). (i) Soon after the Second World War, meetings were arranged between Jews and Christians; and before long, both parties became aware of the presence of large numbers of Muslims in Europe. It was thought that the three faiths would have much in common, and the first annual JCM conference took place in London in 1972, when a British section was formed. The Standing Committee for Jews, Christians and Muslims has branches throughout Europe, and the British section is based in London, with the Sisters of the Sion carrying out the work of the Secretariat.

In 1967, a meeting took place in Berlin between religious leaders and students from the three faiths, and since then meetings and conferences have been held regularly. Jewish-Christian groups and councils already existed in Europe, and it was thought best therefore not to try to alter the nature of these but to form new groups for the three faiths together. The main concerns of the JCM, in Britain as elsewhere, are to educate and promote better understanding: Publications and information are available for schools and other groups.[46]

(ii) Another smaller organisation is "British Friends of Neve Shalom," linked with the community of that name in Palestine, which tries to bring together members of the three faiths.

(iii) The Rainbow Group, which began in Jerusalem, is a private group of Jews and Christians, with a branch in London. In March 1981 the principal speakers were Professor W. M. Watt and Dr. Hasan Askari, each dealing with different aspects of Islam.

(iv) The Council of Christians and Jews (CCJ) was formed in Britain in 1942, to "combat religious and racial intolerance;" it publishes *Common Ground*.

VII. Study and Educational

(1) *Birmingham (Selly Oak) Centre for the Study of Islam and Christian-Muslim Relations*

The organisation most deeply involved with Islam, on a theological, ecumenical and practical basis, is the Centre for the Study of Islam and Christian-Muslim Relations, at the Selly Oak Colleges, Birmingham. The Centre

"Christianity and Islam"

was formally established in 1976, partly as the outcome of an international Christian-Muslim meeting in May 1975, convened by Dr. David Kerr, since 1973 Lecturer in Islam at the Colleges and now Director of the Centre.

This Centre was envisaged as a joint venture of Christians and Muslims, whose concern would be to explore the living traditions of the two faiths in Europe and elsewhere, "in total obedience to their respective faiths and in a spirit of openness to one another and of trust." The Centre has expanded over these five years, and now has both Christian and Muslim members of staff and students.

The programme is broadly divided into three sections:

(i) Teaching: lectures and seminars on Islamic subjects for students at the constituent colleges, which include a College of Education, and for theological students at Birmingham University; programmes of study leading to the MA and the Certificates in Islam.

(ii) Survey Project: to gather and document all relevant information, and make it available to those concerned, on the presence of Islam in Europe; mainly through publication of *News of Muslims in Europe*, of *Abstracts: European Muslims and Christian-Muslim Relations* from the European press) and of occasional *Research Papers*.

(iii) Extension work: "teach-ins" and special courses for groups such as prison officers, health workers, seminars and conferences; outside speaking engagements.

(iv) For the past two years there has been an annual "Summer School" of about two weeks, attended by Christians and Muslims from Britain and overseas.

The Study Centre is in close touch with the Conference of European Churches, with the Catholic Church, the British Council of Churches and the World Council of Churches, and is the main centre for information on any matters relating to Islam in Britain.[47]

(2) *Farmington Institute,* Oxford is a small research centre, which began in 1974 under the aegis of the Farmington Trust (established in 1965): to encourage those whose work is designed to promote an understanding of a Christian involvement in education; its work is expanding especially in the field of religious education. Aims of the Trust and Institute are:

"to support those involved in Christian education; to further an understanding of the spiritual experience of mankind in our schools, and other places of learning; and to encourage the practice of the Christian ethic in the lives of individuals and in society."

An important part of Christian studies is seen to be "not only to examine Christian approaches to other faiths, but also to consider the contemporary critiques of Christianity offered by other religions and ideologies."[48] Work includes the organising and running of conferences and consultations, encouraging and participating in the work of school, college and university groups concerned with religion and education; encouraging a deeper sensitivity to the religious affirmations and experience of adherents of other world faiths. The Institute, through the work of its Director, Dr. Edward Hulmes, takes a particular interest in Islam in its contemporary setting.

The whole question of interfaith, and more specifically Christian-Muslim co-operation and understanding, has to be seen in the wider context of the post-conciliar Catholic church, the growth of the ecumenical movement, the pluriform nature of post-colonial Britain, the changing circumstances in which we live and the varied, and constantly changing, attitudes of those around us. The situation is fluid, events are unpredictable and to a certain extent interact with social, political and economic forces beyond the individual's control.

We leave the last word to the *Report* of the National Pastoral Congress, a Report which one hopes will provide food for thought, prayer and action in every sphere of life, and can sum up the attitude of Christians involved in dialogue in Britain.[49]

"The 1980s are for the Church a time of decision. The needs of the world and the demand of the Gospel, as we have discerned them, will place on the Church and on individual Catholics responsibilities of a magnitude that few have yet grasped...

"Our calling may demand courage; it certainly demands renewal in prayer, in Christian life-style and in fidelity to the Gospel, but it also presents surely the most exciting, enriching and enlivening opportunity given to our church.

"In all humility and in God's grace we accept it."

Organizations: Church and Others

BCC   British Council of Churches, Edinburgh House, 2 Eaton Gate, London SWIW 9BL,
: Committee for Relations with People of other Faiths — CRPOF
: Conference for World Mission — CFWM.
: Community and Race Relations Unit — CRRU

CAFOD   Catholic Fund for Overseas Development.

CBMS   Conference of British Missionary Societies.

CCRJ   Catholic Commission for Racial Justice, 1 Amwell Street, London ECIR 1UL

CIIR   Catholic Institute for International Relations, 1 Cambridge Terrace, London NW1 4JL.

CMS   Church Missionary Society, 157 Waterloo Road, London SE1.

CRC   Community Relations Commission (now CRE).

CRE   Commission for Racial Equality, 10-12 Allington Street, London SW1E 5EH
Concord, Secretary: Dr. P. G. Bell, 19 Gledhow Park Drive, Leeds LS7 4JT.

CSICMR   Centre for the Study of Islam and Christian-Muslim Relations, Selly Oak Colleges, Birmingham, B29 6LE.

DES   Department of Education and Science.

EEC	European Economic Community.
FICS	Farmington Institute for Christian Studies, 4 Park Town, Oxford.
JCM	Jewish-Christian-Muslim
LMP	Linguistic Minorities Project, 18 Woburn Square, London. WC1H ONS.
MC	Methodist Church, 1 Central Building, London SW1H 9NH.
	: Division of Social Responsibility — DSR.
	: Faith and Order Committee.
NMC	National Missionary Council, Holcombe House, The Ridgeway, London NW7 4HY.
NPC	National Pastoral Congress (Liverpool — May 1980).
OXFAM	Oxford Committee for Famine Relief — 274 Banbury Rd, Oxford.
SCIFDE	Standing Conference on Inter-Faith Dialogue in Education, Hon. Secretary: L. Prickett, Little Brunger, Appledore Road, Tenterden, Kent.
SHAP	Shap Working Party, 7 Alderbrook Road, Solihull, Birmingham.
URC	United Reformed Church, 86 Tavistock Place, London WC1H 9RT. Mission and Other Faiths Committee.
WCF	World Congress of Faiths, Executive Chairman: Rev. M. Braybrooke, 28 Powis Gardens, London W11 1JG.
YMCA	Young Men's Christian Association, National Council of YMCA's, 640 Forest Road, London E17 3DZ.
YWCA	Young Women's Christian Association of Great Britain, 2 Weymouth Street, London W1N 4AX.

Organisations: Muslim

—	Ahmadiyya Anjuman Isha'at Islam U.K., S.M. Tufail, 3 Orchard Close, off College Road, Maybury, Woking, Surrey.
—	Ahmadiyya Movement, The London Mosque, 16 Gressenhall Road, London SW18 5QL (Qādiānis).
FOSIS	Federation of Student Islamic Societies in the UK and Eire, 38 Mapesbury Road, London NW2.
—	H. H. The Aga Khan Shia Imami Ismailia Association for the UK, 5 Palace Gate, London W8 5LS.
ICE	Islamic Council of Europe, 16 Grosvenor Crescent, London SW1 7EP.
—	Islamic Foundation, 223 London Road, Leicester, LE1 2ZE.
—	Islamic Institute of Defence Technology (same address).
—	Islamic Cultural Centre, 146 Park Road, London NW8 7RG.
—	Minaret House, 9 Leslie Park Road, Croydon, Surrey, CRO 6TN.
MECC	Muslim Education Consultative Committee, 2A Bowyer Road, Saltley, Birmingham, B8 1ET.

Christians and Muslims in Britain

MET   Muslim Educational Trust, 130 Stroud Green Road, London N4.

—   Muslim Information Service, 223 Seven Sisters Road, London N4 2DA.

—   Muslim Institute for Research and Planning, 6 Endsleigh Street, London WC1 0DS.

—   Muslim Welfare House, 86 Stapleton Hall Road, London N4 4QA.

—   Muslim Youth and Cultural Association, 93 Court Road, Balsall Heath, Birmingham.

NMEC   National Muslim Educational Council (Union of Muslim Organisations).

UMO   Union of Muslim Organisations of UK and Eire, 30 Baker Street, London W1M 2DS.

1)   e.g. *Aide-memoire of Planning Meeting, held in Cartigny, Geneva, October 1976; printed in* Christians Meeting Muslims, *WCC, 1977, p. 143.*

2)   *Unofficial figures are quoted by the British Council of Churches in their* Guidelines *(see n. 34), estimates supplied by the communities concerned: Muslims 1,500,000; Jews 412,000; Hindus 400,000; Sikhs 200,000; Buddhists maybe 100,000; Zoroastrians and Jains, approx. 5,000 each; Baha'is: 167 local assemblies, with several thousand members in all.*

3)   *For more detail, cf.* Research Paper by M. M. Ally, *"The Growth and Organization of the Muslim Community in Britain," Selly Oak Colleges, Birmingham March 1979, and V. Saifullah Khan, "The Pakistanis: Mirpuri Villagers at Home and in Bradford," in* Between Two Cultures, *ed. James and Watson, Oxford 1977.*

4)   e.g. One Year On: A Report on the Resettlement of the Refugees from Uganda in Britain, *Community Relations Commission, London, August 1974.*

5)   e.g. M. Anwar, The Myth of Return: Pakistanis in Britain, *1979 (based on Rochdale), V. Saifullah Khan, "Pakistani Women in Britain," in* New Community *(CRE journal) 5 (1-2). 1976, 99-108.*

6)   Meeting their Needs: An Account of Language Tuition Schemes for Ethnic Minority Women, *CRC, 1977; The Education of Ethnic Minority children ... CRC, 1977; N. Hasnie,* The Way Ahead: A Survey of Asian youth in Huddersfield, *nd.*

7)   *V. Saifullah Khan, 1976, p. 58.*

8)   *J. McIntyre, "Multi-culture and multi-faith societies: some examinable assumptions," Farmington Occasional Paper No. 3.*

9)   Between Two Cultures: A Study of Relationships in the Asian Community in Britain, *CRC, 1976;* Educational Needs of Children from Minority Groups, *CRC, 1974.*

10)   Ethnic Minorities in Britain. Statistical Background, *CRE, 1978.*

11)   Multi-Ethnic Education: the way forward, *by A. Little and R. Willey, Schools Council Pamphlet 18, London 1981.*

"Christianity and Islam"

12)   Council directive, 25 July 1977 (77/486/EEC).

13)   Religions and Cultures: A guide to patients' beliefs and customs for health service staff. *Lothian Community Relations Council, Edinburgh 1978.*

14)   "Health Care of Ethnic Minorities in Britain," Produced by the Mission and Other Faiths Committee of the URC. Cf. "A guide to Asian diets," CRE pamphlet, 1976.

15)   Guidelines, *p. 15.*

16)   D. Shepherd and S.W. Harrison, Islam in Preston, *2nd edn., 1979 (stenciled format; accompanied by slides and materials).*

17)   P. Jeffery, Migrants and Refugees: Muslim and Christian Pakistani Families in Bristol, *Cambridge University Press, 1976.*

18)   Formal opening of the mosque on 28 March 1981, to which were invited representatives of Muslim organisations in Britain, of the UMO, and of civic and political groups.

19)   "Islamic Cultural Centre," illustrated booklet in Arabic and English published by the Centre, London.

20)   For Bradford: E. Butterworth, A Muslim Community in Britain, *Church Information Office, 1967;* Islam in the Parish, *Bradford Community Relations Council, 1973.*

21)   M. Y. McDermott and M. M. Ahsan, The Muslim Guide: For teachers, employers, Community workers and social administrators in Britain, *Islamic Foundation 1980.*

22)   Primers available at the Islamic Cultural Centre include: M. E. El-Geyoushi, Primary Islamic Teachings for Children, *Parts I and II; M. A. E. Siddiqi,* Elementary Teachings of Islam, *published by the MET.*

23) Guidelines and Syllabus for Islamic Education, *UMO 1976.*

24)   National Muslim Education Council: Background Papers, *UMO 1978.*

25)   Quoted from Islam in Preston, *p. 72. Cf. an article "Muslims get their own school" in* New Society, *28 June 1979.*

25a)   Maulānā Muḥammad ʿAlī, The Aḥmadiyyah Movement, *trans. & ed. S. M. Tufail, Ahmadiyyah Anjuman Ishāʿat Islam, Lahore, 1973.*

26)   "Church School Education and Islam in Multi-faith Manchester," paper by the Adviser on RE and the Director of Education for the Diocese, intended for those involved in RE in its Church schools.

27)   Ed. W. Owen Cole, published for Shap by the CRC (now CRE).

28)   S. Crishna, Girls of Asian Origin in Britain, *YWCA 1975.*

29)   "In Search of Identity," Compiled by Ann Meadows for the YWCA, typed format, n.d.

30)   Letter from the Christian Education Officer, National Council of YMCAs, June 1980.

31)   Report compiled by Phyllis Livingstone, 1978.

32)   e.g. the BCC's Community and Race Relations Unit (CRRU), Methodists' Division of Social Responsibility (DSR).

33)   D. Brown, A New Threshold: Guidelines for the Churches in their relations with Muslim communities, *BCC 1976.*

34)   British Council of Churches, 1981.

35)   By K. Cracknell: Why Dialogue? a first British Comment on the W.C.C. Guidelines, *BCC 1980;* Considering Dialogue (Theological Themes in Interfaith Relations 1970-1980), *BCC 1981.*

36) *approx. 27 million, compared with Roman Catholics 4 million; quoted from* Pro Mundi Vita bulletin, *70, January-February 1978. "Aspects of the Roman Catholic Church in England"*

37) *Quoted from "Outreach" material.*

38) *For an account of the early activities of the Secretariat, cf. M. L. Fitzgerald, "The Secretariat for Non-Christians is ten years old,"* Islamo-christiana *1, 87-95.*

39) *Congress Report:* The principal documents of the *1980* National Pastoral Congress of England and Wales, *Catholic Truth Society, London 1980.*

40) The Easter People: a message from the Roman Catholic Bishops of England and Wales in light of the National Pastoral Congress Liverpool *1980, St. Paul Publications 1980, Section 31.*

41) *Information on the National Missionary Council and the Missionary Institute kindly supplied by Rev. J. Brankin, WF, General Secretary of the NMC.*

42) *Published by the Mission and Other Faiths Committee of the URC, nd (1980)*

43) *Published by the Methodist Church, Division of Social Responsibility.*

44) *World Congress of Faiths. Its General Director, the Rev. Marcus Braybrooke, is author of* Inter-Faith Organizations, *1893-1979;* An Historical Directory *(Texts and Studies in Religion Mellen Press USA) 1980.*

45) *Details kindly supplied by Dr. P. Bell, Secretary of Concord.*

46) *JCM:* Newsletter, *first issue July 1972. Cf. L. Blue, "Practical Ecumenism: Jews, Christians and Moslems in Europe,"* Journal of Ecumenical Studies *10(1), 1973; Sr M. Shepherd, "Trialogue: Jewish, Christian, Muslim,"* The Month, *January 1981.*

47) *Literature and information from the Centre for the Study of Islam and Christian-Muslim Relations, Selly Oak Colleges, Birmingham.*

48) *Information leaflet, from the Farmington Institute, Oxford.*

VI

A Joint Catholic-Protestant Consultation on Christian Presence among Muslim Filipinos

Marawi City, July 24-27, 1978

A Communication

At the invitation of the Prelature of Marawi and Dansalan College, we are a gathering of twenty-six Christians from the Roman Catholic and several Protestant Churches who are concerned about and involved in the "why" of the Christian presence in the midst of Muslim Filipinos. We do not speak as official representatives of our denominations, but we do speak as Christians who feel a call from God to live as disciples of the Lord Jesus by a life of faith and hope among our Muslim brothers. We seek with them a solution to the prejudice, hatred and oppression which have for so long marked the relations between Christians and Muslims in this land.

Part One (Addressed to Muslims)

We ask of you, our Muslim brothers, that our presence among you will be welcomed. We are humbled by much that has marked our past history and we ask your forgiveness for our large share of the blame for the tragic past. Now we wish to come with nothing but ourselves—stripped of pretensions and with no ready-made answers to the problems that hinder a fruitful relationship.

We seek a dialogue of life with you. With God's help we sincerely desire to

This Consultation took place in Marawi City, the Philippines from July 24 to 27th, 1978. The text of the Report is reprinted with permission from the Occasional Bulletin (now International Bulletin) of Missionary Research, 3,1. Jan. 79, pp. 31-32.

achieve a more comprehensive viewpoint of His plan that includes all of us as brothers. In any genuine dialogue we realize the vulnerability that we place ourselves in—a vulnerability in regard to many ideas about ourselves and you. This dialogue must lead us to abandon entrenched positions and preconceived ideas.

We, like you, wish to come to a greater appreciation of our own religious tradition and to find a greater security in it, yet we believe that we have much to learn, and hope that through opening ourselves to the riches of your tradition we can return to our own enriched.

We see this dialogue of life as including participation and engagement in the struggle against oppression in all its forms in solidarity with you. When any person is oppressed we too are in bondage.

The full flowering of this dialogue of life between our peoples cannot be completed until all persons are truly free to live according to their traditions and conscience.

We believe that God, the Creator, is at work in history. In His providence we share in creating a more just world order—one in which both Muslims and Christians can live truly human lives in solidarity with each other. Despite the incredible difficulties that are the product of sin, we have a hope that cannot be quenched because it is sustained by God the Fashioner and Finisher of history.

May God, the Merciful and Compassionate, bless our efforts and strengthen us to engage in this task, this dialogue of life through which we pray all may be healed and made whole.

Part Two (Addressed to Christians)

To you, our fellow Chrisitians, we wish to point out that the history of this region where we are at work—Mindanao and Sulu—and the prevailing atmosphere in Christian-Muslim relations here, press us to weigh carefully the implications of our presence among our Muslim brothers. From a Christian perspective a dialogue of life implies at least the following:

- Christians need to take seriously and treat respectfully the Islamic religion and culture of Filipino Muslims. We need to understand and celebrate the fact that Philippines is a multi-faceted and plural society religiously and culturally rich in its diversity.
- Christians repudiate any form of witness or mission which is coercive in character or which deliberately attempts to exploit conditions of poverty, disease or disaster so as to lure Muslims away from their faith and into the Christian religion.
- Christians must repudiate the role of arrogant proselytizers. The "crusading mentality" and all methods of mass evangelism are offensive and threatening to our Muslim brothers. We should be among Muslims as friends and fellow citizens, not as rivals, but as Christians attempting to witness to our faith and to the best in our religion.

- Christians join Muslims as allies in meeting the social, economic and political challenges of nation-building, including the struggle against oppression in all its forms. We must be sensitive to the rights of Muslims to a just share in the natural resources of the whole country and especially of their traditional homeland.
- Christians ought to listen attentively to the Muslims' own articulation of their grievances and encourage serious consideration of the suggestions they themselves offer as solutions to their problems.
- Christians should insist that government officials at all levels deal with Muslim citizens tactfully and justly.
- Christians should insist that the educational system and the media, both public and private, foster positive and respectful attitudes towards Muslim Filipino history, religion and culture.
- Christians ought to regard any injury done to Muslims as an injury done to ourselves and feel that any conditions of injustice or oppression brought about by Christians in relation to Muslims morally diminishes the whole Christian population of the nation.
- Christians of different Churches will express solidarity in the dialogue of life among Muslims. "Going it alone" may be necessary at times but it is not desirable.

Participants in the Consultation

Roman Catholics:

1. Ms. Belo Birondo, Malabang, Lanao del Sur
2. Bishop Fernando Capalla, D.D., Iligan City
3. Fr. Michael Diamond, SSC, Marawi City
4. Sr. Mary Fe Mendoza, R.G.S., Mindanao-Sulu Pastoral Conference Secretariat
5. Fr. Warren Ford, SSC, Dimataling, Zamboanga del Sur
6. Mr. Karl Gaspar, Mindanao-Sulu Pastoral Conference Secretariat
7. Fr. Anton Korterick, O. Carm., Episcopal Commission on Tribal Filipinos
8. Fr. Warren Kinne, SSC, Pagadian, Zamboanga del Sur
9. Fr. Sean McNulty, SSC, Pagadian, Zamboanga del Sur
10. Fr. Eliseo Mercado, O.M.I., Kabacan, South Cotabato
11. Ms. Pet Miclat, Mindanao-Sulu Pastoral Conference Secretariat
12. Sr. Rustica Borja, FMM, Siasi, Tawi-Tawi
13. Bishop Bienvenido Tudtud, D.D., Marawi City
14. Ms. Lindy Washburn, Marawi City

Protestants:

15. Rev. Ricarte Beley, Marawi City
16. Rev. Rudolfo Beley, Zamboanga City
17. Rev. Olimpio Bonotan, Lala, Lanao del Norte

18. Dr. Peter Gowing, Marawi City
19. Rev. Frank Malanog, Iligan City
20. Mr. Mario Mapanao, Program Aimed at Christian Education about Muslims
21. Rev. Felipe Mosot, Iligan City
22. Dr. Robert McAmis, Marawi City
23. Mrs. Fedelinda Tawagon, Marawi City
24. Mrs. Anna May Towne, Marawi City
25. Mr. Howard Towne, Marawi City
26. Rev. Lloyd Van Vactor, Marawi City

VII

Christian-Muslim Relations in Nigeria

BY JOSEPH KENNY

A) Background

Early history of the two communities

The Muslim community in Nigeria is very important. The various census figures are controverted, but all of them list Muslims somewhere under 50%.[1] The Christian total is slightly less than the Muslim. In the states which were part of the former Northern Region Muslims are a little more than half the population. They are heavily concentrated in the extreme north, and are very numerous along the routes to Lagos. The southeastern parts of the country are virtually untouched by Islam.

Islam took root in the Kanem empire in the late 11th century; Kanem (in Chad) absorbed Bornu, the northeast of Nigeria, in the 13th century. Islam spread to the Hausa states in the late 15th century, brought by Malian missionaries. Malian, or "Wangara", traders and missionaries also penetrated the old Oyo (Yoruba) empire and were found along the coast by the Portuguese in the 16th century. Yet Islam was rather stagnant in Nigeria after its initial introduction until the jihad of Uthman Dan Fodio at the beginning of the 19th century. Throughout the 19th and 20th centuries Islam has grown stronger.[2]

Fr. Joseph Kenny, o.p., is a leader in Christian-Muslim dialogue in Nigeria. After he obtained his degrees in Arabic and Islamics (Rome and Cairo), he began his ministry and researches in Nigeria. He is a lector in Islamics at both Ibadan University (Department of Religious Studies) and some Major Seminaries, in order to prepare people to true dialogue. Taken from Islamochristiana 3, 79, 171-192 and reprinted by permission of the publisher.

"Christianity and Islam"

Nubian and Coptic Christianity seems to have influenced Nigeria in the middle ages; so various evidence suggests. Even Benin City seems to have derived its *formée* cross from Nubia via the north of Nigeria and Ida.[3] Written documentation is available for evangelization of the Benin area beginning in 1486 and for missionary journeys across the Sahara to the north of Nigeria in 1688, 1710 and 1850.[4] The solid establishment of the Church in Nigeria, however, had to wait for the second part of the 19th century.

Christian-Muslim relations under the British

The early C.M.S. missionaries were optimistic that the Muslims of the North would easily embrace Christianity.[5] Yet failure met both G.W. Brooke's Sudan Party mission of 1890-92 and Bishop H. Tugwell's Hausa Party mission of 1900. When Bishop Tugwell and Walter Miller began to preach in Kano the Emir told them: "We do not want you: you can go, I give you three days to prepare: a hundred donkeys to carry your loads back to Zaria, and we never wish to see you here again."[6] The missionaries thought that the ordinary Muslims were ignorant and only held to their religion from fear of their Fulani overlords. Evangelization would be simpler, they advocated, if these Fulani rulers were removed.

From 1900 to 1902 the British conquered the north of Nigeria, but they did not depose the Fulani rulers. Instead Lugard instituted the system of indirect rule, and gave the emirs a solemn pledge that he would not interfere with the Muslim religion. Lugard himself was a personal friend of Miller and favored his C.M.S. mission work, but later colonial officers used Lugard's pledge as an excuse to keep missionaries out of Muslim and even some pagan areas, and generally restricted their activities in the North. In the meantime Miller and his associates had a chance to get to know ordinary Muslim people, and were surprised to learn how well they understood Islam and how deeply they were attached to it. They then began to adopt Bishop Crowther's method of the 1870s of patient and tactful contact with the emirs, gaining their friendship in order to preach to the pagan population subject to them.[7]

Apart from British restrictions on Christian missionaries, Muslim leaders themselves discouraged their people from going to Christian schools, which were practically the only schools, and were extremely hesitant about even government schools providing Western education. In the North Christian schools arose among the colonies of Southerners living in the northern cities, and in newly Christian areas in the Middle Belt. The few Muslim students who attended these schools rarely attended Christian religion classes. In a very few instances (such as in the short-lived Catholic secondary school of Gusau) Islamic religion classes were provided for the Muslim students. As a result of Muslim hesitations about Western education there is a great educational imbalance between Muslim and non-Muslim areas of the country today, which Muslims are only beginning to overcome.

In the South Yoruba Muslims had few scruples about attending Christian schools and following the religious instruction as well (from which they usually could be excused), and many Muslim students became Christians as a result. To meet this situation Yoruba Muslim societies, such as the Ahmadiyya, Ansar-ud-deen, etc., opened Muslim schools combining Islamic and Western education.

The government schools of the North, which turned out a small well educated elite of northern Muslims, generally included Islamic religious knowledge in their curriculum. The few Christian students in these schools came under pressure to become Muslims.

During Independence preparations

Muslim and Christian differences affected the independence movement in Nigeria. In the South movements were founded for independence, such as the Nigerian Youth Movement in 1934, the National Council of Nigeria and the Cameroons in 1944, and the Action Group in 1953. In the North, however, the emirs and politicians were not eager for early independence.[8] The response to the demands of the West African Students Union in 1942 for cooperation in gaining self-government was: "Holding this country together is not possible except by means of the religion of the Prophet. If they want political unity let them follow our religion."[9]

A similar response was met by the N.C.N.C. delegation that toured the North in 1946 campaigning against the "Richard's Constitution" drafted by the then Governor of Nigeria. Awolowo openly stated that the fanatical and static nature of Islam was the main force that retarded the achievement of self-government.[10] Replying, Abubakar Tafawa Balewa, the later Prime Minister of Nigeria, threatened that if the Southern politicians, who were all considered Christians, did not stop their attacks on the North, the Muslim North would be forced to continue its "interrupted conquest to the sea," that is, to the South.[11] The Northern leaders amended a motion demanding independence for 1956 to read "as soon as practicable." Their fear of independence was that the more developed South would swamp the North and dominate it.

If the Muslims of the North had trouble dealing with the South, they had equal trouble dealing with non-Muslim peoples in the North, many of whom refused to join the Northern People's Congress (N.P.C.), the ruling party, whose leaders openly identified the party with Islam, despite the N.P.C. motto of "One North, one people, irrespective of religion, rank or tribe."[12] Opposition movements formed, such as the Northern Nigeria non-Muslim League in 1950, and the Middle Zone League in 1951. Later these fused to become the United Middle Belt Congress (U.M.B.C.), which supported Northern Christian interests. Consequently the first Northern Nigerian government in 1951, dominated by the N.P.C., appointed no Christians as ministers and even took steps to curtail missionary activities in the educational and medical fields.[13]

The predominantly Christian Benue and Plateau provinces agitated strongly for a separate state, and the 1957 Constitution Conference set up a

Commission of Inquiry. At the sitting fears of religious persecution, forceful conversion to Islam and discrimination in the North were openly and strongly expressed by Tiv and other minority leaders.[14] No state, however, was created because of the strong opposition of the Muslim rulers and because the British thought that the creation of states would delay the independence of the country.

After the North was granted self-government in 1959, Ahmadu Bello, Premier of the Northern Region, stated on several occasions that the North was for all Northerners, and that his government had no intention of spreading one religion at the expense of the other.[15] Yet it took the Tiv riots on the very eve of independence to bring the Northern government to assure any real pluralism in the North.[16]

The first years of independence

The mood in both the North and the South after October 1960 was to make Independence work. It became a political slogan to "bridge the gap" between the North and the South. After the 1961 election in the North two Christians from the Middle Belt were appointed ministers and another two were appointed provincial commissioners. Moreover Northern Muslims received many appointments in the national administration in Lagos, which they once regarded as a foreign center of power. Both sides made magnanimous gestures of cooperation.

Yet this euphoric mood soon gave way to new tensions. Christian Churches, especially the Catholic, the Sudan Interior Mission, the Sudan United Mission and the Anglican, expanded their mission work among the non-Muslims of the North and achieved tremendous success. The Muslims rulers became afraid that they would lose the upper hand in the North, especially since the Northern Christians had more zeal for education. They therefore began to harrass and curtail the work of the churches in many different ways. Religious feelings were part of the Tiv revolt in 1964 against the imposition of N.P.C. leaders in their area. Ahmadu Bello, the Sardauna of Sokoto and Premier of the North as well as the Vice-President of the World Muslim League, launched a "bloodless jihad" throughout the North, conducting Billy-Graham-style rallies to make on-the-spot mass conversions, and building mosques and Qur'anic schools with grants from Arab states. Promotions went only to leaders who cooperated with the N.P.C. government and its Islamic policies, while areas such as Benue and Plateau province, which did not cooperate, were denied development allocations. To meet strictly religious harassment, the Northern Christian Association was formed in 1965. Also the Protestant organization "New Life for All" launched a counter-campaign to evangelize Muslims.

At that same time in most parts of the country a movement began for the government to take over church schools. In the South this was motivated partly by American secular influences, but the main supporters were groups who felt they were at a disadvantage: the Muslims everywhere, and in particular areas one Christian sect against another. In some places the education ministries were exasperated by the rivalry of one church wanting to set up a school where another church had one instead of going to other places where schools were needed.

A separate and final source of tension was the N.P.C.'s successful effort to have S.L. Akintola elected Premier of the Western (Yoruba) Region in 1965. He himself was a Baptist, but courted Muslim support and was regarded as a tool of the Sardauna. Riots broke out protesting against rigged elections and the imprisonment of Awolowo, and the West remained in a state of conflict until the coup of January 1966. In the North tension grew because of the growing numbers and influence of Ibos who did most of the technical and professional work and had the upper hand in wholesale trade through their national commercial networks. When army officers killed the Sardauna and other national leaders in January 1966 and made an Ibo, J.T.U. Aguiyi Ironsi, the military head of state, the Ibos in the North made no secret of their glee, and taunted the Hausa. The massacre of May, the coup of July which brought Yakubu Gowon to power, and the massacre of September which sent the remaining Ibos out of the North put the Eastern Region in a situation of all but official secession.

The Gowon regime, 1966-1975

One of Gowon's first actions was to divide the nation into 12 states, satisfying Middle Belt Christian aspirations, but also splitting the Eastern Region into 4 states. Chukwumeka Ojukwu refused to let the East be divided, thereby making secession official and creating the proximate reason for the civil war. Ojukwu construed the war as a "jihad of Muslim hordes" invading Christian Biafra. The religious overtones of the conflict had foundation in that the rioters in the North directed their fury particularly against Christian churches and no compensation was ever made or action taken against the organizers of the riots. Moreover during the massacres any Ibo who declared himself a Muslim had his life spared. Yet the federal government was in the hands of Gowon, who was Christian, and the majority of the soldiers and officers of the Nigerian army were Christians. The religious policy of the federal government during the Gowon regime did not fully please either Christians or Muslims, but at least it was even-handed.

During the civil war the necessity of national solidarity made religious tensions in Nigeria drop very low, except for the embarrassing situation of the Catholic Church, which was reputed to be identified with Biafran interests. Yet the war provided the Catholic Church in the North the occasion to develop a viable Northern constituency for the first time, whereas before it was predominantly a church of Southerners living in the North.

After the war evangelism in the North continued quietly; so did Muslim efforts to spread, together with subtle restrictions on Christianity, such as not giving land for building churches in the growing cities. The near total stop put on the entrance of new missionaries (since the civil war was blamed on missionaries) gravely hampered the Catholic Church for a short time, but a vocation boom followed, together with a rapid indigenization of the episcopacy.

A Universal Primary Education (U.P.E.) scheme was introduced in 1975; at the same time religious education was made an obligatory subject in all primary and secondary schools, with the Muslim and Christian teachers paid by the government but chosen by their respective religious leaders. The spoils of this move were the vast numbers of pagan children who effectively were herded into either Christianity or Islam. As a whole, the Muslims were better prepared and took greater advantage of the situation, even though universal primary education has not yet been fully realized, and many schools do not have religious teachers. One result of the new educational policy is to see religiously mixed student bodies and teachers of both Muslim and Christian religious knowledge in the same school. In assessing the benefits of pluralism, exchange and dialogue in such schools, however, we have to remember that government schools usually have poorer discipline and academic achievement, and the students do not receive a good formation in understanding and living their own faith.

In Yorubaland the government took over all schools, but let religious bodies continue to administer them. These schools usually teach only the religion of the denomination, either Christian or Muslim, yet the administration has no control over the intake or the appointment of teachers, and the quality of these schools has gone down. There has been strong pressure to take away the denominational character of such schools entirely, but lately a strong counter-pressure has developed to return the schools to complete denominational control.

Since independence Yoruba Islam has become more politicized, and Muslim groups have become more vocal in protesting against any form of discrimination. A very strong protest was made in 1967 by the Muslim Students Association in a paper entitled "Case for unbiased religious education in our schools."[17] They complained that the government policy gave Christianity an advantage over Islam, that Christian religious instruction and worship were forced upon Muslim students and no provision was made for Islamic instruction and worship; even public holidays declared for Muslim feasts were not observed by Christian schools. The students concluded by demanding the government to take over the schools. Since 1967 most of these grievances have been remedied, but Muslims still allege that discrimination is rampant in the South.

Christian-Muslim polemics have been another source of the hatred, fear and suspicion which still exist between Muslims and Christians, at least on the organizational level. Polemics carried on by Christians in the South (It would be impossible for them in the Muslim dominated northern states) is principally the work of the Jehovah Witnesses and various Aladura preachers, who spare no blows in attacking and ridiculing the teachings of Islam. The Anglican lay preacher Fawole in Ibadan and the Apostle Adetoro in Lagoso quote the Qur'an and Hadith in Arabic and translation, and equate with paganism such Muslim practices as the use of charms and amulets and the sacrifice of rams.[18] The Scripture Union, strong especially among university students, openly preaches and tries to convert Muslims. They have had some success, but Aladura rallies with emphasis on healing, such as those of Prophet Obaderi (from the Christ Apostolic Church of Ilesha), attract more converts.

Muslims on the other hand, both in open *wa'z* sermons (such as those of Alhaji Ajabgemokeferi) and writings, ridicule Christian teachings and attack the foundations of Christian belief. Alhaji Bolaji Akwukewe's *True light* (1965) and Alhaji A. Dirisu Ajijola's *Myth of the cross* (Lahore, 1975) are particularly hostile. They utilize not only 19th century rationalist arguments against Christianity, but also those developed by the Ahmadiyya and other Pakistani groups, such as attacking the person of Jesus as described in the gospels. As a matter of fact, wherever Muslim books are sold literature printed in Pakistan is abundant.

The final years of military rule

Muslim Christian relations took a new turn after Gowon was ousted in July 1975. Murtala Muhammad came to power in a bloodless coup and carried out many needed reforms which made his regime popular; moreover he established diplomatic relations with the Vatican, a move that the Christian Gowon, even though Protestant, could not make without risking charges of partiality by the Muslim community. Rumors that Murtala Muhammad had plans to promote Islam in Nigeria never could be verified.

After the assassination of Murtala Muhammad in February 1976 Olusegun Obasanjo, a Baptist, was appointed Head of State, but the general impression was that Shebu Yar'adua, a Muslim from Katsina, was really running the country. Since the assassination party, which failed to gain power, was composed of officers from Plateau, Gowon's home state, reprisal measures were taken against any Plateau leaders who were implicated or could be charged with any form of corruption. Church hospitals were suddenly taken over without consultation, and the policies of the state government gave the Christians a feeling that they were being punished. The creation of an unreal myth around Murtala Muhammad and the simultaneous condemnation of Gowon without trial strengthened the impression that Islam makes the difference for being an acceptable head of state.[19] The government built a mosque and Qur'anic school in Kano in memory of the deceased head of state, but no Christian monument. Only the retaining of Joseph Garba, a Catholic, as foreign minister softened the anti-Christian impression. Nevertheless tensions subsided after a short time, and even disturbances later on in Jos, the Plateau capital, resulting from street preaching by Muslims and Christians, did not develop into a crisis situation.

The next event was the debate about providing for federal Shari'a courts in the new constitution. Although a few Muslims, such as Yusufu Bala Usman[20] and A.B. Ahmad,[21] argued against establishing such a court on grounds that it would be giving a special preferential position to Islam in the coutnry, the prevalent Muslim voice supported Shari'a. A typical moderate opinion was put forward by the Etsu Nupe, Umaru Sanda Ndayako,[22] who maintained that the Shari'a courts simply provide for the needs of the Muslim community and do not place Islam in a privileged position. He added that Nigeria, as a secular state, should respect the needs of all groups and care should be taken that Muslims do not infringe on the rights of non-Muslims.

The more official viewpoint was expressed at the National Seminar on Islam and the Draft Constitution at the beginning of August 1977, and the National Conference on Freedom of the Press and the Shari'a at Minna at the end of the same month.[23] At these meetings demand was made for Shari'a *in toto*, not just for religious matters (a "truncated Shari'a"), but all matters of life. A Muslim, it was said, is subject to no other law than the Shari'a; the Constitution is valid only in so far as it reflects the Shari'a, while any other law (imported English law, based on pagan Roman law) is alien and has no binding force for a Muslim. This is true even for a Muslim minority, but while the 1963 census says that Muslims are 45%, the National Seminar on Islamic Law said they are 75%.[24] Accordingly at the Minna seminar Malam Ma'aji Shani suggested that the Shari'a should be made the law of the land, and Sheikh Ahmed Lemu suggested that the Constitution should make Islam the state religion, with the Shari'a applied *in toto* to any citizen who believes in God and the Qur'an.[25] The Draft Constitution in fact opened the door to total Shari'a in nos. 184 (3) e and 186 (2) with the phrase "any other question." This was one step to the declared ultimate objective of making the full Shari'a the supreme law of the land.

In public debate the discriminatory provisions against non-Muslims in the classical Islamic treatises on Shari'a were passed over in silence. Yet not only were the treatises of Māwārdī, and Turtūshī at the basis of Uthman Dan Fodio's jihad of 1804,[26] but Christians in the North today still experience what Shari'a discrimination means in practice. Only ignorance or hypocrisy could have led the former British colonial officer Martin Dent to argue in favor of Shari'a in Nigeria, saying that it concerns only personal law between Muslims.[27] Elsewhere, Dr. Shittu No'ibi argued for total Shari'a as if it were not prejudicial to the rights of non-Muslims, and pointed out what a concession the Muslims were making by demanding at this time only the limited provisions of the Draft Constitution.[28]

When the Constitutive Assembly came to vote on the Shari'a question in April 1978 the proposal for a Shari'a court at the federal level was defeated. The states, however, were allowed to provide for Shari'a courts as they saw fit. Most Muslim members walked out and boycotted the Assembly for a time, but in the end agreed to abide by the new Constitution for the time being, with the hope of reviving the issue in the future. In the politicking for the national elections in 1979 the political parties left the question of Shari'a in the background, because it was too inflammatory.

In the meantime many aspects of Shari'a were being introduced at the state level. For instance there is a Sokoto State bureau to control the orthodoxy of preaching, and threats of police action have been made against preachers who do not abide by the Qur'an and Hadith. At Ahmadu Bello University in Zaria the Muslim Students Association was very vocal during the Shari'a debate and threatened an armed jihad if the provisions of the Draft Constitution were not passed.[29] Immediately after the Shari'a provisions were rejected by the Constitutive Assembly demonstrations took place at many universities protesting the introduction of certain fees. At Ahmadu Bello University the demonstrations were suspected to be connected with circulars distributed at the same time calling for an attack on Christian establishments and the army was called in; several students were killed. In April 1979 the A.B.U. Muslim Students Association attacked the Kegites, a palm-wine drinking club, in order to ban liquor from the campus; they even burned down the Vice-Chancellor's house. Various ulterior motives were ascribed to this action, but it had widespread support simply because it was done in the name of Shari'a. Nevertheless the student leaders were punished, and the public statements of the political candidates reflected the desire of most people to see religious strife averted.

Passage to civilian rule

The political parties campaigning for the July-August 1979 elections kept religious issues strictly in the background. All parties were required to have a national rather than a regional, tribal or religious constituency; so only five qualified. Nevertheless much of the electorate was persuaded that Shagari's Sokoto based N.P.N. (National Party of Nigeria) represented conservative Islamic interests, even though it won Benue, Cross Rivers and Rivers states, where the Muslims have no political influence. P.R.P. (People's Redemption Party), based in Kano, represents Aminu Kano's Islamic-Socialist tendencies; Waziri Ibrahim's Maiduguri based G.N.P.P. (Great Nigeria People's Party) has a populist Islamic appeal, and won Bornu and Gongola states. Nnamadi Azikwe's N.P.P. (National People's Party) was mainly supported by the Ibos and the Plateau Christians. Obafemi Awolowo's U.P.N. (United Party of Nigeria) won most of the Yoruba vote, except in the northern-looking Muslim area of Ilorin in Kwara State; it also won Bendel State. The declaration that Shagari won the presidency was based on a surprise post-election interpretation of the rules. It remains to be seen how an acceptable civilian government can take over and assure justice and peace in the country.

B) Efforts at Dialogue

Protestant initiatives

The Anglican and Methodist Churches in 1952 sponsored a survey of Islam in West Africa carried out by J.S. Trimingham; the results were published in

"Christianity and Islam"

the pamphlet *The Christian Church and Islam in West Africa* (London: SCM, 1955). He made another visit in 1961, and published as well *Islam in West Africa* (Oxford: Clarendon, 1959) and *A history of Islam in West Africa* (Oxford: Clarendon, 1962). Kenneth Cragg also visited and conducted workshops in many places in West Africa; the report of his visit was published as "West African Catechism," *Muslim World,* 48 (1958), pp. 237-247. As a result of these visits several Protestant churches met in 1968, and in 1959 launched the "Islam in Africa Project" in order to assist the churches to understand Islam. Dr. W.A. Bijlefeld was the first director; others who dedicated themselves to this project were Dr. Robert Stade, the Revs. John Crossley, Hans Haafkens, E.O. Oyelade and T.A. Akinlade. A Northern branch was led by P. Ipema, Emory Van Gerpen and E.M. Smith.

The Islam in Africa Project always aimed at peaceful relations with Muslims based on a positive and accurate understanding of Islam, but to gain the widest cooperation of churches with many different views the project subscribed to no theological position concerning Islam. For the same reason the project is not part of the World Council of Churches or any national council. But such neutrality proved to be a liability, since neither the government nor the churches were much in favor of an international organization that was not responsible to the Nigerian churches. Since 1977 the study center in Ibadan has been closed. Its library was moved to the Institute of Church and Society, and any further activities are hoped to come under the Institute's auspices. The problem of ideology will remain for some time, because the Northern Nigerian branch is oriented towards ways of converting Muslims, while the all-African leadership meeting in Legon in 1977 was strongly latitudinarian in tendency.

The Institute of Church and Society in Ibadan has been interested in Islam since it was founded by the Nigerian Council of Churches in 1964 and has sought the cooperation of the I.A.P. study center for its own seminars. At the one on evangelism in 1973 Rev. Oyelade presented the paper "Christian-Muslim involvement in evangelism." In March 1974 at a seminar on "Christianity in Independent Africa" Rev. Oyelade with J. Kenny, O.P., presented a paper "Changes in Christian-Muslim relations since independence." The Institute of Church and Society has also hosted several W.A.A.T.I. (West African Association of Theological Institutes) meetings, which have included discussion on Islamic studies. At the August 1979 meeting J. Kenny presented a paper "Muslim use of Christian Scriptures," and a workshop on Islamic studies was held with Protestant, Catholic and Muslim participation.

One strength of Protestant involvement in Christian-Muslim relations is the presence of lecturers on Islam in university faculties of religious studies, such as S. Babs Mala at the University of Ibadan, E.O. Oyelade at Ife, G.O.M. Tasie at Jos, and T.A. Akinlade at Abraka College of Education, University of Benin. The University of Ibadan Religious Studies department (under Methodist leadership) has been particularly interested in promoting inter-religious dialogue at the academic level. It sponsors an annual Religious

Studies Conference, considering Christian, Muslim and Traditional Religion approaches to a particular theme. The papers of these conferences are usually published in the department's journal *Orita*.

Catholic initiatives

In 1961, during the Second Vatican Council, the Apostolic Delegate to Nigeria, Archbishop Sergio Pignedoli (now the Cardinal head of the Vatican Secretariat for non-Christians) toured the North and took special interest in the problem of relations with Muslims. One of the things he noted among the clergy of the North was the absence of any specialists on Islam and the general lack of knowledge about Islam and the Nigerian Muslim situation. His efforts to remedy this situation resulted in two achievements:

First Victor Chukwulozie, a young priest of the (now) archdiocese of Kaduna, who for some time was interested in relations with Muslims, was encouraged to organize two meetings between Catholics (with some other Christians) and Muslims. The first took place in Kano on 11 October 1962, and the second, on «Ecumenism and the undergraduate», at Ahmadu Bello University, Zaria, on 7 March 1963.[30] These meetings were between private individuals on both sides, and neither side was sponsored or had official backing by its higher authorities. Fr. Chukwulozie went to Oxford for Islamic studies in 1963 and returned to Nigeria in 1970, when he took up the post of lecturer in the Department of Philosophy and Religion at the University of Nigeria, Nsukka. He is also the national Correspondent with the Secretariat for non-Christians.

The second result of Archbishop Pignedoli's efforts came from his contact with the Dominicans who since 1953 staffed the Prefecture Apostolic of Sokoto. Archbishop Pignedoli asked the Prefect, Msgr. Lawton, O. P., if the Dominicans could provide personnel to conduct research and dialogue as the Dominicans in Cairo were doing.

Msgr. Lawton then asked the Cairo Dominicans to send someone to look at the situation and make recommendations. Fr. Anawati was to come, but could not get an exit visa. In July 1963 Fr. Jacques Jomier came and recommended that at least two Dominicans be trained in Islamic studies. While visiting his home country in January 1964, Msgr. Lawton spoke of his needs to the Dominicans of his province and was promised that Fr. Joseph Kenny, just finishing his theological studies, would be sent. In November Fr. Kenny came and spent two years in Nigeria before leaving for studies in Rome, Tunisia, Cairo and Edinburgh, where he obtained a Ph.D. in Arabic and Islamic studies. In 1967 Fr. James Kelly was sent to London to do an M.A. at the School of Oriental and African Studies in the area of African Islam. Fr. Kelly returned to Nigeria in 1969, and Fr. Kenny in 1970.

In the meantime a significant step was taken at the major seminary of Sts. Peter and Paul in Ibadan. In 1966 the rector, Fr. L. Nadeau, O. P., introduced courses on Islam taught by lecturers from the University of Ibadan Department of Arabic and Islamic Studies. In 1967 the introductory courses became

121

part of the program of the external diploma in religious studies offered by the University of Ibadan Department of Religious Studies; a pastoral course on appraisal of non-Christian religions was also provided for the final year. When the major seminary of St. Augustine was founded at Jos in 1967, the same diploma program was adopted. The courses on Islam at Ibadan and Jos have been taught by university lecturers such as Drs. El-Garḥ (Egyptian), Abdul, and Shittu Nǫibi (both Nigerian), and Frs. Kenny and Kelly. The Bigard Memorial Seminary at Enugu and Ikot-Ekepene, with its 800 some students, as yet does not offer any courses on Islam.

Courses on Islam are also taught at other Christian institutions, such as the National Institute of Moral and Religious Education at Lago (Project T.I.M.E.), which was started by Catholics and is now run jointly by Catholics, Protestants and Muslims, and at the Catechetical Training Institute for the northern dioceses at Malumfashi.

Efforts to promote Christian-Muslim relations have been helped by the visits of outside Catholic specialists, such as Fr. Jacques Jomier, O. P. (in 1963, 1971, 1973 and 1975), Fr. Franz Schildknecht, W.F. (at the invitation of Msgr. Lawton in 1966), and Fr. Jacques Lanfry, W.F. (in 1971).

Some Catholic bishops have had personal contacts with Muslim leaders, but official overtures, in the North at least, have been disappointing. For instance, greetings sent to emirs on the occasion of Islamic feastdays are not acknowledged or reciprocated. The bishop of Sokoto has brought many visitors to see the Sultan, but no Muslim official has ever set foot on the Church compound, and invitations are ignored. Only when Archbishop Jatau was ordained in Kaduna in 1972 was a high ranking Muslim present; Archbishop Jatau spoke special words of greeting and good will for the Muslim community on that occasion. Bishop Sanusi of Ijebu-Ode, who has Muslim parentage, is another noted supporter of Christian-Muslim dialogue. He and Fr. Kenny attended the Vatican-Lybian dialogue at Tripoli in February 1976.

More has been accomplished in relations with Muslims at an informal level, especially through medical services while there were Catholic hospitals and dispensaries, and later when sisters were working in government hospitals. Discussions between priests and Muslim religious leaders have not gone very far; Muslim reserve, especially in the North, is evident whether the Christian representative is a foreigner or not, but the fact of being a foreigner is a particular obstacle. When some local Muslim officials attended the Church wedding of an army officer in Yelwa in 1975, the Fathers were privately amazed at such a historic event.

The first "Official" Christian-Muslim dialogue was organized by Fr. Chukwulozie on 28 November 1974 at the Pastoral Institute in Ibadan, under the joint chairmanship of Bishop F.A. Job of Ibadan and Dr. Lateef Adegbite, the Western State Attorney-General and Commissioner of Justice.[31] Several papers were given on the dignity of man and the role of religion in society, and an interesting discussion took place. A defensive atmosphere which built up at the beginning was broken when one lawyer said that in his long experience in court a Muslim or a Christian swearing on the Qur'an or Bible could perjure himself without scruple, but let him swear by Ifa (a Yoruba divinity) and he will never tell a lie. At the end of the meeting a committee of five was set up to continue dialogue activities, and the journal *Nigerian dialogue* was launched to publicize the content of dialogue meetings. The committee never met, although two issues of *Nigerian dialogue* have appeared under Fr. Chukwulozie's editorship, and a third is at press.

Another attempt at dialogue took place in December 1978 at Jos, where under the auspices of the National Catholic Bishops' Conference Fr. Chukwulozie organized a dialogue on a national level, involving especially Northern Muslims. Many prominent Muslims were invited and accepted, but all of them either sent excuses or did not show up. The 15 or so participants (8 of them Dominicans), however, discussed the papers that were presented by the Christian representatives.

Muslim initiatives

It is not surprising to find more Muslim participation in dialogue in the more open Yoruba society than in the North of Nigeria. One of the most prominent Muslim spokesmen in Muslim-Christian relations has been Dr. M. O. A. Abdul, of the University of Ibadan Department of Arabic Studies. His pamphlet *Islam and Christianity United* (Lagos: Islamic Publications Bureau, c. 1971) was somewhat simplistic in suggesting that Christians should stop worshipping Jesus etc., but he developed a more nuanced approach to Christianity later. He attended the W.C.C. sponsored Broumana dialogue in 1972, and was co-chairman of the W.C.C. Legon dialogue of July 1974, where he delivered a paper "A community of religions." He participated in the Catholic sponsored dialogue in Ibadan in November 1974, where he presented a paper "The dignity of man vis-à-vis Islam." Only confusion in the airline baggage department prevented him from taking part in the Islam in Africa Project seminar in Legon in July 1977. He has attended various inter-religious international meetings besides these, and taught for several years at Sts. Peter & Paul Seminary, Ibadan.

Dr. I. A. Balogun was another lecturer at the University of Ibadan Arabic department who has shown an interest in Muslim-Christian dialogue. Originally an Ahmadiyya member, he welcomed Fr. Kenny to speak in his mosque. He also addressed a gathering of Christians at Agbeni Methodist Church, Ibadan, in 1972, reading a paper "Has Christianity failed in Nigeria?" Now head of the Department of Religions, University of Ilorin, he organized a dialogue between Muslims and Christians under the auspices of his department at Ilorin, 7-11 August 1978.[32] At the University of Ibadan Religious Studies seminar of February 1979 Professor Balogun delivered an interesting paper "The concept of '*ahd* in Islam," relevant to the political situation in Nigeria. In the discussion he emphasised a Muslim ruler's duty to abide by his electoral commission rather than to impose Shari'a on unwilling subjects.

"Christianity and Islam"

Dr. D. O. Shittu No'ibi lectured for a time at Jos University and returned to Ibadan in 1978. His involvement in Muslim-Christian relations took practical shape when he substituted for Dr. Abdul (who was in Saudi Arabia on sabbatical) in teaching "Introduction to Islam" at Sts. Peter and Paul Seminary.

In the North a number of Muslim lecturers in Islamic, historical or cultural studies have shown a genuine personal interest in cooperating with Christian researchers and in dialogue, but the delicate political situation of the Northern states has prevented any public exchange from taking place.

Among political or traditional rulers some can be characterized as appreciative of and friendly to the Christian churches, while others are simply just and proper, and still others are opportunists or definitely hostile. Over the years the Sultan of Sokoto, Abukabar III, has shown himself not only just, but genuinely concerned to curb fanaticism and protect the interests of all who live in the North and particularly in Sokoto. His son, Muhammadu Maciddo, who has held various high posts, is likewise respected by Christians. Sheikh Ahmed Lemu, now chief *qāḍī* of Niger State, has, in spite of his stand on Shari'a, been open to contact and cooperation with Christian groups.

We should not pass over non-Nigerian Muslims who have been in the forefront of dialogue. The first of these is the Egyptian Dr. M. S. El-Garh, head of the department of Arabic Studies at the University of Ibadan. He was the first lecturer on Islam at Sts. Peter & Paul Seminary, and at any private or public occasion where Muslim-Christian relations have come up he has shown himself to be very judicious and sensitive, reflecting his own deeply interiorized Islam. Another spokesman is the Indian Dr. Abdurrahman I. Doi, who was in the department of Religious Studies at the University of Ife from 1967 to 1977, when he moved to the Institute of Administration at Zaria. He was a founding member of the Conference of Muslim Lecturers and Administrative Staff of Nigerian Universities, and has edited its journal, *The Nigerian Journal of Islam*, beginning in 1970. Notable articles, from the standpoint of dialogue, have been his review of the Vatican Secretariat for non-Christians' book *Guidelines for a dialogue between Muslims and Christians* (1:2, January-June 1971), and the article he invited Fr. Kenny to write, "Towards better understanding of Muslims and Christians" (2:1, July 1971 — January 1972). Dr. Doi has also written with sympathy about Yoruba traditional religion and its interaction with Islam and Christianity.[33]

Present problems in dialogue

Dialogue so far has been restricted to a very few formal meetings and personal contacts of interested individuals. Most often it has taken place without close involvement or encouragement from the leaders of the respective communities. Dialogue, in the sense of mutual listening and speaking in order to achieve greater understanding of the other without the immediate aim of winning the other to one's own side, has received more encouragement

124

from Catholic leaders, especially because of pressure from Rome. The preoccupation of most Christian and Muslim leaders is to defend their own side and if possible conquer the other.

While a limited amount of dialogue has been going on among intellectuals and university people, a great amount of practical dialogue goes on among the ordinary people in their daily lives. Most ordinary people are defensive about their religion, if only because it marks them off in a social category. Yet when they are in a situation where they must share their lives and work, they quickly make practical accommodations, without any guiding principles, in all sorts of matters affecting religion. Intellectual leaders are often unaware of the day to day interaction of Muslims and Christians, and the theoretical knowledge they have which could guide the people does not reach them.[34]

Besides these problems strictly concerned with dialogue, there are problems affecting general Muslim-Christian relations in the country. One the Christian side there is the fear that Muslim political power is becoming the predominant force on the federal level. In the North, besides the well known difficulties that the churches continue to experience, the take-over of their institutions has often resulted in replacing their Christian character with an Islamic one, starting with their names. For instance, the Baptist Teachers' College, Minna, is now Ahmadu Bahago College (after an emir of Bida), while Queen of Apostles College, Kaduna, is now Queen Amina College (after a 16th century queen of Zaria, but echoing Muhammad's mother). At an education meeting in Sokoto which I attended, the Christian primary schools of the state were all given new names, but the Ansar ud-deen school in Chafe was left with its original name. Christian religion is still not taught in many schools in the North; a complaint of this to the state governments was made by the National Association of Bible Knowledge Teachers of Nigeria at its meeting in Jos in 1976.

Government Arabic schools are established throughout the northern states, and there are departments of Arabic and Islamic studies in the universities at Ibadan, Kano, Zaria (A.B.U. Institution of Administration, for Islamic law), Sokoto and Maiduguri. These are in fact government seminaries for Islamic religious leaders; private Islamic training institutes are very few. Religious studies departments, combining Islam, Christianity and African Traditional Religion, exist in Ibadan, Ife, Nsukka, Jos, Ilorin and Calabar; one was organized for Ahmadu Bello University, but canceled when a Muslim vice-chancellor took over after the coup ousting Gowon.

Christians also complain that many northern states still proceed as if they were Islamic states governed by the Shari'a, and that they give official encouragement to Islam and its spread. The amount spent by the Federal government to finance Pilgrims' Boards and provide free amenities for the annual hajj is also seen as official encouragement of Islam.

On the Muslim side, the whole idea of dialogue is suspicious and seems only a subtle attempt to convert Muslims. Muslims in Yorubaland complain that Christianity is favored by the state governments, and note that Islamic

"Christianity and Islam"

religious knowledge is still not taught in most primary and post-primary schools, especially in former Christian schools. Some Muslims insist that Christians must drop certain doctrines such as the Trinity, Incarnation and Redemption if dialogue is to be possible, and complain of misrepresentation of Islam on the part of Christians. During 1977 and 1978 many Muslims voiced severe criticism of Christians who opposed the inclusion of federal Shari'a courts in the Constitution. Yet the aftermath of the revolution in Iran in February 1979 has been a cause of embarrassment for proponents of Shari'a.

In spite of these drawbacks on both sides, the good will of many people gives reason for hope in the future. Neither side advocates complete secularity in the government; their complaints have been directed rather against unequal treatment. True equity can only be guaranteed if the government is neutral with regard to religion as such, not trying to judge the theological worth of any religion, but concerned only with the rights of citizens to whatever conveniences are necessary for the practice of their religion.

Various manifestos have been issued about what needs to be done to promote dialogue in future years. The dialogue meetings at Ibadan in 1974 and at Jos in 1978 made statements; recommendations were made in other papers. All such statements include: 1) the necessity to understand and be committed to one's own religious tradition, 2) openness to understand sympathetically and accurately the other's religious tradition, 3) the promotion of toleration and equitable treatment of the nation's religious communities, together with inter-religious cooperation involving people at every level, 4) the need for an organism to identify and voice complaints about statements, publications or actions which aggravate tension between the religious communities, 5) the need for a similar mechanism to promote cooperation in facing problems of the nation as a whole and to provide opportunities for common research and dialogic exchange.

1) Cf. I. I. Ekanem, The 1963 Nigerian Census, a critical appraisal *(Benin City, 1972), 64-66. On pp. 163-6 he points out that the increase of the Muslim population in the North between the 1953 and 1963 censuses was 1.457%, while that of the Christian majority in the East and West in the same period was only 144.5% and 112.9% respectively. See also Joseph M. Cuoq,* Les musulmans en Afrique *(Paris, 1975), pp. 254-7; note his confusion of "Middle Belt" with "Midwest Region."*

The following figures are taken from Appendices 3 and 4 *in Guy Arnold,* Modern Nigeria *(London: Longman g.p., 1977, 176 pp.).* Census comparisons *(millions):* Lagos *(1952-53 census: 0.50; 1963 census: 1.44; 1973 census [provisional]: 2.47),* Western *(4.36; 9.49; 8.92);* Mid-Western *(1.49; 2.54; 3.24);* Rivers *(0.75; 1.54; 2.23);* East-Central *(4.57; 7.23; 8.06);* South-Eastern *(1.90; 3.62; 3.46);* Benue-Plateau *(2.30; 4.01; 5.17);* Kwara *(1.19; 2.40; 4.64);* North-Western *(3.40; 5.73; 8.50);* North-Central *(2.35; 4.10; 6.79);* Kano *(3.40; 5.77; 10.90);* North-Eastern *4.20; 7.79; 15.38).* Total *(30.41; 55.66; 79.76).*

Seven States have changed their names: North-Central *to* Kaduna *(capi-*

Christians and Muslims in Nigeria

tal: *Kaduna)*; Kano *to* Kano *(cap.: Kano)*; Rivers *to* Rivers *(cap.: Port Harcourt)*; Mid-Western *to* Bendel *(cap.: Benin)*; South-Eastern *to* Cross River *(cap.: Calabar)*; Kwara *to* Kwara *(cap.: Ilorin)*; Lagos *to* Lagos *(cap.: Ikeja)*.

And other *States have been divided:* Western *into* Ogun *(cap.: Abeokuta)*, Ondo *(cap.: Akure) and* Oyo *(cap.: Ibadan)*; East-Central *into* Imo *(cap.: Owerri) and* Anambra *(cap.: Enugu)*; North Western *into* Niger *(cap.: Minna) and* Sokoto *(cap.: Sokoto)*; Benue-Plateau *into* Benue *(cap.: Makurdi) and* Plateau *(cap.: Jos)*; North-Eastern *into* Bauchi *(cap.: Bauchi)*, Borno *(cap.: Maiduguri) and* Gongola *(cap.: Yola.)*

2)   *Cf., among many works, S.J. Hogben & A.H.M. Kirk-Greene,* The emirates of Northern Nigeria *(London: O.U.P., 1966).*   .

3)   *Just some indications are: 1) archeological: the brickwork style found in ruins in Bornu State, such a cross found near Lake Chad, which was in the Lagos museum in 1966, 2) tradition, such as that related by Muhammad Bello in his* Rawḍat al-afkâr *concerning a Coptic origin for the Gobir Hausa; on such a tradition among the Batta people see Margaret Nissen,* An African Church is born *(Denmark: Purups Grafiske Hus, 1968), pp. 57-8; on other vague reports and influence on the Jukun people see Richard Gray, ''Christian traces and a Franciscan mission in the central Sudan, 1700-1711,''* Journal of African History, 8 *(1967), 383-393.*

4)   *I plan to publish, with translation, the documents directly concerning Nigerian Christianity from 1486 to 1850.*

5)   *Cf. J. W. B. Kelly, O. P.,* Two views of Islam: that of the Muslim reformers and that of the Christian missionaries in Hausaland during the 19th and early 20th centuries *(M.A. thesis, S.O.A.S., University of London, 1968), pp. 26-38.*

6)   *Walter R. Miller,* Walter Miller: an autobiography *(Zaria, 1949), p. 35; cf. P. T. Crampton,* Christianity in Northern Nigeria *(Zaria: Gaskiya, and in O. Kalu, ed.,* Christianity in West Africa, the Nigerian story, *Ibadan: Daystar, 1978), p. 44.*

7)   *Cf. E. A. Ayandele,* The missionary impact on modern Nigeria 1842-1914 *(London: Longman, 1966), p. 141 ff. See also Sonia Graham,* Government and mission education in Northern Nigeria 1900-1919 *(Ibadan University Press, 1966).*

8)   *See Ahmadu Bello,* My life *(Cambridge University Press, 1962).*

9)   *Cf. Obafemi Awolowo,* Path to Nigerian freedom *(London: Faber, 1947), p. 51.*

10)   Ibid.

11)   *Cf. B. J. Dudley,* Parties and politics in Northern Nigeria *(London: Cass, 1968), p. 22*

12)   *Cf. ibid., p. 143.*

13)   *Cf. S. Babs Mala, ''Christian-Muslim dialogue in Nigeria'' (ms paper, May 1977).*

14)   *Cf. J.I. Tseayo, ''The emirate system and Tiv reaction to 'Pagan' status in Northern Nigeria,'' in G. Williams (ed.),* Nigeria, economy and society *(London: Collings, 1976), pp. 76-89.*

15)   *Cf. E. O. Oyelade & J. Kenny, O.P., ''Changes in Christian-Muslim relations,'' a paper for ''Christianity in Independent Africa'' seminar, held at*

127

"Christianity and Islam"

Institute *of Church and Society, Ibadan, 6 March 1974.*

16) Cf. B. *Nkemdirim,* Social change and political violence in colonial Nigeria *(Devon: Stockwell, 1975), chs. 7 & 8.*

17) The Nigerian Sunday Sketch, *10 December 1967, pp. 2, 3, 7, 9.*

18) Cf. E. O. Oyelade, op. cit.

19) Add to this the continued veneration of Balewa's memory, and more so that of the Sardauna, as fostered by some British adulators, e.g. Rex Niven, The war of Nigerian unity *(London: Evans, 1970), p. 77 etc.*

20) See New Nigerian, *29 March 1977.*

21) See New Nigerian, *15 September 1977.*

22) See New Nigerian, *1 August 1977.*

23) See New Nigerian, *7 April; 15, 22 July; 2, 3, 5, 6, 30 August; 13, 28 September.*

24) See New Nigerian, *12 April 1977.*

25) See New Nigerian, *30 August 1977.*

26) See his Bayân wujûb al-hiira 'alâ l-'ibâd *(edited by Fathi Hasan El-Masri, Ph.D. thesis, University of Ibadan, 1968).*

27) West Africa, *24 April 1978, reprinted in* New Nigerian, *28 April 1978. Neither publication would print any rejoinder.*

28) "The Nigerian Draft Constitution and the Sharī'ah controversy," NATAIS, Journal of the Nigerian Association of Teachers of Arabic and Islamic Studies, *n. 1 December 1977), 88-121.*

29) See the full text of their letter to the Supreme Military Council of 1 March 1977 and another undated Press Release signed by Ibrahim Ya'qub, secretary-general in Appendix 1 and 2.

30) Cf. V.C. Chukwulozie, "Christian-Muslim relationship in Nigeria," a paper at the "Christianity in Independent Africa" seminar, Jos, September 1975.

31) Cf. ibid.

32) The proceedings were published by the University of Ilorin under the title Religious understanding and cooperation in Nigeria.

33) E.g. "Syncretism in Yorubaland: a religious or a sociological phenomenon?", Practical Anthropology, *16 (1969), 109-113; "Some further aspects of Yoruba syncretism."* Practical Anthropology, *16 (1969), 252-256; "A Muslim-Christian-Traditional saint in Yorubaland,"* Practical Anthropology, *17 (1970), 261-268.*

34) A similar assessment of dialogue problems was made by S. Babs Mala, op. cit.; *see also his "Christian-Muslim dialogue: its historical perspective in West Africa," a paper at the "Christianity in Independent Africa" seminar, Jos, September 1975.*

128

VIII

Opportunities and Limits of Organized Dialogue

BY EDITORS: PRO MUNDI VITA BULLETIN

1. Thoughts on the recent history of organized dialogue

A. The participants and their initiatives

The Christian participants in these colloquia, meetings, and visits were either representatives from specialized bodies of the WCC and the Catholic Church, or, in the main, academic people and intellectuals from faculties of theology. Sacred Scripture or literature. In either case they have always stood aloof from and independent of political power.

It has not always been so with the Muslim partners, and certainly not so at the Tripoli Congress organized by the Arab Socialist Party of Libya. Very few leaders or members of institutions officially representative of Islam have actively participated. They have sometimes had to fall in with the wishes for dialogue expressed by the political authorities. Most Muslim participants have been academic people and intellectuals from faculties of literature or

This essay, a joint report by the Editors of the Pro Mundi Vita Bulletin, whose offices are in Rome, is reprinted by permission of the Publisher: 74, Sept.-Oct. 7F, pp. 35-52.

philosophy, and have been profoundly influenced by French or English culture. They have always made it clear that they spoke on their own behalf, preferring to give personal witness rather than proclaim a communal position. At many congresses, however, quite a number of high-ranking leaders from Ministries of Religion or Walfq-s have been present as official delegates, representing the Islam recognized by the political power of their country.

Many initiatives have come from the Christian side, few from the Muslims. Almost always, however, a joint commission, with an equal number of members from either side, has prepared the dialogue, smoothed away difficulties, and done everything possible to ensure success. It must be admitted that not infrequently the participants were persons new to dialogue. This gave the unfortunate impression that each encounter was the very first of its kind and that it was necessary to keep to rather general matters acceptable to all but binding on none. While many of the Christian participants were already prepared for dialogue and anxious to get to know their partner better, the same could not be said of the Muslims. To this difference in readiness and openness was often added a disparity of method, mainly due to very different intellectual demands and cultural forms. The fact is: an Arab partner who speaks but one language does not act or react in the same manner as one who is at home in both the Arab and a European culture. Many a colloquium has suffered from this very marked difference among the participants as regards the requirements of scientific method and information.

On the Christian side every tendency has been represented, thanks to the immense spread of the WCC, the catholicity of the Secretariat's delegates, and the growing co-operation between the two specialized bodies (which, however, reserve the right not to participate in any given colloquium). But, on the Muslim side, no great participation seems to have come from the Chi'tes, nor has ecumenism between Sunnites and Chi'tes played any great role. No Muslim organization has been set up with responsibility for dialogue: all arrangements for "organized" encounter still have to pass through the local Islamic authorities of any particular nation. In certain cases it would seem that Muslims bent on dialogue are found more often in the political and cultural world than in that of theologians or religious leaders.

Another question arises at this point. What exactly are the partners in these Muslim-Christian colloquia looking for? It is no secret that among Christians and also among Muslims there are fundamentalists, reformists, "orthodox", and liberals. If dialogue is to be honest, all people of all these tendencies should be able to participate or at least feel that their views are represented. There is a great temptation in dialogue to look for "easy" partners who will readily respond to one's viewpoint, but who do not really represent their community of faith as a whole. Merely belonging to the culture of Islam or Christianity (or political membership of a country that is traditionally Muslim or Christian) is not necessarily a qualification for "organized dialogue". The difficulties that have emerged during colloquia have arisen because individual Christians and/or Muslims were not of the same "spiritual group" and because these groups themselves, both in the Christian world and the Muslim *umma*, are often tempted to cut themselves off from each other.

There have been colloquia at which some participants were intent only on proclaiming their own convictions without taking the partner and his sensibilities into account: a misuse of the time allowed, as there was no attempt to explain the propositions to those who could not understand them. Generally, however, speakers have expressed their ideas in a manner more or less adapted to the questions in the partner's mind, once they were known. In some cases they were bold enough to compare, to correct, to wonder about their own positions and finally to arrive at an exchange of ideas. This attitude was more common in interdisciplinary colloquia, but it would seem, in fact, that the Muslim theologian is less inclined thereto than the Christian theologian. Whatever their explicit or implicit intentions, the participants have always been considered true believers, even though this fact is appreciated and measured in different ways within the Muslim and Christian traditions. Even though the relations between faith and research were regarded differently, the dominant qualities of the majority of the participants always were a living, convinced faith, sincerity towards God and man, and a desire for encounter and exchange.[1]

Intentions apart, the attitudes of the participants were usually more in line with the spirit of dialogue. In this everyone was supported by his tradition of hospitality, by his own intellectual curiosity, by his fundamental honesty, and by the many occasions the colloquia offered of sharing in "community life". Even if a mutual lack of knowledge showed itself quite frequently in the discussions, and even if sensibilities were often hurt by the strange, if not irrelevant and therefore aggressive, guise of someone's exposition, it has to be admitted that the quality of faith on both sides became apparent in the very capacity to forgive shown by many participants on more than one occasion. Often the Christians gave full rein to healthy self-criticism. Some colloquia could have been much better if the Muslims had done likewise.

B. *Themes and contents of the colloquia*

The Muslim-Christian colloquia of the last few years have tackled a great number of diversified topics. The very variety is, in a way, a sign of the will to explore many avenues. A preliminary balance-sheet can be made since the themes fall easily into two categories — specifically religious topics or action programmes realizable more or less immediately.

Many colloquia treated of the Muslim-Christian dialogue itself. The aim was to point out the possibilities and promises, to specify the content and the spirit, to guarantee seriousness and depth, to develop the necessary vocabulary and specific attitudes. At this level, the partners sometimes went along parallel paths without any convergence. Nevertheless, the experience has gone on, and Christians and Muslims have reached the point where they can tell each other how they envisage eliminating the serious bones of contention that have piled up over thirteen centuries. Is it possible for a Muslim to explain Christianity to his brethren in such a manner that a Christian can accept it? Can a Christian do the same thing vis-á-vis Islam and Muslims? Often this twofold theme gave rise to heated discussions. Still, it had led to a better understanding of what, in each religion, can be grasped and perceived by the other, and consequently to a less imperfect delineation of the essential elements, on either side, which still remain a mystery and basically inaccessible to the other. On this level, many Christians have discovered that the other side had a poor knowledge of Christianity as regards its fundamentals and its authentic sources. Thus both sides have complained of being misunderstood, or badly known, and have insisted on prejudices and misunderstandings being got rid of as soon as possible through action that is both critical and pedagogical.

In order to improve the opportunities for dialogue there has been frequent insistence on the need for peaceful coexistence and encouragement of all forms of true cooperation. More than one colloquium therefore has studied the relations between communication and the concrete situation of minorities in the hope of a *modus vivendi* emerging, despite the different designs Islam and Christianity have for organizing and inspiring society. This important theme has been treated both from the historical viewpoint (the mutual implications of political expansion and religion) and the sociological and economic point of view. It would be useful if it were treated also from the juridical and anthropological angle. Sometimes there have been discussions on the plurality of cultures and the possibility of a "pluralist society", which is not seen in the same manner by everybody.

If, in these two domains, dialogue has reached deeper levels it is because the colloquia have again and again made it clear that Muslims and Christians in their faith and action have a common heritage, even if some people unduly extend or reduce its content. The discussions have always brought out many slight differences and stressed how very different meanings can be covered by apparently similar theological terms. It would seem, however, that the texts of Vatican II give a rather good description of this heritage; and this account many speakers have tried to clarify in detail and to develop in the sense of an experience of God that sometimes goes further than its official expression by both religions. Apart from the essential points of the contents of faith (adhesion to the One, Living and Subsistent God, Creator of heaven and earth, who loves man, forgives him and shows him mercy, who is worthy of praise and glory, who sends prophets and speaks through them, who raises the dead and summons souls to their reward) and apart from action (in the service of life, justice, freedom, peace, brotherhood), the participants have begun to understand the importance of a better analysis of their own personal response. For there are also common religious attitudes which it would be well to develop together and enrich from either side by sharing religious experiences. Every revelation is an approach to truth and demands obedience. Every believer must inquire into the mystery of the Word of God and of Sacred Scripture. All worship requires prayer, meditation and liturgy, and all education in the faith demands suitable ways of teaching. All the foregoing has been experienced by both sides and been discussed at length.

At the level of joint action, based on the same theological vision of the value of creation and of the dignity of man as a privileged creature. Christians and Muslims have often discussed fundamental themes that look to the future. They have become aware that together they have something to say to present-day man about the relationships of faith to science and technology, the answers religion can offer to life's new problems (mastery of demographic growth, for example), to cultural problems (faith "limited" or "strengthened" by the achievements of the human sciences) and economic problems (unequal development of nations and States, a new international economic order). For the past ten years they have been trying to state and to unify the content of that message. Both sides know that social justice derives from faith and that respect for the created world depends on ecology: their religious message is the vehicle of a common hope for the modern world. The validity of religion and the credibility of faith is enhanced when believers constantly and everywhere fight for human rights. This is the general framework of the common answer of Christians and Muslims to the challenges of modernity in the context of the effort to build up a new international community.

Finally, there are the definite divergencies and irreducible truths about which Christians and Muslims show themselves quite different, if not opposed, to each other. They have been bold enough in some colloquia to pursue discussion to that point and to run the risk of a difficult confrontation on thorny themes which, of course, serious dialogue cannot overlook. Among topics that have been discussed seriously and in depth might be mentioned a reconsideration by Christians of the religious aspects and merits of Mohammed, the common attempt at a better understanding of what both sides can see and admire in Jesus, a common recognition of the duty of the apostolate (*Mission* and *Da'wa*) in the context of respect for religious freedom and a rejection of proselytism of any kind. In view of the fact that these themes sometimes caused tensions and often showed that the partners were unaccustomed or disinclined to listen to or understand what the other side thought about them, one concludes that colloquia should tackle such subjects only at the end, when the participants are convinced that they have many common values and that nothing is likely to lead to a split. The difficulty the Muslim sometimes has in listening to and understanding what a Christian says is due to the fact that he is bewildered by the method and framework of thought.

C. *Working methods*

How have the Muslim-Christian colloquia developed all these themes, whose extreme variety required that every participant should be competent and qualified in several disciplines? Their preparation, progress and achievement must be looked into before a tentative general appreciation is made. What place was given to prayer, meetings, and exchange, in and apart from working sessions? Tomorrow's methodology must take account of all this if Muslim-Christian dialogue is to get away from mere repetition and paths already well trodden.

1. Preparation

This work was often done by a joint commission, sometimes at very short notice (e.g. four months for Tripoli). While, generally speaking, topics were decided on fairly early, it was not always easy to distribute them among the speakers. Normal delays, including that of the postal services, were not the whole explanation. There was sometimes a vagueness and indecision about looking for participants, keeping to commitments and dates, and even about participation itself. While the secretaries of preparatory commissions often managed to keep the situation in hand, many would-be participants rightly complained about a lack of information regarding the names and qualifications of their partners and the topics and contents of their papers (e.g., at Tripoli and Córdoba II, where some Christians did not know who the majority of the Muslims would be). Often participants did not even have time or opportunity to consult together beforehand. Some colloquia thus had the air of being improvised: this led to uncertainty, repetition, a lack of convergence, and disregard of the rule of dialogue. Not knowing the exact qualifications and personal needs of their opposite numbers, some participants restricted themselves to generalities, being afraid to draw up a fully documented and detailed paper that might hurt an "unknown" audience. It is then, all the more to the credit of the preparatory commissions that in such circumstances they usually succeeded in completing the translation of papers that had already reached the secretariat.[2]

2. Proceedings

To some degree the principle of parity was often broadly respected, each topic being treated by a Muslim and a Christian, with rotation of chairmen and of priorities. The result was frequent and pointless repetition, particularly when both sides dealt in generalities. Generally speaking, in discussions, in so far as there were two chairmen, equal opportunity was given to both delegations. Speakers were seen to stick more readily to time-limits under a chairman of their own religion. Whenever the one chairman was a Christian, Muslim interventions always obtained extra time. The more observers there were, the more requests were made by them for permission to speak in order to get out of their position of silence and marginality. Observers, if there were many of them, soon became participants and their interventions became full-blown conferences.[3] It was often noted that Muslim participants easily gave in to the temptation to be long-winded, their papers being so long they could not be read in full in any one session. The choice of participants would therefore seem to be a real problem. As Prof. Abdelmajid Charfi from Tunis said: "Nothing is more unpleasant than having to put up with endless talk from 'dialogue professionals' whose only concern it is to please this group or that, in complete disregard of the fundamental principles of intellectual honesty".[4]

More serious, in most of the colloquia, was the attempt to deal with too many topics (as, for example, at Tunis). Seeing the wide scope and complexity of the themes before him, Prof. Abdelmajid Charfi hoped that in "subsequent encounters" account would be taken "of this complexity (in order to) limit each meeting to just one or two problems, thereby avoiding programmes that were too heavy and not very conducive to calm and systematic reflection."[5] Colloquia devoted to one theme only, treated from both points of view, were the exception.[6] Very often there was a tendency to treat of everything and to allow time for a great number of secondary papers. Although some of these were of great importance to serious dialogue, others dealt with matters that were too marginal. Here is where guidance of the convening committee, of delegation secretaries and of chairmen becomes decisive and difficult. Drawing a line between strictness and anarchy is not easy. Generally speaking, the conveners never made cuts in the programme but they did admit quite a lot of extra papers and allowed public exchanges and discussions to go on far too long. Thus the colloquia suffered from too heavy an agenda, and participants had little free time for interpersonal dialogue. Indeed, the importance of a Muslim-Christian dialogue depends also on the many possibilities it offers to participants to meet at meals and have longer discussion, to have friendly chats during walks in a park or in some quiet corner, to relax on some touristic or cultural outing. This presupposes, of course, that the participants can meet one another frequently through living in the same surroundings and having enough free time.

What about the tone of the papers and the climate of the public discussions on the conditions and on the themes described? There is no denying that both sides discovered the advantages of a common language that developed through respect, esteem, attention to the other's vocabulary, and the effort to understand and get closer. Those who took part in the most difficult of the colloquia are the first to recognize that there is in the dialogue a dynamic that grows, willy nilly, when dialogue really takes place, even though for a long time dialogue amounts to two monologues that are more or less polemical and critical. Does that mean that there has always been freedom of expression? One could not go that far, for the papers from both sides immediately reveal enduring problems and long-lasting touchiness. Every individual has *his* own way of life, a particular way of expressing *his* tolerance, *his* understanding, and *his* "openness". Sometimes Christians had to put up with listening to the same accusations being repeated, accusations stemming from the past with its prejudices, errors and injustices on both sides. Simultaneous translation, even when good, was not always perfect. It brought out the deep difference in vocabularies and was often the unwitting cause of many misunderstandings.[7] At a deeper level, however, the discussions revealed religious sensibilities that were very different and readily susceptible to hurt or offence, for no apparent reason. In the end the Christian suffered in silence and felt a lack of understanding when he realized from the talks of the Muslim partners that his own Scriptures were judged to be inauthentic or false. On the other hand, the Muslim found it difficult to listen to a Christian scientific or theological discourse on the person of the founder of Islam so different from his own view. All these difficulties are not only limits but also reasons for speaking and dialoguing more and for attempting to pray together.

Has prayer found its very natural place in these colloquia of believers? Here too Christians and Muslims have shown themselves heirs of their respective religious traditions. It is well known that entrance to the mosque is often forbidden to non-Muslims, and very seldom are they allowed to be present as guests or spectators at Muslim community prayer. Because of its exceptional location and situation, Córdoba made is possible for both partners to be present at the other's official liturgy. In other places, this would be very difficult. On most occasions there was the chance, at the beginning or the end of the congress or even daily, of standing silently to listen to a reading or singing of a meaningful passage from the Holy Books of both religious traditions. It was more difficult to arrange for a time of silence during which each participant might address his own preferred prayer in his heart to his Lord. On this point also religious customs are different; smaller groups may succeed but larger gatherings will only produce noise.

3. Achievement

At the end of most of the colloquia, conclusions or memoranda were drawn up in which their activities were recapitulated, points of agreement listed, and action programmes proposed. At some colloquia this was not done, or only very short texts were produced, for it is no secret that in the most important congresses there was political interference connected with Sionism and the Palestinian problem, which merely complicated matters and led to lasting misunderstandings. Some conclusions suffered from being drawn up in a hurry, especially if they were lengthy, as at Tripoli. Ambiguities and a regrettable lack of clarity arose out of the differences in the representative character of the partners, and also from the mixture of literary styles in the making of joint declarations, the expression of wishes, resolutions and decisions, and in bilateral or unilateral recommendations — all these being fundamental elements in "a common programme," which we shall deal with in a later section. While the Christians at the meetings tended to be brief and to the point on precise topics, the Muslims sometimes tried to encompass a whole mass of problems at once. The varying degrees of care with which the conclusions were prepared also affected their value and credibility.

The tasks of publishing the reports and carrying out the recommendations were often given to a committee. The existence of specialized bodies for dialogue, of official institutions and public associations usually made these tasks easier. Gradually a small collection of Proceedings of Muslim-Christian Dialogue has been amassed where many texts can be found, though few colloquia have published or summarized the general contents of the discussions. There remains also the delicate problem of implementing in real terms the wishes and desires expressed at the colloquia. In all fairness it should be said that some Christian participants, particularly those of Córdoba,[8] have been bold enough to do so. It is hoped that in the future the specialists in this dialogue will profit from the ample "common Muslim-Christian experience" reflected in the many conclusions referred to above, always respecting, however, the great principle of parity. This perhaps is the area where some "conclusions" reveal shortcomings; for example, in their demanding too much from the Christian partners. Only the strictest equality in contributions, commitments and forbearance will encourage Muslims and Christians to continue this dialogue in a fair way as responsible persons with similar rights and obligations.

D. Preliminary balance-sheet of the organized dialogue

At the end of the Tripoli Seminar, Sheikh Subhi Sâlih from the Lebanon stated: "A page of a dark past has been turned over for ever," because the members of the two delegations "have surpassed themselves and spoken of duties before thinking of rights, being, above all, intent on objectivity." This led another Muslim, Prof. 'Utba to say: "The seminar has opened up a road to a future in which relations between Muslims and Christians will be characterized by understanding and harmony". On the Christian side, Fr. A. Mandouze, a Frenchman, declared: "At Tripoli both sides have drawn much courage and honesty from one another, a beginning has been made in mutual knowledge and acknowledgement of one another, it will be impossible from now on to present an image of the other which does not correspond to the living facts, it will be impossible to judge without listening."

After the many colloquia and encounters of the past ten years, that is mainly what Muslims and Christians repeatedly refer to: "they have been ready to take the trouble to meet, to speak, and to live together in friendship" for they know "that the page has been turned, past conflicts are past and a completely new step in history is beginning to take form" — to quote the words of two other participants at the Tripoli Seminar. The fact is that within the global framework of reconciliation between religions, in a period of ecumenism among the Christian Churches that holds much promise, Christians and Muslims have decided to put their old apparatus of polemical arguments and ideological theses into the archives or on the scrap heap. It is a sign of the times, perceptible to all true searchers after God, that they are to meet, speak, explain themselves to one another, accept mutual differences, and to work together, the better to face the challenges of the modern world. That is the first balance-sheet of this "organized dialogue," imperfect as it may be, and of the many forms of day-to-day dialogue which it authorizes from now on at all levels. The recent visit of Cardinal Pignedoli to Cairo at the invitation of the Great Imâm, Sheikh of al-Azhar, even though a very formal one, can be regarded as a symbol of this.

Thanks to this "organized dialogue" in limited colloquia, research seminars, or the bigger congresses, hundreds of Christians and Muslims have learned to work, to think, and even to pray together, while public opinion has begun to get accustomed to a new vocabulary in this matter. Opposition has changed to encounter, to friendship, even to fraternizing. Many prejudices and misunderstandings are now tending to disappear and this had led many Christians and Muslims to change their views about the other. Many Muslims have recognized that Christians are true monotheists, authentic witnesses to God, and loyal servants of the Gospel, free from dreams of power and wealth. Many Christians have come across modern educated Muslims who are aware of their faith, free from any complex, able to listen and to understand the Christian partner. The growing number of such encounters has, without any doubt, created a new climate of understanding which today is encouraging dialogue at the level of daily life all over the world.

Whether they have participated as privileged witnesses in these colloquia or live the open friendship of believers at the grass roots, Muslims and Christians can henceforth consider as definitive the conclusions prepared by the Christians present at the Tripoli Congress, and can join them in saying: "We have become aware of the fact that our common faith in God, Creator and Judge of man and of history, has been and remains a revolution in the process of human development. This faith has raised man to his dignity of 'deputy' of God on earth. It also implies and demands respect for the dignity and freedom of man. This same faith, although superior to ideologies, is actually their life-giving source, providing man with the motivation and energy that enable him to find his right place vis-á-vis God, his brethren, and the cosmos. Without this same faith in God, it is impossible to guarantee man his full freedom and full dignity.

"All the sons of Abraham have the obligation to ensure that their common religious heritage leads them to a rediscovered mutual trust and renewed love of one another, and to have the courage so to act that their life and work inspire them to cooperate as brothers in the service of the human family.

"Faith in the One God demands that we recognize all men as brothers, that we look into ourselves when we see all the injustices existing in our respective societies, and that we personally become converted in view of the demands of justice and the appeal of the poor and the oppressed. The Prophets have reminded us of the fact that sincere worship involves the establishment of justice among all God's creatures. Whatever the level at which we appeal to our sacred scriptures — and on this point we take different positions — we are in almost complete agreement about what social justice demands in practice.

"As there are many difficulties in the way of dialogue (prejudices, suspicions, mutual fear and differing sensibilities), and as we are still in the first stages of our search for a mutually intelligible language on prophetic mission, we are invited:

— to learn the lessons taught by history in order to retain the fruitful experiences and to avoid the errors of the past
— to see to it that each side comes to know the other as it wants to be

known: revision of religious textbooks, utilization of the mass media, increase in the number of professorships in Islam and Christianity, and cooperation between them

— to be fair enough, on either side, to guarantee to all religious minorities all the rights and obligations the majority enjoys

— to recognize each religion's "duty of apostolate" and the authentic witness each must give, while respecting human liberty — which involves the condemnation of any kind of proselytism

— to define more clearly the exact scope and methods of dialogue."[9]

This appears to be the charter for Muslim-Christian dialogue today. Its philosophical and theological implications, as well as its practical and mystical demands, need to be examined. The colloquia of the last ten years have also given the opportunity to Muslims and Christians to respect and get a better view of their profound differences within a common heritage of faith and action. Little by little, both sides have found out — with the intent of avoiding — the dangerous snags of an easy syncretism and of apologetics, whether contentious or irenic. In fact, only authentic Christians and true Muslims can take part in profitable dialogue. Prof. Mohammed Aziz Lahbabi admitted after Córdoba I: "the dialogue presupposes partners are different: the other is other because he is not me. There should be no apologetics nor proselytism; to make concessions or to demand them from the other would be a betrayal of the spirit of dialogue."

On their part, the Christians involved in the dialogue have learned much from it. Not only have they found out a bit more about what the living faith of Muslims is, and what Muslim theology has said about the approach to the mystery of God, they have also learned to meditate, in a still more Christian manner, on the importance of creation, of "cosmic revelation" and of the interventions of the Spirit of God in history. From being at times overattentive to the marvellous consequences of the incarnation of the Word, they have been led by this dialogue to restore to its full greatness the transcendence of the ineffable God and the total gratuitousness of the Father's revelation to us in the person of his Word, Jesus Christ. The dignity of man is always the marvellous reflection of God's perfection. That is the reason why, in the long run, Christians are enriched by it: they have been humble and repentant, able to admit their past errors and their responsibility for the evils the modern world is suffering from. They have found occasion for joy, for being coherent and enterprising in loyalty to their full identity and in their esteem for the faith of others. It would seem that many Muslims have experienced a like enrichment in so far as they were seeking, along with Christians, the "face" of God and His mysterious will, in a spirit of utter unselfishness.

2. Today's opportunities for dialogue

A. The political and cultural situation

More than ever before, circumstances invite Muslims and Christians to a

"Christianity and Islam"

dialogue of faith and action because there has never been such a good opportunity of applying the principle of parity. Both sides have denounced the politico-religious undertakings of the past (conquest and crusades) and settled the awkward disputes of the colonial period. Within the present framework of independent nations and cultures "in dialogue" (UNO and UNESCO), Christians and Muslims are relatively equal in power and prestige. While one side has the advantage of advanced technology and a developed economy, the other has major economic assets, such as oil, and is in full process of development. States treat one another as equals and cultures meet and enrich each other with no sense of superiority or inferiority, thanks to generalized education going hand in hand with the multiplication of universities and research centres. The Arab language itself has become one of the major international languages.

Muslim and Christian communities are found everywhere. There is no Muslim country without a Christian minority, made up of either local citizens or foreigners, and there is no country with a Christian tradition without a long- or recently established minority. There is, then, no longer any equating of Muslim-Christian dialogue merely with relations between the Arab world and the West. The very venues of the colloquia and congresses are proof enough that the dialogue is an international reality of interest to the whole world. There is Muslim-Christian dialogue going on among the Filipinos, among the Indonesians, among the Senegalese and in every country with a de facto or de jure pluralist society.

More than ever, too, Christians and Muslims feel bound to the human community (especially that of the Third World) and at the same time trustees of a common heritage to which they have to bear witness. One particular Muslim writer sees it as a "community of communities" and is anxious for the development of this "spirit". Never before have there been so many and such widespread means for getting information and spreading it. Newspapers, books, radio and television enable believers to learn more about the faith and worship of other people, and about the problems of their community and its concrete achievements. Travel facilities increase the universality of modern culture and lead all men to enquire more into the religion of others, then into their own religion, within the framework of what is now an openly pluralist society.

B. Renewal of attitudes

The evolution of Christian Orientalism, the renewal of theology, the texts of Vatican II and the constant efforts of the specialized bodies of the Catholic Church and of the WCC have been of great help to Christians of all schools and denominations in coming to a positive view of the great historical religions and in giving a privileged place among them to Islam as a monotheism that is mysteriously linked to biblical tradition. As Prof. Abdelmajid Charfi stressed: "The time is past when a Muslim was looked on by the Christian as a potential convert, if not as an enemy unworthy of respect. No longer is a

140

Christian, in Muslim eyes, a victim of diabolical machinations, to be brought back to the true religion, if need be by force". Many Muslims have, in fact, reconsidered their concrete appraisal, if not their theological definition, of the Christian they have met and respected because of his evangelical values. They regard him as a monotheist, who is to be ranked among the "People of the Book" and deserving of salvation in his own religion. They have grown accustomed to making a distinction between Christianity and the West, seeing that Christians have ventured to challenge the West and to criticize it. They have discovered that it is possible to be a Christian while being likewise an Indian or an African, that is to say, unconnected with Greco-Semitic philosophy and the historical disputes of Mediterranean peoples.

All societies alike are in danger of becoming severely dehumanized by the worldwide demands of modern technology; and to this danger religions cannot remain indifferent. Materialism is advancing on all fronts and across all frontiers. Whether practical and of liberal origin, or theoretical, stemming from Marxism, materialism threatens both Christianity and Islam in a society where wealth and well-being are endangering true values. There is no need to resort to some "Holy Alliance" of spiritual forces in order to repel these attacks, but the fact of identical dangers threatening Christianity and Islam is surely an incentive to both religions to see if they have not one and the same message, or analogous remedies, for salvaging the dignity and happiness of man as well as the honour and greatness of God. Momentous questions are facing both religions, which they have no right to overlook: how can freedom be guaranteed without allowing laxity to corrupt and how can socialization be achieved without dictatorial communism gaining around?

All the more should such questions involve the two religions since monotheistic religions (and the great philosophies, too) are not innocent in the eyes of history. Sometimes they have minimized the importance of economic and social injustices, if they have not made them possible or legitimated them. Sometimes they have denied to man the practical exercise of his dignity and the freedom of scientific research. They have sometimes not cáred about the depths of man's psychology, his capacity for heroism, and the claims of his quest for power. For that reason all so-called "modern sciences" are, in their eyes, "suspect": are historicism, Marxism, psycho-analysis, existentialism, and structuralism to be rejected as criticisms destruction of faith or welcomed as agents that purify that same faith? Today, Christians and Muslims, being "in the same boat", are questioning one another, the better to help one another to face all these challenges of "modernity". For Muslim believers, it is of interest to know how Christians have renewed their exegesis and how they face today's demographic problems, while Christian believers will be interested in how Muslims envisage greater social justice, with, perhaps, interest-free loans!

D. Demands of action

In the present situation, Muslims and Christians, finding dialogue easier by reason of its international scope in a climate of relative equality, and finding themselves inspired by a new spirit, being inclined to more understanding attitudes and up against the same challenges that modernity poses to all religions, have no choice and can no longer hesitate: they have to speak, to make their position clear to others, and to give common witness if they want faith to be credible and God better honoured. This dialogue has to be started or developed without more ado, despite the objective difficulties arising from the fact that people are not prepared for it.

The very urgency of the problems faced by all prohibits any delay. Ecology calls for awareness, and religions have a lot to say, jointly, on this. The new international economic order awaits a new declaration by religions on their views of man and his use of the riches put at his disposal by God. Muslims and Christians must forthwith become involved with culture (UNESCO), food (FAO), health (WHO) and children (UNICEF) at all levels of their societies in order to bring into play all the fundamental values that are part and parcel both of their ancient moral code and of the present-day charter of nations. Moreover, even where believers from a minority (in Christian or Muslim countries with a laicist regime or in countries with Islam or Christianity as the State religion) it is out of order for them to constitute independent or autonomous "confessions." They are called upon to live together in pluralist societies, which will only become more respectful towards persons and the communities that make up those societies through dialogue between Christians and Muslims.

3. Present-day limits to organized dialogue

The preliminary balance-sheet of organized dialogue is therefore positive, and present possibilities for bold coherent development are numerous. There are, of course, difficulties: personalities, methods and themes. Some difficulties arise from a lack of preparation, from improvisation, or the casualness of participants, but others are more fundamental. It is important that these be taken into consideration, for they may well be limited areas within which dialogue can successfully develop. If we deny them or overlook them we could perhaps be demanding more from the Muslim-Christian dialogue than it can promise or effect. For it to be as successful as possible, it would be best to delimit the area, not go beyond it, lay down rules and observe them. The more we are aware of the limits to dialogue, the better will we be able to develop it along the lines proper to it, thus avoiding vain hopes and early disappointments.

A. Is the dialogue too official?

The dialogue has been criticized by some, and not without reason, as being too official, formal, and far removed from daily life, which after all is what really counts. What else could be expected from "doctors of the law" or "official representatives of religion"? — an exaggerated objection, for many people took part in the colloquia in their own name and as believers, though it is also true that many encounters, because of the presence of "official delegations" became "performances" and were treated as such by radio and television. There is always the real danger of people thinking that by the end of the meeting the main exercise is over and they can go home with no further thought of conversion or reform. Many of the "conclusions" seem to have remained a dead letter: only now and then has there been any sign of their being put into practice, and in most cases it has been the Christian partner that has taken them seriously. There is also the danger of a "dialogue of official representatives" developing, separate from that of the "elites" and quite unrelated to the "day-to-day dialogue of ordinary "silent believers." Tomorrow's dialogue should embody and harmonize all the different levels of encounter and sharing, a task that is far from easy.

B. *Polemics, irenicism or dialogue?*

People remain what they are, often being prisoners of their past: they do not change their ideas in a mere ten or twenty years. It will take one or two generations of persistent effort on either side to get rid of prejudices, renew attitudes, and deepen spiritualities. We are far from this at present. And since, time and again, at such encounters new participants turn up, we have to resign ourselves to a period of polemics. During this time an attempt should be made, in all serenity despite the hurts and mishaps, to acquire the language, gestures and sentiments of true Muslim-Christian dialogue through untiring inquiry and ungrudging, continuous information. The opposite extreme would be to give in to facile irenicism, repeating the same old urbanites about being "brothers," about dialogue being easy and the goal being near, all problems being solved. The danger of practical syncretism and of theological concordism is obvious. A polemical spirit and a complacent irenicism are ever present dangers when Christians and Muslims engage in dialogue on the level of religious experience. The former is the greater threat, because. as Prof. Abdelmajid Charfi said: "The dead weight of the past is still with us, holding together our defensive reflexes, our feelings of self-satisfaction, attitudes of ignorance, mistrust and contempt."[10]

C. *Dialogue with political dimensions?*

Arising out of the view each side has of the relations between religion and society, there is the other danger of such meetings for organized dialogue being used for ideological, if not political, ends. There are too many recent examples of this for thinking they will not crop up in the future. Here the Christian must make a great effort to understand and accept his partner's view, bearing in mind Cardinal Pignedoli's remark: "One of the greatest hindrances to dialogue is political intervention in religion. Some people do not make the Gospel's distinction between what is Caesar's and what is God's, and people's minds are, moreover, troubled by local tensions or fear of losing their freedom".[11] Without losing sight of these realities, those who take part in religious dialogue must venture to distinguish without, however, separating the spiritual from the temporal. In some countries, where religious communities have hardened into political entities, dialogue between Christians and Muslims is at times impossible, due to the unyielding position on both sides when religious, social and political elements are lumped together: that is when dialogue runs up against the confessionalistic, defensive attitude of Christians and the excessively theocratic, fundamentalistic demands of Muslims. Such attitudes can only lead to controversial apologetics. Real dialogue must be aware of these very real dangers and allow them no opening, lest the barely dormant demons of the past be re-awakened.

D. Are the partners impartial?

Even if the above-mentioned dangers are avoided, there are still other and greater difficulties. Both sides are tempted to use two lots of weights and measures. Muslims and Christians alike imperceptibly become over-critical of the others and are apt to be lenient towards their own people. When someone presents a good paper on the common heritage of the monotheists, he is criticized for not stressing the differences. When he speaks of Jesus, pointing out what to him, seems to be common on the level of prophetism and what is specific to Christianity, he is criticized for lacking a spirit of dialogue. There is no need to expect perfect impartiality, but at least the principle of parity should apply: the recent history of dialogue is proof enough that this is still difficult even for the most intelligent people. There are exegetes who criticize, in others, literary styles that are not in line with science, while the same styles are found in their own Holy Scriptures.[12] Then, of course, there is the genius of each language. Whereas French is suitable for Cartesian analyses and English treats problems in a pragmatic manner, Arabic can strike the mind and the heart by its affirmative and incantatory power. Participants in dialogue would do well to remember that not all languages have the same kerygmatic force, nor the same inclination to serenity.

E. Is it really possible to listen?

There is still another limitation, more objective than the foregoing, which the Christian must bear in mind. Whereas he can already, with relative ease, listen and accept a Muslim view on Christianity and repeated criticisms of Christians, the Muslim partner is not always equally inclined to listen to a Christian view on Islam or to criticism of its historical achievements. There are many reasons for this attitude, and the Muslim is excusable in so far as his attitude is a healthy, defensive reaction to the past excesses of Orientalist criticism. However, many colloquia have been timely reminders to Christians that Muslims are deeply conscious of already possessing, through their religion, a ready-made and "orthodox" view of Christ and Christianity. Very often their only criterion of judgement in this matter is the Koran itself. It seems difficult for many Muslims to admit that Christianity as actually lived by Christians, and as expressed by the whole Christian tradition, is "legitimate" Christianity. The same holds for Judaeo-Christian scriptures: they are continuously suspect, since the basic sources of Muslim thought maintain that they have been falsified, transformed, and altered. This is a real difficulty, which limits the scope and the methods of dialogue once it starts dealing with fundamental values in both religions.[13] Finally, at the level of attitudes, the Christian is likely to feel uncomfortable when a colloquium or encounter is organized in a "Muslim country": he has the impression of being the victim of his partner's theological superiority complex. The Muslim partner unwittingly tends to treat him as belonging to the minority, and repeatedly assures him that Islam is tolerant and guarantees the rights of "protected persons (dhimmi-s), oblivious of the fact that the Christian simply wants to be treated as an equal, as a full citizen in his own right. Some Muslims are aware of this and can overcome it, but they are in the minority. Any serious dialogue should re-educate these deep-seated attitudes, and it should exact absolute equality in every respect.[14]

F. Is it possible to transcend one's outlook?

Besides these difficulties, some other problems should be borne in mind. Organized dialogue is something too recent to have solved them all. Ignorance about the other side is still all too common. More effort is needed to spread information in order to lessen and eliminate prejudices and to help both sides to know one another "in truth."[15] When Muslims and Christians think they have reached this stage, they find there is no lack of re-interpretations as they look at each other in the light of their own theological system. It is difficult for a Muslim who has a good knowledge of Christianity not to apply his view of "revelation-as-divinely-dictated- without- any-human-input" to Jewish and Christian Scriptures. Likewise, it is hard for a Christian with a good knowledge of Islam to abandon his concept of inspiration in his study of the Muslim understanding of the Koran.[16] Apart from these dangers, which can be avoided by people who are aware of them, there are others, more subtle, that are almost impossible to overcome. Christians and Muslims together should agree on what are the exact differences of meaning in a religious vocabulary which appears to be common to both. In a theological system everything hangs together, and each element derives its full meaning from the whole. For example, to the Christian, creation implies hidden, preparatory links with the incarnation of the Word, whereas for the Muslim there is only the magnificent act of the transcendent bounty of God, without God being "involved" in his creature. Beyond these different theologies that explain, in a sometimes diametrically opposed sense, certain realities thought to be common to both sides, there are religious sensibilities that react differently to certain words in the "spiritual" vocabulary. Would it not be possible for participants in the dialogue, in a spirit of friendship, to explain clearly to one another what these fundamental differences are, so that all confusion may disappear from the exchanges and everyone be recognized in his ultimate identity? They would need to have the courage and patience to draw up a list of the misunderstandings and false problems, and the honesty to recognize, while regretting their lack of present solutions, the points of contention and the "signs of contradiction."[17]

G. Ecumenism, dialogue, or mere encounter?

Our purpose, in stressing the many difficulties that still remain as obstacles to the future of organized dialogue, is to help this absolutely necessary dialogue to gain in realism, clarity and authenticity. If many disappointments are to be avoided and more supporters recruited among believers on both sides, the language spoken must be that of truth, realism, and essential requirements, thus making clear what exactly are the objectives and methods of organized dialogue. There is too much ready talk about wider ecumenism with the People of the Book, in the mistaken idea that Muslims and Christians are intent on unity and common truths after the manner of Catholic-Protestant-Orthodox ecumenism. This only does harm, because the aims and methods of Muslims and Christians are thus confused with the brotherly and evangelical exchange between various Christian communities. While dialogue should be marked by the same ecumenical spirit, based on respect, understanding and reconciliation in prayer, the difference between dialogue and ecumenism needs pointing out. Muslims and Christians together will never envisage any kind of reunion or unification. Though together able to honour God and proclaim the dignity of man they know that, for all, Jesus Christ remains the "sign of contradiction" and therefore of absolute difference. The Muslim-Christian dialogue can never be equated with ecumenism.[18] The very word "dialogue" is ambiguous: some people prefer to use the word "encounter". It would seem, however, that over the last ten years Muslims and Christians have got used to "dialogue" in a vague sense, a sense which they can make richer as progress is made in their exchanges within the framework of "holy rivalry" proposed by the Koran to the People of the Book.[19] In the meantime, they are certainly called upon by God to discover what values lie in the difference, while they give common witness that God alone is great and that it is an honour to serve him by fulfilling in a perfect manner man's mission today.

4. Conditions for better "organized dialogue"

All the foregoing facts about organized dialogue, its opportunities, and its limitations, show quite well how necessary and urgent it is for Christians and Muslims — now more than ever. It also shows the need for Muslims and Christians to free themselves from all complexes and self-complacency in order to respect each other, while remaining faithful to their own tradition and open to the religious experience of the other. There is reason to hope that the time of parallel monologues is definitely over and done with. Experience has shown that not everyone who wants to can engage in dialogue, and that "encounter" demands discipline and method, scientific preparation and theological insight, as well as real sympathy and kindness. Indeed, Muslims and Christians should not overlook the fact that they often come from very different backgrounds and cultural levels. How, then, can they plan their "organized dialogue" for the immediate future?

A. *Participants and the format of encounter*

The Muslim-Christian colloquia of the last ten years fall more or less into two types: private meetings of well-qualified select groups, and public congresses at which speakers and audience hoped to foster the spirit of dialogue by catching public attention. This suggests the twofold aim of organized dialogue in the future: scientific inquiry into the values of faith and action, and the more practical aim of changing mentalities and attitudes. Hence the need to envisage two quite different kinds of encounter in respect of aims and the people attending. There should be more large congresses, that is, mass meetings with a different audience each time and a nucleus of specialists in dialogue. Speakers and audience should be as representative as possible of tendencies and institutions at local, regional, national and even international level. Catholic, Reformed and Orthodox Christians should be present with both Chi'ite and Sunnite Muslims. there should be fundamentalist, liberal, run-of-the-mill as well as very spiritually minded persons from either camp, all fully part of the community of faith, along with authentic and responsible representatives of church or believing community. The Muslims and Christians should be from all levels of the population so that, besides specialized theological explanations, the many and varied testimonies of believers practicing dialogue during their daily round may be heard.[20] Several languages should be allowed, to illustrate the international dimensions of the dialogue. The ultimate goal being to arouse public awareness and to stimulate among the participants the virtues needed to start dialogue, only truths and values that are obviously common to both sides would be dealt with, while as much information as possible and effective witness in favour of dialogue would be given. Press, radio and television would have full access to these open events, in the hope of widespread publicity being given to the topics, the new spirit, and the practical conclusions.

Parallel to these meetings, a great number of workshops should be set up to pursue scientific research and an in-depth exchange of views, at regular select meetings, without publicity, at local, regional and national level. Reserved to academics, theologians, experts, and actively committed persons, this kind of meeting would study a few themes fundamental to dialogue, in all their theoretical and practical implications, due regard being paid to the demands of scientific work. This work, as Prof. Mohammed Arkoun admits, "requires long preparation on both sides and the ability to take account of the feelings and, even more, the mind of the other side" [21] It would be well to employ only one language in each group, while bearing in mind the language each side uses to express its faith. Such meetings, held in a spirit of mutual esteem by partners who have become real friends, would be equal to the task of thoroughly studying very important theological problems, working out "specialized vocabularies" for dialogue, and eliminating the false problems that are still an obstacle to dialogue. Publications and reviews would, of course, be needed to disseminate the results among circles responsible for the dialogue.

B. A common charter

Muslim-Christian dialogue, in big or small groups, should be based on a common charter equally binding on both sides. Recognizing one another as monotheistic believers with Abraham as the model of their faith, Christians and Muslims would have to regard their sharing in common fundamental truths and values as definitely established. Every new declaration should refer to them by way of introduction so that this joint heritage becomes common knowledge: they are in fact the truths and values the Second Vatican Council recognized as being shared by both partners. To this should be added some common explanatory considerations that would become the practical rules of a jointly developed Directory for Dialogue.

This implies, first, that both sides be explicitly resolved to explain themselves to each other in a friendly manner based on mutual respect, to accept each other as different and worthy of esteem, to learn more about each other's faith, to help each other more in daily life, to make an effort to react generously to the demands made by each one's conscience, and, finally, to encourage one another to become better believers searching after the will and the face of the Lord. These attitudes should often find expression in recommendations and appeals that bind both Muslims and Christians. Is it too much to imagine both parties agreeing to subscribe to the following propositions about the prophets and Sacred Scriptures?

Since Christians believe that the "fullness of prophecy" was realized in Jesus Christ (admitting, however, that the spirit of prophecy continues to show itself in each generation), and since Muslims regard Mohammed as the "seal of the prophets" (while insisting that the life and message of Jesus are of an exceptional character), an authentic dialogue calls for mutual respect in matters on which they differ from one another. The Christian should not demand of a Muslim the recognition in the Messiah of all the qualities Christianity ascribes to him. Likewise, the Muslim should not demand of a Christian that he recognize in Mohammed all the qualities Islam attributes to him. While maintaining that there are the same differences regarding the Holy Scriptures, Christians and Muslims could perhaps assert that God's Word, entrusted to men through the ministry of the prophets in very different ways, should be read unceasingly, meditated and commented on, so that believers may discover the "obvious" and the "hidden" sense. They should, of course, be aware that the Koran has the same importance for Muslims as Christ, the Incarnate Word, has for Christians.

If such recommendations can be made on themes that are so difficult, it is surely desirable that specialists in dialogue show themselves resolved to devote joint efforts to the drawing up of a practical directory — awaited by many — of points of agreement between Christians and Muslims and the

Ten Years of Christian-Muslim Dialogue

attitudes they should have towards each other. The many "conclusions" of the colloquia provide copious material for this. Once the way is marked out, false problems eliminated, and rules of conduct laid down, dialogue can then progress seriously and safely thanks to strict methodology and well-defined themes.

C. Method

What has been said about the methods used in recent colloquia suggests what improvements are desirable. Future encounters should be prepared more seriously — which presupposes planning far ahead and a strictly observed time-table. Participants should have an opportunity to know about one another, their partner's personal research and interest in the dialogue, the title of the papers, at least, if not their contents. It would be good also if each side were informed, in respect of the proposed topic, how the other sees the problems, what vocabulary will be employed and its relation to the language used. Finally, encounters should be boldly postponed when partners will not keep to the strict preparation dialogue requires an equal contribution by both sides in the way of papers, etc., and parity in exchange of views and information.

Throughout congresses and colloquia the same principle of parity should be applied all around and to all participants. For papers, communications, and testimonies, the same amount of speaking-time should be allowed to Christians and Muslims. Only the presence of two chairmen, one Muslim and one Christian, can guarantee the observance of this fundamental rule. The principle of alternate chairmen and interventions should be respected as far as possible, bearing in mind the rules of "hospitality." This is of great importance if participants and, eventually, observers, are to be freed from all complexes of inferiority (or superiority!). Any committee set up before, during or after the colloquium to draw up conclusions, give information to the press, publish the report, etc., should be obliged to keep strictly to this absolute rule of equal representation from both sides. When the number of languages allowed requires translations to be made, in advance or simultaneously, the conveners should engage specialized personnel, Muslims and Christians, qualified in religious and theological matters. Translations made in advance should be checked by both sides, speakers should be required to speak slowly and to use the original texts of the Sacred Books. Finally, more attention should be given by all concerned to the drawing up of the conclusions: all haste should be resolutely avoided, there must be a readiness to re-read, if need be, several times; brevity and clarity should be the order of the day in view of eventual translations having to be made. All and any of these conditions should be repeatedly emphasized whenever necessary.

These encounters, particularly of small groups, should provide greater opportunity for prayer and silence, meditation and exchange. They should therefore be held near places of worship, or rooms for "silence" should be made available. There should be readings of the Holy Books: the "presence" of the participants during official worship on both sides should be prepared and explained; and working sessions should take place in a quiet atmosphere. To know one's partners more as believers and as "searchers for God" will be to the advantage of everyone. Participants should have more free time so that they can sit together after a meal, meet together, or organize small groups for "fraternization". Timetables should make it easy for Muslims and Christians to meet outside the working sessions or larger public sessions. Finally, efforts should be made to effect rapid publication of the final report, the papers and the subsequent discussions. The latter often become the most important documents leading to deeper reflection on the real dimensions of the dialogue.

D. *Appropriate themes*

Here it is well to return to the distinction between public congresses and colloquia for ten to twenty participants; whereas the former should be limited to a superficial, general treatment of general themes, the latter should take up more precise themes and study them deeply in all their aspects. In either case, it may be useful to concentrate for a long time to come on the common heritage of faith and values held, more or less, by both Christians and Muslims, as has often so been done, even if it amounts primarily to studying parallels and comparisons.

Both sides have a lot to say to each other on the mystery of God, the assertion of his existence, and the approach to a knowledge of him. This would provide many topics that could be treated in themselves or in connection with spiritual life and personal experience. One could envisage a colloquium on the Beautiful Names of God: their scriptural sources, the contribution of different traditions, the development of theologies about them, their importance in worship and liturgy, their special place in individual piety and popular devotion. Another meeting could deal with the relations between Faith and Reason in Christianity and in Islam: the realities of "nature", "grace", and "divine satisfaction"; the respective role of proofs "from tradition" and "from reason" in theology; methods and aims of theology itself; the problems of inspiration/revelation; the "stages" of scientific and mystical knowledge. Likewise a common reflection could be devoted to the "vision of God" as proposed in the two religious traditions: what is to be found about it in Scripture, and in dogmatic, ascetical and mystical theology? what is thought about it or expected of it by the "people" and the "spiritual" elite in their quest for God? what are its limits?

Another point of convergence for research by believers is Man, his dignity, values, and undertakings. They could inquire into the sources and demands of human dignity: contributions from the respective Scriptures and traditions, developments by theology, by civil and religious law, the historical shortcomings of religions; the universality of this dignity (those who enjoy it and those who guarantee it); its concrete expression in more precise terms in codes and laws. On the other hand, there are mankind's saints and heroes.

Ten Years of Christian-Muslim Dialogue

There is no obligation to a common study of Abraham, model of faith for both Muslims and Christians: his place in their scriptures and authentic traditions; exegetical and theological explications: the interiorization of the model through worship and liturgy and in popular piety and devotions. Finally, believers should surely meditate on the convergence between wisdom and sanctity in the building up of perfect man, in answer to the ever increasing and anguished desire of modern man to surpass and transcend himself. What do scriptures and their orthodox traditions have to offer by way of answer to the quest for perfection by the wisest and the greatest of "God's fools"? What is a saint in Islam and in Christianity, and what are his greatest virtues? Is his nature transcended or transformed? By his own means or by God's intervention? What would be the ultimate stage of sanctity?

Daily activity in the service of God and of man is another field open to both Christians and Muslims: there are many new problems to solve, and forms of worship to be renewed or interiorized. As believers, in imitation of the living God who is Just and the Giver of Peace, are called upon to work to unite mankind, to defend and promote life, justice, peace and brotherhood, Christians and Muslims should surely reflect together on topics that are fundamental for the future of mankind. To be more specific as regards the service of life: how can its dignity be guaranteed in the early stages (contraception and abortion) and at the later stages (suffering, death, euthanasia)? How can meaning be given to sickness? What is the meaning of therapeutic research and what the implications of medical ethics? The ultimate demands and the many aspects of social justice could be considered, ranging from the proper use of worldly wealth (a blessing or a curse?) to war, racism, and the modern idols: the State, productivity and consumerism. In his service of God, the better to encounter his brethren, man finds a need to pray, fast, give, and return to the sources. There is no reason why Christians and Muslims should not inquire into the role of worship, almsgiving, and pilgrimages. It would certainly be enriching to have exchanges about their respective forms of prayer, the scriptural sources and recognized traditions, liturgical developments, privileged forms of prayer (personal or common), literary styles and forms of expression (litanies, hymns, psalms, etc.). there is every chance here for believers to share their age-old experience.[22]

E. Spirit of dialogue

Christians and Muslims are in the first place believers, and therefore they must meet and speak together as "People of God" and as "seekers of his Face". In the words of an African imām of the Peulh tribe: "When two persons agree to walk together part of the way, God joins them as a third." Indeed, those who have been really involved in some of these Muslim-Christian encounters have experienced the "divine presence" that leads both parties to mutual forgiveness in order to be "closer to one another." The first requirement of any religious dialogue is the knowledge that people are gathered together "in the name of God" and that they have to give witness together "for the glory of God". Faith is capable of many miracles because it counts on the light and the power of God to help the darkness and weakness of our intelligence and will. Hence, the more room Muslim-Christian dialogue makes for prayer, the better the chance of its taking place "in the sight of God."

The spirit of dialogue requires three very simple virtues which, however, are hard to practice: those of knowing how to keep silent, how to listen, how to be moderate. Engaging in dialogue implies, first of all, creating silence within oneself and putting aside preconceived ideas, knowing that the partner will show himself to be different from what one already thinks him to be. Christians and Muslims should practice keeping silence before speaking together: useless monologues would then be avoided, because in that silence they would recognize the "sacred space" where God already brings them together and joins them in a common destiny. Engaging in dialogue, then, is to accept the other just as he shows himself and expresses himself — what he is and what he wants to be. This presupposes a capacity to listen for a long time until the "moment of grace," when the individual no longer asserts himself in opposition to the other but reveals his authentic face and unveils his secret "dreams of sanctity." Finally, dialogue implies questioning one's own knowledge and former assertions so as to see what are the chances of conversion through the mere sharing of experiences communicated in this fashion. Striking declarations, blunt assertions, and long-winded conclusions are the outcome of a pride that forgets that people live in the current of history, amid what is provisional, and in sin. Is not every believer expected to become humble in the face of "God's Judgement"? It is modesty and meekness alone that gives full efficacy to each one's efforts rendering them concrete, lasting, and "open to grace."

Muslims and Christians can find in their Scriptures much advice particularly useful for the dialogue. The Koran reminds the Muslims that the "closest in friendship are those who say 'we are Christians." That is because there are priests and monks among them and because they are not puffed up with pride" (5:82). Hence their wise directive: "Be courteous when you argue with the People of the Book" (29,46)[23]; and again a famous *hadith* says: "No one among you will be a true believer as long as he does not desire for his brother what he desires for himself." On their part Christians have Paul's dictum: "Finally, brothers, fill your mind with everything that is true, everything that is noble, everything that is good, and pure, everything that we love and honour, and everything that can be thought virtuous or worthy of praise" (Ph 4: 8). They should therefore follow some of his recommendations: "far from passing judgement on each other" *(Rom.* 14: 13), "I want to urge each one among you not to exaggerate his real importance. Each of you must judge himself soberly by the standard of the faith God has given him" *(Rom.* 12: 3); "avoid getting into debt, except the debt of mutual love" *(Rom.* 13: 8). Encouraged by these invitations on both sides to address themselves to the other in very respectful terms, they may expect God, who already brings

Ten Years of Christian-Muslim Dialogue

them together and inspires their silence, attention, and moderation, to inspire also the thoughts and sentiments required by an open and serious dialogue.

F. The spirituality of the Christian partner

A Christian engaged in Muslim-Christian dialogue, either on the level of daily life or in colloquia and congresses, must fully live all the demands of his faith and at the same time, be near to and different from his Muslim partner. He must be close to him in his uncompromising monotheism (to be restated untiringly in the liturgy), in his undying sense of transcendence (to be referred to in his "sober" worship), and in his effort to give the "greatest service" (love also is a "commandment"). To God alone is due power, praise, and glory: and it is an honour to be called to serve and obey him.

In this perspective, he will reflect on the possible similarities between the very great God of the Muslims and the God-Love of the Christians. Is not the divine mercy, which is expressed by many a Beautiful Name in Islam, a first manifestation of Him who is gift, exchange, and sharing, in Himself and beyond Himself? The Muslim's esteem for the Word of God can lead the Christian to a deeper reflection on that Word who expressed the fullness of the Father and reveals it in time to man: the ever effective presence and ever living challenge of the Word. Also, admiring the Muslim's respect for the prophets, the Christian, conscious of all the "spokesmen of God" in his own tradition, can discover the continuous intervention of the divine Message and his duty to live again the "prophetic condition" even today. Finally, the strong solidarity of the Muslim *umma* reminds the Christian — should he have forgotten it — that he is part of a fraternal, ecclesial, and supranational community, which, from within, is inspired by the communion of saints in which God extends ever more the "space of his Tent." Did Jesus not proclaim that "anyone who does the will of my Father in heaven, he is my brother and sister and mother"? (*Mt.* 12: 50).

Paradoxically, it is by deeper reflection on the spiritual meaning of his dialogue with the Muslims that the Christian, in amazement, discovers unexpected extensions to his love of God, Father, Son and Spirit. Indeed, this Son is the Word who is "creator and unifier" of history. His unceasing activity makes it possible for the religious traditions of mankind to remain alive and to express a great many spiritual values, which are so many "seeds" awaiting germination and fruition. Thus He who is the Way, Truth, and Life reminds the Christian that he is not at the end of his quest, and that many others also are searching for the same face hidden behind these three mutually linked terms. Therefore Christians and Muslims must, in greater unity, continue their pilgrimage, however long the way and however few the resting places.

It it not the Spirit — intervening before any encounter, presiding over it and guiding it to fruition — who causes these seeds to grow and guarantees the trail towards this unutterable goal? The Christian is, therefore, called upon to untiringly discover the fruits of the Spirit in the life of men, the culture of nations and the religion of believers. If a Catholic, he cannot but marvel at the endless variety of God's gifts to the nations, even though he admires His Word as their first and total achievement. He knows very well that the perfect Christ will appear only at the end of history, and therefore that he cannot aspire to the full knowledge of this well-beloved Christ as long as Christ has not gathered all to offer all to his Father. Every Christian, then, as soon as he tries to live the Muslim-Christian dialogue in all its demands and implications is finally called to a more profound dialogue with Jesus Christ himself. The most mysterious demand will be that the Christian conform himself at times to Christ on the cross because he alone has been given the privilege to know the truth about it and to experience its weight. The dialogue is also a long "passion" involving much suffering, for, as a Muslim has said, "there are no roses without thorns" — to which Christians can answer: there is no Easter without Good Friday.

CONCLUSION

In trying to present an account of how Muslim-Christian dialogue has developed over the last decade, this Bulletin has given a brief description of current relations between the Church and Islam after thirteen centuries of difficult confrontation, and of Islam itself in its present-day reality, with its twofold design for temporal civilization and spiritual adventure. It is impossible for us to grasp the difficulties or the chances of dialogue today if we are unaware of the fact that Muslim-Christian relations of times past still weigh heavily on men's minds, or that Islam still claims to pursue a double design whereas the Church has given up its dreams of Christendom in order to be at the exclusive service of the Gospel. Nevertheless, in the light of the decisive changes made by most Christians in their relations with Muslims, following the lead of the competent bodies of the Catholic Church and the WCC, and in the light of the varying degrees of openness displayed by many Muslims from all schools and tendencies, it can be said that Muslim-Christian dialogue has now entered upon a new period, of which we have witnessed only the very beginning.

Our historical survey of the various official and semi-official manifestations of organized dialogue gives much food for thought. One fact has been established: Christians and Muslims are boldly going out of their way to meet and speak together in order to get to know each other better and to cooperate more in bearing better witness to faith in our day. The best way for Islam and Christianity (and Judaism, too) to refute the accusation that religions create divisions among men in the name of God is by showing that religions can also bring believers together, because it is God who calls us together, reconciles, and unifies, and breaks down the barriers separating men.

The greater part of this Bulletin, therefore, has been devoted to a rough balance-sheet of this decade of encounters and colloquia, in order to evaluate successes and failures, strengths and weaknesses. There is a simple and clear rule: only by engaging in dialogue can one learn how to do it. Progress has indeed been made, and this is a good thing. Still, Muslims and Christians should take the exact measure of the possibilities and limits of dialogue, for it is only by taking both into account that one can work out what the ideal circumstances for the future may be. This Bulletin has attempted this, freely mixing experience, wisdom and optimism. It is hoped that the proposals put forward may help both sides to prepare better for this dialogue and thereby improve the "organized manifestations" of the next few years. Of course, these proposals are based on Christian thinking that tries to make allowance for the views of the partner, while remaining none the less coherent in itself and ready to go on to the ultimate consequences. Hence, the Bulletin, after describing what the common "spirit of dialogue" could be, has suggested exactly how the Christian partner should live this spirit, in line with the mystery of his own vocation and the model God himself has given him.

Decisive words have been uttered and irreversible actions have been taken regarding the new relations Christians and Muslims can and must develop among themselves from now on. The Muslim-Christian dialogue is an adventure in which both sides have much to learn, to discover, and to suffer, by accepting the trials and errors and tentative steps as well as the bold and sometimes extreme steps of the most generous among them. Reality demands that they know and accept that they are very different one from another, that they accept for the time being a deep cleavage between religious sensibilities, between the general theological backgrounds and contexts, and the temporal implications of faith. Reality demands that they do not despair about reaching better mutual understanding, beyond prejudices finally overcome, yet have no illusion about the real possibilities of an immediate "coming together." There are two possible kinds of dialogue: the irenical, easy dialogue governed by protocol and politeness and the "dialectical," vigorous dialogue in which each partner is very demanding towards the other, because finally it is a quest for truth, for God, for greater respect for the other. The best among Christians and Muslims are well aware that they must opt for the second kind, even if it is more difficult and requires long scientific preparation and demands very patient research.

Does that mean the dialogue should be limited to some exceptional experts? This would be to overlook the fact that dialogue is, first and foremost, an encounter of hearts and souls before becoming an encounter of intellects and ideas. Experts must continue their difficult task in select colloquia, but in constant contact with their community of faith and in the effective service of the mass of silent believers, who are the humble makers of dialogue at the level of daily life. The latter is the only important one, because it is at this level, the level of families, of neighbourhoods of work that people meet, hearts speak, and experiences are shared. This Bulletin had to throw light on the initiatives of the specialized bodies, but it should be kept in mind that these bodies are *at the service* of grass-roots communities and local Churches. These communities and Churches bear the main responsibility for dialogue: the Secretariat for non-Christians and the DFI sub-unit of the WCC have stated repeatedly that their only desire was to give information, to support, and to coordinate the initiatives of Christians who, living together with Muslims in natural communities, have there to foster common service to all men, the special friendship that exists among believers, and the paying to God of the special honour due to him alone. The aim of the "organized dialogue" in its various forms is precisely to help these initiatives to grow in number so that they may bear even greater fruit to the joy of Christians and Muslims alike.

1)   Professor Abdelmajid Charfi writes in Islamochristiana, *no. 1 (1975): "It is a question of pursuing (or restoring) the meaning(s) of Scripture, taking account of the legacy of the past and of Tradition, on the basis of today's general situation and problems, using the indispensable though ambiguous tools of the human sciences, their means of investigation and their areas of inquiry. For some, this interdisciplinay research is based on a preliminary given whose meaning has to be continually rediscovered. For others the meaning comes at the end of the road. But for almost everyone there is today no expression of faith which can do without continual research."*

2)   English, French and Arabic are the languages normally used at these meetings – Spanish also being used at the Congress of Córdoba. At some meetings the translation was bad and this misled some of those present as to the exact content of the speaker's thought. It is not within the capacity of a run-of-the-mill translator to translate theological, exegetical, juridical, mystical or simply technical vocabulary. This is a real difficulty, though not insurmountable: highly qualified personnel should be employed – and they should be well recompensed: something not all the colloquia can afford.

3)   This happened at Tripoli and Córdoba. It is at spectacular colloquia with official delegations (often national and Muslim) that there is danger of the floor being monopolized by the heads of these delegations, by the reading of endless messages, telegrams and communiques. At Tripoli and Córdoba the Christians showed admirable patience, if not holy resignation, in the face of an overwhelming disparity in the use of speaking time.

4)   "Nothing is more disagreeable than putting up with categorical affirmations from people who possess the Truth about everything under the sun. While a very wide confrontation of tendencies, spiritual families and ideologies is a good thing, the demands of dialogue cannot be brushed aside" (Islamochristiana, *no. 1 (1975), p. 119).*

5)   Ibidem, p. 119.

6)   For example, the religious personality of Mohammed, at Córdoba II.

7)   Simultaneous translation quickly comes up against insurmountable problems in this kind of meeting: the technical nature of the language, the modality of the language, the structures of thought. It would appear to be difficult for religious minds to see the sacred texts translated roughly, and thus "manipulated" without due respect. Translators having "official translations of the holy books" at their disposal would only partially solve the problem. In view of the jealous care with which the Muslims regard the very letter of the Koran, the problem seems insoluble. At Córdoba II, the Muslims present intervened at every hand's turn to correct any error in quoting from the Koran, no matter who the Muslim speaker was.

8)   As regards what is taught about Islam and its founder in the primary

Ten Years of Christian-Muslim Dialogue

and secondary school textbooks, see the account of Fr. E. Galindo Aguilar at Córdoba II. It is clear that participants who are only personally involved feel far less responsible for this "implementation" of the conclusions: hence, some people think, the importance of representative bodies.

9)   *These conclusions added, by way of example, other gains of this organized dialogue. "The Christian delegation solemnly stated that it asked pardon of the Muslims for all unjust or hurtful things said by Christians throughout history concerning the person of Islam's revered prophet. The Christians took note that the Muslim delegation recognized Christians as monotheists, our difference being not over monotheism itself, which is common to both, but its theologiccl content. The Christian delegation urgently asked the Muslim delegation to pursue serious historical and exegetical research into the real value of the Christians' sacred scriptures" (see Islamochristiana, no. 1 (1976), pp. 159-160). The content of these "common conclusions" matches the "propositions islamo-chrétiennes' frequently suggested by Fr. Y. Moubarac and printed in* Concilium, *no. 116 (June 1976), pp. 139-141.*

10)   Islamochristiana, *no. 1 (1975), p. 115.*

11)   Bulletin, *no. 36 (1977), p. 95.*

12)   La Bible, le Coran et la Science *(Paris Segher, 1976) by Dr. Maurice Bucaille, much publicized in Algeria and Tunisia, is an example of this tendency to have double standards: in it the Bible is criticized for speaking of the "days of creation" (contrary to science!), whereas the Koran is open to the same criticism, for it says repeatedly that God "created the heavens and earth in six days" (7,54: 10,3: 11,7: 25,59: 32,4: 50,38: 57,4: 58,4); the genealogies and ages mentioned in the Bible are scoffed at, while it is forgotten that the Koran says that Noah "lived there one thousand years less fifty" (29,14); and the Bible is said to confuse names, ignoring the fact that Mary is called the "mother of Jesus and sister of Aaron" in the Koran.*

13)   *Islam has always maintained (Koran: 4,46; 5,13; 5,41; 2,75) that Jews and Christians have falsified their scriptures* (tahrif) *even as regards the actual text (those who confine this accusation of falsification to the "sense" of the interpretation given them are few). But whereas all Muslims maintain they believe in four revealed books – the Torah, the Psalms, the Gospel (in the singular), and the Koran – they also say that the first three have long since disappeared, since what the Jews and Christians call sacred scriptures are only a falsified version. As for the Gospel, another argument is brought forward: none of the four biographies of Jesus contains the announcement of the prophet Mohammed, as the text of the Koran affirms (61,6). All the scientific explanations concerning the thousands of ancient manuscripts and the discoveries of Qumran change nothing in the situation, whereas the pseudo-Gospel of Barnabas (which in its present form seems to be a forgery going back to the 16th or 14th century) is welcomed by many Muslims, since it presents a Jesus who quite fits in with what the Koran and Islamic tradition says.*

14)   *It is well to recall here that on the basis of certain verses of the Koran (especially 9,29) Islam has constructed a whole theory about the "Muslim State" in which Jews and Christians find themselves protected and separate, respected in their cultural rights and their personal status (juridical and*

judicial autonomy), a national or provincial minority kept in their status quo with no possibility of increasing in numbers or in the institutions they possess.

15)   *The Christians should be patient and delicately try and explain to their partners what is meant for them by the mystery of the God who is Love, expressed in his Word and revealed to men in that incarnate WORD, Jesus Christ, so that all men may have access to "divine" promotion, which renders them like unto Christ through the mystery of a "new creation" in which his death and his Pasch are of universal efficacy. The Muslims on their side could inform their friends how meditation on the mystery of the Oneness of God has led them to unexpected discoveries, and how the Mohammed of history, having become the Mohammed of faith, now ranks as the unique model to love, to follow and to imitate.*

16)   *In this the Christian will think always of the divine, principal author and the human, secondary and instrumental author (in line with his "vision" of inspiration) while the Muslim will apply to the Jewish and Christian scriptures his criteria of "heaven-sent divine dictation" by the one and only author of all revelation. Mohammed Arkoun in* L'Islam, hier, demain *(Paris, Buchet/Chastel, 1978), p. 219, puts it this way: "La croyance traditionnelle commune aux sociétés du Livre (: soumises à l'autorité des Ecritures saintes) veut que la religion soit un enseignement révélé par Dieu, 'descendu' (tanzil) du ciel selon la métaphore coranique."*

17)   *One of the most urgent tasks of the Muslim-Christian dialogue is the joint development of a* vocabulary of master words in Scripture and theology in the two religious traditions. *The Christian would then see how the ultimate identity of Jesus Christ is at the heart of the debate, a real corner stone on which everything is built and structured.*

18)   *See Fr R. Clément in "Le Colloquie islamo-chrétien de Tripoli,"* Etudes *(November 1976), pp. 557-566; and M. Lelong,* J'ai rencontré l'Islam *(Paris, Cerf, 1975), p. 146. "The dialogue between the Church and Islam cannot have the same ultimate goal as rapprochement among separated Christians. Muslim-Christian dialogue does not aim at unifying the two communities but at bringing them closer in friendship and in awareness of their differences, as well as in the certitude that they have things to say to each other and also to say together."*

19)   *"Had Allah pleased, He could have made you one nation: but it is His wish to prove you by that which He has bestowed upon you. Vie with each other in good works, for to Allah you shall all return and he will declare to you what you have disagreed about" (Koran, 5,48).*

20)   *There are witnesses from Muslims and from Christians which seem sometimes to solve the most stubborn difficulties and contradictions by the very simplicity of their sincere quest for God; let us not forget that the Spirit is at work in each one and makes use of the "little" ones to teach the "great." These are real challenges which force each one to surrender to the truth.*

21)   *See* Le Figaro *of 22 February 1976, p. 4.*

22)   *Dare Christians and Muslims enter in the very near future on a debate in which exchange is difficult about realities on which there is such a great difference of views. Only well prepared select groups can venture to do so provided there is among the members of the group profound esteem and friendship to guarantee each and every one against the danger of a rupture.*

Ten Years of Christian-Muslim Dialogue

Even so Prof. Mohammed Talbi of Tunis issued a warning: "Apart from any consideration of how much preparation the participants may have done, certain themes are, and will for a long time to come be, difficult to tackle in common ... The Koran speaks with respect and veneration of Jesus, son of the Virgin Mary, and Word of God ... this veneration is found in many a contemporary work, but, despite the sympathy present in these works, a Christian will not recognize in them the Christ God of the mystery of the Incarnation and the Redemption. It is likewise difficult for a Muslim to find in the many lives of Mohammed, often written in the West with sympathy, the Seal of the Prophets bringing mankind the perfection of the ultimate message of God. How is one to dialogue usefully with a Christian or a Jew on the nature of the Koran? Corresponding to the mystery of the Incarnation of Christ and of his Redemption there is in Islam the no less difficult mystery of the concretization of the Word of God, consubstantial with Being – and therefore eternal – and yet descended (tanzil) *into the world of contingency and phenomenology. It is perhaps no mere chance that in the Middle Ages such heated disputes arose within Christianity and Islam about the nature of Christ and the nature of the Koran" (see "Islam et dialogue: réflexions sur un thème d'actualité". p. 42 and note 27 supra).*

23)   *The verse continues: ... "except with those among them who do evil. Say: 'We believe in that which is revealed to us and which was revealed to you. Our God and your God is one. To Him we surrender* (muslim) *ourselves.' "*

''"Christianity and Islam"''

IX

The Second International Muslim-Christian Congress Of Cordoba (March 21-27, 1977)

BY EMILIO GALINDO AGUILAR

"Cordoba, the Jerusalem of the West, House of Peace and Understanding, which creates a spirit of fellowship where Muslims and Christians can meet in peace." This was how Dr. Abdelaziz Kamel described Cordoba, the scene of the Second International Muslim-Christian Congress (March 21-27, 1977). Like the first congress[1] it was organized by the *Asociacion para la Amistad Islamo-Cristiana* (A.I.C.) of Spain.

This type of congress is history in the making in the context of the hopes of both Muslims and Christians. The spirit which animates them, which has come to be known as "the spirit of Cordoba", the freedom enjoyed by the organizers, Muslims and Christian alike, the international participation which implies support as well as being an honour, all this goes to make of Cordoba a clear symbol and a concrete realisation of dialogue and friendship between Christians and Muslims. The following account wishes not merely to present an accurate report on the events of the Second Congress of Cordoba but also to bring out its real achievements and the prospects it holds for the future.

Fr. Emilio Galindo-Aguilar, w.f., Ph.D., is at present director to the DAREK NYUMBA, which under his leadership and experience has become a focal point for the promotion of respect and understanding among Christians and Muslims in Spain. The center, situated in Madrid, has contributed greatly to the advancement of dialogue among the Spanish speaking public. Since 1972, Fr. Galindo has been also editor to the monthly publication Encuentro, *which aims at improving Muslim-Christian dialogue.*

This essay is taken from Vol. 3, 1977, pp. 207-228 of ISLAMOCHRISTIANA, *the publication of the Center for Studies for Muslim-Christian Dialogue in Rome and is reprinted here by permission of the publishers.*

"Christianity and Islam"

All the paths of history lead to Cordoba

The opening session, held in the presence of the civic authorities of Cordoba, had as its setting the Hall of Mosaics in the Alcazar of the Christian Kings. Altogether there were about 200 participants in the congress coming from about 20 countries. The following countries sent official delegations: Algeria, Kuwait, Libya, Morocco, Mauritania, Palestine, Syria and Tunisia. The official delegations from some Arab countries were absent, although they had accepted the invitation to attend. It would seem that this absence was due to a last-minute communication from the Shaykh al-Azhar on behalf of the Committee for Islamic Research of Al-Azhar University. In this communication he declared that he was opposed to this type of congress as he could see no utility in it as long as the official Church did not change its attitude, towards Islam and Muhammad, and above all as regards the activities of missionary congregations involved in evangelization. This declaration, probably due to reasons internal to Egypt, explains the absence of some Arab countries as also that of the Shaykh al-Azhar himself who had accepted to give the opening address.

It is worth mentioning, as something new and a decisive development of this congress, the full support given by the Episcopal Conference of Spain, represented by its president, Cardinal Tarancon, Mons. Briva Miravent, the president of the episcopal commission for ecumenical relations, and Mons. Cirarda, bishop of Cordoba. Worthy of note also is the presence of official delegations from the Arab League's office in Spain, from the Hispano-Arab Institute of Culture, and from the World Council of Churches. The latter only served to underline even more the inexplicable absence of the Vatican.

A good number of journals, both Spanish and foreign, as well as press agencies, sent correspondents to Corboda to cover the congress.[2]

The Mayor of Cordoba, his excellency Sr. D. Antonio Alacron Constant, welcomed the participants saying: *"Welcome to Cordoba, this ecumenical and open-hearted city. The history of this city is like a carpet in which has been woven the best of its heritage. Cordoba, gentlemen, is a city of dialogue, understanding and collaboration. And because all the paths of history lead to Cordoba, I ask you to keep Cordoba in your heart the way she keeps you in her soul."*

The Theme of the Congress

Dr. Gomez Nogales, the Christian co-chairman of the congress, in his speech of welcome, declared: "We are conscious of the great responsibility that history places upon us by our having made Cordoba once more the arena of a movement which no one can sustain, but we rely on and are inspired by *'the spirit of Cordoba.'"* He went on to outline the aims of the congress:

1) to strengthen the *"spirit of Cordoba."*

2) to attain to a high academic level and thus give to the world *"a tangible proof that these topics can be treated by Muslims and Christians with the*

162

The Second International Congress of Cordoba

courtesy required of them by their religious conviction, namely that they adore one and the same God."

3) An effort to follow through strictly the programme of the congress. That is why, as if fearing outside interference of unforeseen problems, he added: *"Any theme of a polemic nature or falling outside the programme should be left for another occasion apart from the congress."*

It would seem that such a precaution was justified, because in fact there were attempts made to raise the question of the Mosque of Cordoba, as had been done in one of the conclusions of the Tripoli Congress.[3]

Having been warned against outside influence and invited to maintain an atmosphere of serenity and a high academic level, the participants were able to dedicate themselves entirely to the study of the central theme: *"Positive esteem for Muhammad and Jesus in Christianity and Islam."* An *"apparently dangerous and difficult theme,"* as Cardinal Tarancon of Madrid admitted, yet one which is at the root of historical prejudices and the constant animosity between Muslims and Christians. There was certainly a risk in proposing such a theme. That is why some people, including the Vatican Commission for relations with Muslims, were apprehensive, thinking that the time was not ripe for a public discussion of this topic. The organizers of the congress, more in contact with reality perhaps, relying also on the experience gained from the first congress of Cordoba and on its *"spirit,"* and above all free from any temporal commitment, confident moreover in the workings of the Spirit, thought that not only was it possible to discuss this theme but that it would be a positively liberating experience for all, especially for the Christians. The reason for this was given by Prof. Miguel Cruz Hernandez in his conference the following day:

"Perhaps no religious man in history has met with so much abuse and contempt as Muhammad. Likewise there has never been an accusation based on politics and so little on religion as that levelled against Islam."

That is why Dr. Gomez Nogales considered that it would be a great achievement of the congress if it could bring about a change in the attitude of Christians with regard to Muhammad.

"May one who has been considered evil, worthy only of contempt, be given a place of honour and respect among the founders of great religions. If we were to look upon him with the same respect that Muslims have for Jesus we would have taken a tremendous step forward in the encounter with Islam."

The organizers were prepared to take the risk but not to *"tempt the devil."* In this case the temptation would have been to improvise. That is why, in 1974, a group of experts belonging mainly to Comillas University, Madrid, and to the faculty of Muslim theology in Tunis, formed a planning committee to arrange the programme. As regards method they took a fundamental option: both the figure of Muhammad and that of Christ would be treated by

Muslims and Christians from the point of view of their respective faiths. We wish to discover in the faith and theology of the interlocutors the basis for a positive appreciation in the face of the prejudices and animosities of history concerning Jesus and Muhammad. No one, by this very fact, could feel disturbed if the belief of each one did not coincide with his own. With a new spirit and with mutual understanding we wanted to study these topics which until now had been taboo.

The theme was to be studied by means of sixteen lectures, eight from the Muslim point of view and eight from the Christian point of view. Twelve would be dedicated to different aspects of the figure of Muhammad and four to Jesus. This mathematical inequality obviously did not imply any value-judgement. It arose simply out of socio-historical conditions. Christians have a greater need to reevaluate the figure of Muhammad. There are certainly fundamental differences between the Muslim vision of Christ and the Christian vision. Nevertheless, as is well known, the esteem of Muslims for Christ has been and still is constant, to such an extent that it is unthinkable for someone to be a true Muslim and not to have a great veneration for Jesus and Mary.

The inspiration of the Spirit which has to be followed

After the greetings to the participants on the part of each of the official delegations coming from Muslim countries, Dr. Mustafa Kamâl al-Tarzi, the head of the Tunisian delegation, and head of Religious Affairs in his country, pronounced the opening address on behalf of the Muslims present. He underlined the role of Muhammad as the Seal of Prophecy while being at the same time in continuity with previous prophets. He emphasised the importance of a congress such as this *"to clarify points of doubt in religious matters, to remove barriers and feelings of fanaticism, especially in an era characterised by a lack of religion, atheism and sionism."* He ended his speech by inviting all believers to be united to combat the forces of evil which assail us.

Then followed the speech of Cardinal Tarancon, Archbishop of Madrid, president of the Episcopal Conference of Spain. With the simplicity of a believer he gave his witness before his brothers. This was followed with much interest by both Muslims and Christians. When the time comes to write the history of Muslim-Christian relations, not only in Spain but in the whole world, the presence of Cardinal Tarancon at Cordoba and the words he spoke will have to be considered as of decisive importance. All the more so because of the position of the Cardinal and, why should it not be said, because of the reservations expressed by the Vatican Secretariat for non Christians with regard to the Congress and in particular to its theme. These reservations, known to Cardinal Tarancon, raised a moment of doubt in his mind, but he overcame this, understanding that the Congress and the *"spirit of Cordoba"* were a *"movement of the Spirit which had to be followed."* The Cardinal's gesture in attending the Congress was highly appreciated by the ambassadors of Arab countries represented in Madrid who delegated the ambassador of

The Second International Congress of Cordoba

Tunisia to express their gratitude. This same appreciation was snown during the congress, especially by the Muslim participants. In fact Dr. De Epalza, the organizing-secretary of the congress, was able to affirm that the Cardinal's gesture was *"half the success of the Congress. He set the tone and gave guide-lines, directing the Christians and provoking the admiration of the Muslims. Moreover this (his speech) is an ecclesial document which will have repercussions throughout the Christian world."*

The first point to note in the Cardinal's speech is the support given to the Congress by the Spanish hierarchy, support which the first congress of Cordoba lacked.

> *"I express to you the support and interest of the Spanish bishops for all efforts in our country towards better understanding between followers of different religions."*

He then gave his definition of the Congress:

> *"It is not only a friendly gathering, an experience of brotherhood and understanding, but a working session in order to promote this understanding between Christians and Muslims, by seeking for that which can unite us, choosing for examination those areas in which something can be achieved. For the 'spirit of Cordoba' is a spirit of work in common for mutual understanding, respect and love, a movement of the Spirit which all Catholics should obey. May this be understood by all members of the Church in Spain and may we be helped in this by our Muslim brothers."*

Coming to the actual theme of the congress the Cardinal went on:

> *"We have to forget the past and show respect for the Prophet of Islam. To insult Muhammad, whether publicly or not, is an offence not only against historical and religious truth, but also against the respect and charity due to our Muslim brothers. To insult someone is certainly not the way to show love, the basic Christian virtue."*

He then referred to the step forward the Congress wished to take in the appreciation of Muhammad:

> *"On the basis of our Christian faith and the methods of our theological tradition concerning religious values outside Christianity,* (according to modern theology) *the Christian must acknowledge the values Muslim belief about Muhammad contributes to Islam as it is lived today by hundreds of millions of believers."*

Finally the Cardinal asked:

> *"How is it possible to appreciate Islam and Muslims without showing appreciation for the Prophet of Islam and the values he has promoted? Not to do this would not only be a lack of respect, to which the Council exhorts Christians, but also neglect of a religious factor of which account must be taken in theological reflection and religious awareness."*

165

"Christianity and Islam"

Leaving further developments to Christian experts and theologians at the Congress, Cardinal Tarancon highlighted two positive values concerning Muhammad:

> "His faith in one God and his concern for justice. His faith in one God is integral to his message and his life. This is the most important belief which he left to his community. This witness to the unicity and sovereignty of God, in which Christians also believe, is of real importance in the world of today, especially for believers. His call to justice is also relevant today. We do not wish to enter into the details of his prophetic preaching and political reaction. We call attention only to the equality of all men and women as God's creatures and the justice due to them. Any religious message can be watered down, but the call for justice and respect for human dignity is a prophetic cry which cannot be drowned, neither by us who are inspired by the Spirit of Jesus nor by those who consider Muhammad as a model and teacher for humanity."

At the close of the opening session Sr. D. Manuel Santolalla de Lacalle, the head of the delegation of the civic authorities of Cordoba, expressed his great hopes for the congress.

This opening session was more than a mere exercise of protocol. It created a spirit, provided a method for work, and, without false irenicism, opened doors for a dialogue on a theme considered by many as taboo.

Muhammad. A historical figure

The following section will consist of an analysis of the papers presented to the congress.

Dr. Muhammad Haykal (Egyptian, Director of the Institute of Islamic Studies, Madrid, cultural attaché at the Egyptian Embassy in Spain, co-president of the Amistad Islamo-Cristiana and of the congress) spoke on the theme: **Muhammad as a historical figure.**

He declared: *"Muhammad is a great historical figure because of the admirable character of his life, because he has changed the course of history, and set an example of moral life for humanity of all time."*

To prove this assertion he proposed *"to go back to the original sources of the life of Muhammad,"* especially *"to the persons who lived with him and who were conversant with what he did."* He also suggested that we must be aware of Muhammad's environment, the spirit and traditions of his age, the customs of his people.

On these bases Dr. Haykal gave a lively and well-documented account of the different stages in the life of Muhammad.

Dr. Mikel De Epalza (University of Comillas, Madrid) spoke on the theme: *Muhammad, a historical figure and his values, from a Christian point of view.*

The Second International Congress of Cordoba

The first part dealt with Christian principles. De Epalza emphasised that every human person is deserving of respect. This includes respect for his family and relations. Furthermore there is a religious aspect to every human life, and this holds good for Muhammad too. Every human life, including that of Muhammad, has been saved by the blood of Christ. Respect for a person implies respecting his options, the way his freedom has been expressed. In the final analysis God alone knows the mystery of each person. Therefore no-one can judge another. These moral principles can be reduced to three basic points: 1) objective knowledge; 2) appreciation for what we have in common; 3) appreciation of diversity.

The second part was *"a kind of Christian reading, positive and appreciative, of the biography presented by Islam."* It insisted on the sympathy which has been lacking in the Christian approach to the Prophet of Islam. *"This personal witness of friendliness and affection towards the prophet is perhaps the greatest value a Christian can express to his Muslim brother."* De Epalza then dwelt on different aspects of the life of Muhammad, his integrity, sincerity, poverty and generosity, the model quality of his family life, the way he fulfilled his prophetic role. Finally he expressed a wish: *"May the knowledge of Muhammad, the great Prophet of Islam, and appreciation of him, grow among Christians."*

Points from the following debate

Dr. Perez Ramon (Bilbao) asked if there is a difference between the prophet of faith and the man of history.

Dr. Haykal replied: *"In Islamic thought there is no difference. We believe in Muhammad as a prophet and as a historical figure. We believe in Muhammad as a historical figure through our faith. His message and his example can only be known through faith."*

Muhammad. Prophet and Apostle

Dr. Ahmad Bekir (Dean of the Faculty of Theology, Tunis).

His conference was on *Muhammad, Prophet and Apostle. Divine origin of the Qur'ân.*

This paper proved to be a disappointment. It consisted mainly in a series of unrelated affirmations and did not really develop the theme proposed. It was apologetical in tone, lacking in critical awareness and relying too much on arguments from authority.

Points from the following debate

Dr. Ibrahim al-Ghuwayl (Libya): Although modern youth has a tendency towards rationalism and mu'tazilism, we have to remember that knowledge of God does not come from human reason, but from the light God instills in the heart of the believer.

Dr. Maurice Borrmans (Rome): He suggested that a distinction should be made between three different levels: faith, theology and modern criticism, in

"Christianity and Islam"

order to give autonomy and freedom to faith. He asked for clarification concerning the use of *hadīts* in the biography of Muhammad, in particular as regard's the Prophet's impeccability.

In reply Dr. Bekir gave a brief expustion on the historical sources for the life of Muhammad. He went on to say:

"Every prophet must be absolutely infallible and therefore impeccable". Here we touch upon one of the crucial points in the development of Islam and the possibility of Muslim-Christian dialogue.

Prof. Gregorio Ruiz.

He treated the theme *In what sense can Muhammad be considered a prophet by Christians?*

He distinguished three types of prophet:

1) in a *sociological sense:* the one who revolts against his environment and despite its hostility is able to influence it;

2) in a *biblical* sense: includes a call from God, rejection on the part of those who surround the prophet, criticism both from the religious and social points of view.

3) as *revealer:* one who bears new truths which conform to the deposit of revelation or reform it.

He then applied these categories to Muhammad.

1) There is no difficulty in recognizing Muhammad as a prophet in the *sociological* sense. This can be proved from history.

2) On examination we find that Muhammad fulfils the criteria for recognition as a *biblical* prophet. He was called, rejected, and his mission was an authentic criticism, both religious and social.

3) It is admitted that God can raise up prophets outside of the visible Church and that these play an important role in the plan of salvation. Nevertheless the Christian finds it difficult, if not impossible, to accept Muhammad as a prophet in the third sense, i.e. as one who bears truth of universal import which have to be accepted *sub specie discrimine salutis*. It is difficult to accept contradictory affirmations as leading to the same eschatological truth.

Prof. Ruiz ended by saying that the fact that we cannot accept Muhammad as a prophet in this last sense does not mean that we cannot accept his incomparable role in the history of salvation. He was in fact a providential instrument to lead his people to the adoration of God and to encourage a spirit of prayer and love of neighbour, together with total submission to the will of God. This is a role given by God and accepted by Muhammad and carried through against opposition - as in the case of the prophets of the Old Testament. For us believers, whether Christians or Muslims, what is important is that word of God should be a reality in our lives.

Prof. Ruiz's conference was listened to in complete silence, as if heralding a storm. The reactions from the Muslim side came quickly. In general the Muslims felt offended, although some young Muslim theologians congratulated Dr. Ruiz for his clarity and his scientific approach, and for his recognition of the prophetic character of Muhammad. The negative reactions were perhaps due, as Dr. Ruiz himself pointed out in the ensuing discussion, to a lack of attention to the actual subject of the talk which was a presentation of the *Christian* point of view.

Some points from the afternoon debate

Dr. Ahmad Hamani (head of the Algerian delegation) put forward a conservative point of view. It is not necessary to deepen these problems. Christians and Muslims should abide by what they believe and not lose sight of what the word of God tells them.

Dr. De Epalza (Madrid) declared: *"Not only do we apologize for the incident, but we look for a solution in harmony with spirit of the congress".*

He proposed three solutions:

1) Dr. Ruiz was prepared to correct his text, if necessary, with the help of Muslim experts.

2) For greater clarity criticism would be accepted.

3) We would request a Muslim brother to deepen the study of the points on which the Islamic faith and the Christian faith differ with regard to prophecy.

Dr. Haykal (Madrid) expressed the opinion that the paper was neither clear nor accurate regarding the Qur'ân. He also felt that it strayed from the spirit of the A.I.C. The aim of the A.I.C. is not to force conversion on someone. Rather we should try to fight against our common enemies, political, cultural, religious. He supported the solutions proposed by Dr. De Epalza.

Calm returned, but the debate continued on the following day.

Dr. Bekir (Tunis) said that Dr. Ruiz should have come to prior agreement with Muslims. These cannot tolerate that Muhammad be compared to sociological prophets such as the Buddha or Marx. Dr. Bekir then dealt at some length with Christ's announcement of the Paraclete, understood as referring to Muhammad. Finally he said that there was no need to get worked up about an incident such as this, though he would have liked hurtful words to have been corrected.

Dr. Raja Sassi (Director of Religious Affairs, Libya) expressed the opinion that the Torah is not the norm of prophecy, because of the immoral aspects found in its prophets. He also alluded to contradictions in the Gospels, which throw into greater light the Gospel of Barnabas. But finally, he said, we are not in a position to judge the prophets chosen by God.

Dr. Ibn Abboud (Marocco) praised the A.I.C. for its spirit of openness which is one of the signs of future success, namely better understanding between Muslims and Christians. He felt that the paper read by Dr. Ruiz, although controversial, could nevertheless provide a new starting point for this process.

Dr. Taieb Salama (Tunis) suggested that the A.I.C. should look for points of agreement. Disputed questions should be left to small groups of specialists outside the congress. He remarked that Dr. Ruiz had treated prophecy from a particular angle. He had not dealt with the Islamic idea of prophecy.

"Christianity and Islam"

Dr. Abdelaziz Kamel (Egypt) concluded the debate. He praised the seriousness of Dr. Ruiz's work. He did not see any great difference between the position he proposed and that of Islam. Positive results should come from conflicts. We must be careful not to interpret the speaker's words according to Islamic categories, but try to understand them according to his own position.

Despite this conclusion the debate was reopened on the following day. To our way of thinking it was taking up a disproportionate amount of time.

Dr. Lahbabi (Marocco) congratulated the speaker for raising the intellectual level of the debate. In any dialogue it is necessary for the partners to say what they believe. Dr. Ruiz had every right to express his own theory. For instance, Muslims say that Christ was not crucified and was only a man. We know that this does not concord with Christian beliefs, but it is not for all that an attack on Christianity.

The spirit of tolerance and open-mindedness shown by these words met with long and loud applause.

Dr. Mustafa Cherif (a lecturer in sociology from Algeria) presented *"some remarks of a young Muslim for future understanding"*. It cannot be expected of Christians that they speak like Muslims. Yet it is very important that the body of Christians give Muhammad a place in the history of salvation. The *šahâda* cannot go against Jesus of Nazareth. God's revelation, as the speaker mentioned, is not closed with Christ but continues. If Muhammad is recognized as a biblical prophet, close to God, to call him a sociological prophet only creates confusion. Dr. Cherif also referred to a difference between Christians and Muslims as regards the understanding of revelation. When God speaks to His chosen one he dictates his word to a heart virgin of knowledge, like the absolute Word of God in the womb of the Virgin. Muhammad, the *ummi* (in the sense of "unlettered") received the word offered by God for all men. The subtle distinction between revelation and personal word - introduced by Christians - would mean that God speaks no absolute and sacred word. We Muslims do not accept this relativity of the Word of God. This is the fundamental difference between Christians and Muslims.

Dr. De Epalza pointed out that Muslims speak in order that we may have a direct witness to their faith. For the portrait of the Prophet this spiritual tradition will provide us with better knowledge of the Prophet of Islam.

Prof. Ruiz apologized for having hurt anyone's feelings. He felt nevertheless that difficult topics should not be avoided nor left to small groups of specialists. Rather they should be treated openly. In reply to many objections he pointed out the difference in the understanding of revelation. For a Christian, man's appropriation of revelation is gradual. The discovery of God is progressive. Therefore it is less difficult to consider the Bible as the work of a people and thus subject to revision. In Islam, on the other hand, it is not the people who fashioned the Qur'ân that fashioned the people. A Muslim will feel that revelation has been given once and for all and will find it difficult to accept that revelation is progressive. He then answered specific objections:

— The Torah is a norm of prophecy for Christians, not for Muslims. Therefore Christianity accepts prophets despite their defects. The centre of our faith is the crucified Christ, for where sin abounded there grace was superabundant.

— In speaking about Muhammad as a sociological prophet he was only making use of contemporary language. He did not compare Muhammad with Marx.

— The political role of Muhammad was not considered as an objection. Even biblical prophets engaged in politics.

Dr. Hamani (Algeria) made a severe criticism of Dr. Ruiz, *"if he does not know anything about Islam, as he has said, why should he speak about it"?* He went on to treat a great number of points, but because of the late hour and because his rapid delivery made translation impossible, his words fell on deaf ears.

Fr. Basetti-Sani (Italy) gave a communication entitled *"Comment puis-je reconnaitre comme authentique la mission prophétique de Muhammad?"* He took as his starting point the Pauline-Scotist conception of the incarnation of Christ as the centre of divine activity *ad extra*. Through God's revelation Muhammad became the spiritual guide for a humanity which was ignorant and weak in its progress towards God. He gave new meaning to life: as a witness to the absolute sovereignty of the God of Abraham, Moses and Jesus, and by bringing the Arabs into the movement of history. *"Islam which comes after Christ enters the history of salvation thanks to the movement of reintegration inaugurated on the Cross"*. Therefore Fr. Basetti-Sani concluded by *"recognizing Muhammad as a true prophet in the history of salvation which is centred in Christ."*

Muhammad, exemplar and model of virtues

Prof. M. Aziz Lahbabi (Morocco, former Dean of the University of Rabat, advisor on scientific research to the Ministry of Higher Education, Algeria) gave a paper on *Muhammad, a man of commitment.*

The most striking feature of this paper was its form. Lahbabi imagined a journalist interviewing Muhammad and questioning him about his personal identity, his mission, his family, the problem of Christians, and Jews, liberation from slavery, the nature of his message, the problem of Jesus, holy war, etc. From the point of view of the content there was nothing new, yet through its style the paper achieved its purpose, namely to arouse sympathy for Muhammad.

The method followed by the speaker displeased many of the Muslims present.

Dr. Lahbabi replied that it was the message that mattered. He said he drew his inspiration from modern methods of communication. Young people today, whether we like it or not, go through a religious crisis. Few follow the

"Christianity and Islam"

precepts of Islam. Therefore we change our method of presentation so that they can be encouraged to listen.

Dr. D. Miguel Cruz Hernandez (Director general of Popular Culture, islamicist and professor of Arab philosophy and history) spoke on the theme *Muhammad, exemplar and model of virtues.*

His conference was a complete success. Muslims were heard to say: *"we never thought that a Christian, taking his own faith as his starting point, could recognize so many virtues in Muhammad."*

First Dr. Cruz Hernandez developed the various factors which have contributed to the West's false image of Muhammad. He then went on to describe the virtues found in Muhammad: individual virtues, monastic (fortitude, temperance, prudence and justice) and theological virtues (faith, hope and charity). He paid particular attention to the prophet's environment in order to bring out the exceptional nature of Muhammad.

Muhammad, politician and founder of a political community

Dr. Abdelaziz Kamel (former vice-president of Egypt, professor at Cairo University, considered by all as one of the pillars of the Congress of Cordoba) addressed the theme *Muhammad, politician, founder of a political community and of a just and humanitarian social order.*

Dr. Kamel's paper was notable for its good documentation, its moderation and serenity, and its religious spirit. It was a real example of the *"spirit of Cordoba."* It was a liberating speech because it helped to destroy many prejudices. Dr. Kamel went over the various stages in the life of Muhammad: his preparation (40 years), his first preaching and his first exercise of responsibility (13 years), his organization of the state (10 years). He concluded by underlining the importance of Islam in Medina. The community there set an example for the world of belief in God, love for men, esteem for work and science, an appeal to turn to God for peace and protection.

Dr. John B. Taylor (World Council of Churches, Geneva) spoke on *Muhammad and his community, for Christians.*

In the first part of his paper he presented *principles for Christians and Muslims in their common search for community.*

1) Mutual respect in community relations, and a respectful curiosity about the faith of the partner in dialogue.

2) Recognition that dialogue means appreciating both the similarities and differences, and that mutual recognition is not static but is an on-going process.

3) Understanding and common study, within the framework of dialogue, and for the service of the community, especially in the field of history.

In the second part he dealt with *specific demands made on Christians living amongst Muslims.*

These demands concern respect for Muhammad, recognition of the values enshrined in Islamic tradition and by the Muslim community.

Christians must understand not only the Muslim experience of revelation

172

given by God in the Qur'án, but also the response in obedience.

Christians and Muslims were invited to build community on the basis of hospitality: to receive, not only to give; to listen, not only to speak; to learn, not only to teach; to enter into each others suffering and joys. Sharing means invitation and offer without forcing anyone to accept.

In all this it is important to recognize that faith is a gift from God. Hence both Christians and Muslims can turn together towards God. This is the real meaning of *"conversion"* in the context of dialogue. In this way the community can bring about a reconciliation between Christian mission and *da'wa*.

Muhammad, a religious figure

Prof. Eusebio Gil (University of Comillas, Madrid) gave a paper on *Muhammad, the religious man and his message*.

Speaking as a theologian Prof. Gil brought out points of convergence and divergence between Christianity and Islam. This can help both Christians and Muslims to be faithful to the demands of their respective religions.

He analysed the function of Muhammad as messenger and warner. He brought out the main points of his message: unicity of God, creation, man's response in faith on the model of Abraham. He touched upon Islamic spirituality and mysticism. He ended by declaring that theocratic legislation does not exclude tolerance which he defined as follows: *"the attitude of one who knows that in the final analysis only God can move hearts."*

Dr. Eva de Vitray Meyerovitch (French Muslim and university lecturer) dealt with the theme of *popular devotion to Muhammad*.

As a framework for her talk Dr. Meyerovitch drew from the Qur'ân three characteristics of Muhammad: his humanity, his nobility of character, his mercy and compassion. The Prophet is therefore a model for the members of his community. She then went on to talk about his role as intercessor, a role given to all the prophets, basing her presentation on extracts from Sufi writings.

Muhammad and Christianity

Prof. Muhammad Hamidullah (Paris)

In his absence Prof. Hamidullah's paper on *Christian misunderstandings about the Prophet of Islam* was read by Dr. Mustafa Cherif. It centred the misunderstandings on the following points: the life of Muhammad, his political activity and his personal behaviour, the question of the prophetic role of Muhammad, the tension in history between Christians and Muslims.

The paper was unfortunately marred by many inaccuracies which the reader, Dr. Cherif, felt obliged to disavow.

Dr. Yoakim Moubarac (Paris and Louvain)

Dr. Moubarac had planned to present a paper on the *Traditional Christian objections against Muhammad. An attempt at a reevaluation*. In fact he gave a short twenty-minute speech in which he reminded his listeners of the dramatic situation in the Lebanon. He invited them to meditate on the tragic death of the leader Kamâl Joumblat and encouraged both Christians and Muslims to persevere in their efforts to bring about a rapprochement, despite the accumulation of obstacles and the almost inevitable incomprehension. He expressed the wish that the former should try to live a *"muhammadan polarisation (istiqtâb)"* in order to grasp better Muslim religious experience, and the latter should make the effort of developing a *"christic (or better 'îsâwî) polarisation"* in order to perceive more clearly the heights to which Christian religious experience tries to attain.

His speech was given in an excellent Arabic. He expressed the regret moreover that his paper, written in French, had suffered badly in being translated into Arabic. This was why he had decided not to read it in public. He requested the secretariat of the congress to distribute the French text only.[4]

The figure of Jesus in Islam

Dr. Ibrahim al-Ghuwayl (Libya) presented *the Qur'anic portrait of Jesus.*

For those familiar with the Qur'ân this long paper presented nothing new. It dealt first with prophecy in general and then treated explicitly the particular case of Jesus, Messiah, son of Mary, Word, Spirit. Dr. al-Ghuwayl ended with two observations on points of difference. First the expression *"Son of God,"* which for him was equivalent to what the Jews meant by *"servant."* The second concerned the crucifixion in which, according to the Qur'ân, someone took Jesus' place.

An additional paper was presented on the same topic by Dr. Mustafa Kamâl al-Tarzi (Tunis), but again without throwing new light on the subject.

Dr. Maurice Borrmans (Rome) spoke on *Christian reactions to the Islamic presentation of Jesus.*

This was a difficult and delicate subject. The speaker, conscious of this, began by·indicating the spirit and limitations of his paper:

> *"I intend to respect entirely the faith of my Muslim brothers and their dogma, just as I would ask them to appreciate at its proper worth the faith of Christians in this Jesus who divides us while at the same time being common to us."*

He outlined the different reactions of Christians to the Islamic presentation of Jesus. These can go from *profound joy* on account of the positive statements about Jesus found in the Qur'ân and the Sunna *(first part)* to a *great sadness* on account of the change in the name of Jesus (from *Yasû'* to *'Isâ)*, the repeated negations concerning the nature of Jesus and the doubt cast upon the good faith of Christians and on their monotheism *(second part)*. This can evolve into a *great hope* on account of the admirable place that Muslim mystics give to Jesus and the renewed interest of many contemporary Muslim thinkers in the life and message of Jesus *(third part)*. This·hope however is *dimmed* when one bears in mind the little value attributed to such as these by official Islam and when one considers the sources of information used by "*men of religion*" for their knowledge of Jesus.

This paper was well-articulated and displayed the care and scientific competence for which Dr. Borrmans is noted. Nevertheless it provoked a strong reaction. It should be noted however that it was not its contents that were questioned but rather whether it was opportune. In this context it is worth noting the remarks made by Dr. Abdelaziz Kamel: "Does dialogue mean merely polite conversation and diplomacy? Must not questions be raised in all honesty and charity if we want to progress together in dialogue?"

Points from the ensuing debate

Prof. Sassi put a series of questions, on the crucifixion and Paul's understanding of it, on baptism and communion, on Christ as God, on the importance of the Gospel of Barnabas.

Prof. De Epalza tried to restore calm to the assembly. He pointed out that the theme originally chosen for the congress had been the figure of Muhammad. It was the Muslims who had asked for the figure of Jesus to be included. We must remember, he said, that we are dealing with the Jesus of the Qur'ân, and that the congress does not have to say everything about Jesus. We should also recognize that our methods are different.

Dr. Michel Lelong (Paris) declared that he disagreed completely with the way in which the paper had been presented. Rather than engage in polemics we should build up mutual confidence on the following foundations: search for the truth, struggle for international social justice, conversion to God in recognition that we are poor and sinful.

Dr. Outbah (Libya) stated that conflict should be avoided and that an effort should be made to seek what unites.

Dr. Abedlaziz Kamel (Egypt) gave some indications on the methodology to be followed in such meetings. It is important, he said, for Muslims to say what they believe on the basis of the Qur'ân and for Christians to share what they believe on the basis of the Gospels. He went on to distinguish three areas of contacts:

1) the area of specific beliefs. Here there can be no dialogue.

2) the area of common ground, v.g. belief in the unicity of God in the context of present-day athesim.

3) the area of practical cooperation.

Awareness of these distinctions will be an important element of the "*method of work*" of future congresses. He also pointed out that human words are subject to revision, but this does not apply to the Qur'ân and the Sunna.

Dr. Kamel's speech met with warm applause.

Dr. Bormans thanked Dr. Kamel for his remarks. He recognized the difficult nature of dialogue, and in particular of the subject he had been asked to treat. He had based it on a scientific analysis which did not exclude, however, respect and appreciation. But can there be any true dialogue, he

"Christianity and Islam"

asked, without some suffering being caused? He then added that he was willing to correct his text according to the rules of dialogue.[5]

Mons. Henri Teissier (Bishop of Oran, Algeria) gave a paper on *the universal message of Jesus according to Christianity*. He reminded his listeners that he was speaking explicitly as a Christian, basing himself on the Gospels and the Epistles. He dealt with three main points:

1) Jesus and the prophets before him.
2) The Christian view of the relations between God and Christ.
3) The conception of human life brought by Christ.

The most important point, he declared, is the unity of all men in Christ.

Communications to the Congress

Apart from the sixteen papers on the theme of the congress a certain number of communications were presented on particular topics.

Prof. Ignacio Hernaiz (Madrid University): *The need for more study on the founders of great religions*.

Dr. Michel Lelong (Paris): *Recent changes of public opinion in France concerning the Prophet of Islam*.

P. Giulio Basetti-Sani (Naples): *How can I recognize the authenticity of Muhammad's prophetic mission?* (see above).

Prof. Gómez Nogales: *The contribution of the theology of religions to an understanding of Muhammad*.

The Spanish Muslim Association: *The historical importance of Muhammad*.

Dr. Rafael Jimenez Pedrajas (Cordoba): *The Mozarabic martyrs of Cordoba*.

Dr. Emilio Galindo Aguilar: *Report on the revision of secondary school text-books with regard to the presentation of Islam*.

Mr. Guy Harpigny (Belgium): *Contemporary positions regarding the prophethood of Muhammad*.

There were a great number of other communications, many of which suffered from a lack of preparation or merely repeated what other speakers had said. Some written communications were however cut short by the secretary of the congress, perhaps with too great severity, such as that of Mons. Ibrahim Ayad (from the Latin Patriarchate of Jerusalem and member of the O.L.P. delegation) and that of Br. Martin (Palestine/Egypt) on *Reflections of some Muslim writers on Islam and Muhammad*.

Highlights of the Congress

We must not forget that the foundation and the goal of the congress was God, since it was above all a meeting between believers. This attitude of faith was clearly expressed in two moments of prayer.

On Friday the *Ṣalât* was celebrated by the Muslims in the ancient Mosque of Cordoba, in the presence of a large group of Christians. It did not however

The Second International Congress of Cordoba

cause as much of a stir as during the first congress. His Excellency Mahmud Fawzi al-Gariani (Ambassador of Libya) donated a valuable Persian carpet to be used on such occasions. The Bishop of Cordoba, together with other ecclesiastical dignitaries, welcomed the Muslims and the rest of the participants in the Patio de los Naranjos. Shaykh Ali al-Schwiter (Libya) gave a short address of welcome from in front of the *mihrâb*, thanking the Christians in particular for their presence. The *hutba* was given by Dr. Tarzi (Director of Religious Affairs, Tunis).

On the Saturday the Eucharist was celebrated in the Cathedral-Mosque. it was concelebrated by the bishops of Cordoba, Astorga and Oran and a good number of priests. The most important texts were read both in Spanish and in Arabic so that the Muslim brothers could follow more easily. Similarly the homily, given by Mons. Briva, bishop of Astorga, was also read in Arabic by Mons. Teissier.

To pray in Cordoba is to *pray twice*. It means to bring together what theologians and men of learning would appear to separate. It means to live a deep unity between Christians and Muslims symbolized by the harmony of stone and faith found in the Mosque-Cathedral of Cordoba.

The closing session

This was held on the morning of Sunday, 27th March, in the headquarters of the civic authorities who were present for the occasion.

As at the first congress the Mozarabic community of Toledo presented a number of Labaros for ecumenism.

There followed various speeches. Dr. Rasjidi (Indonesia) spoke on behalf of non-Arab Muslims, Dr. Kamel (Egypt) on behalf of Arab Muslims, Dr. Lelong (Paris) on behalf of non-Arab Christians and Mons. Ayad (Beirut) on behalf of Arab Christians. For the Arab countries there was a speech given by Dr. Tuhamy, head of the Madrid information office of the Arab league. He suggested that a section for the study of Arabic should be opened in Cordoba University. Then Mr. Fernando Ayape, general secretary to the congress, gave an account of the activites of the A.I.C. since the first congress of Cordoba and outlined future projects. After this Mons. Briva, president of the Spanish Episcopal Commission for Interconfessional Relations, proposed that theological dialogue should be complemented by practical cooperation. Dr. Haykal, co-president of the A.I.C., thanked all the participants for being present and taking an active role in the congress. The final speech was given by his Excellency Sr. Santocalla, head of the civic authorities of Cordoba. He pointed out that the Mosque of Cordoba had been built not by artists but by people who while working on it praised God. He assured all present that Cordoba was always ready to welcome them. A dinner, offered by the civic authorities, closed the congress.

Looking to the future

It can be said in conclusion that the Second Congress of Cordoba was an authentic religious encounter, honest yet friendly. Free from facile irenicism and empty formalism, it brought together in sincerity two groups of believers. We can take note of progress in the capacity for listening to each other and in the effort to understand each other's faith. To deal with the very delicate theme of the congress was a true miracle of faith in the Spirit.

A decisive advance in the congress was the wholehearted support given by the Episcopal Conference of Spain, especially through the presence of Cardinal Taracon whose speech had such an impact.

The discrete but efficient work of the A.I.C., which contributed so much to the success of the congress, should not be overlooked. They constitute a small group of people who by the sole means of great faith in dialogue have succeeded in creating a movement and a spirit which have made an indelible mark on Muslim-Christian relations.

For the future attention will have to be given to the suggestions made by Dr. Kamel concerning the method of dialogue. It might also be necessary for the participants in future meetings to be drawn not only from the ranks of theologians and men of learning, officials and representatives of tradition. More opportunity should be given to younger Muslims engaged in research who would represent a more dynamic outlook and a greater spirit of freedom. As a further suggestion it would be better to have two chairmen, a Christian and a Muslim. This would make it possible for speeches which run over time to be cut short without embarrassment. The sole chairman of the congress, a Christian, in fact allowed the Muslim participants far more time than their Christian counterparts. Papers should also be thoroughly prepared beforehand. This hard but necessary discipline will be a guarantee for the progress of dialogue.

(Adapted from the Spanish by
    Justo Lacunza Baldo and Michael Fitzgerald)

1)   For a report with full bibliographical details see Emilio Galindo Aguilar, Cordoue, Capitale califale du dialogue islamo-chrétien, in Islamochristiana, 1 (1975), pp. 103-114.

2)   The communications media was represented by Spanish Television (TVE), Arab broadcasting corporations and local radio stations. The following publications sent correspondents to follow the congress: Ecclesia, Vita Nueva, Cambio 16, Al-'Arabî, La Vanguardia (Barcelona), Ya (Madrid), Cordoba (Cordoba). There were also correspondents from EFE press agency and from Egyptian Radio and TV.

3)   For an excellent and exhaustive account by an active participant see M. Borrmans, Le séminaire du dialogue islamo-chrétien de Tripoli (Libye) (1-6 février 1976), in Islamochristiana, 2 (1976), pp. 135-164.

4)   Here are the main points of Dr. Moubarac's prepared paper. He distinguished three main categories in the objections which Christian polemicists have levelled against Muhammad, namely objections concerning the moral life of Muhammad, objections concerning the signs of prophecy, and objec-

tions against the Qur'ân. He likewise distinguished three bases for these objections: political, cultural and racist.

As a positive reaction against these opinions he presented four examples, two from the Middle Ages (Timothy I and Abelard) and two from modern times (Louis Massignon and Olivier Clément).

He then asked whether Christians could simply recongize the prophecy of Muhammad. He felt that what was most important was a spiritual approach which would bring about a proper evaluation of Muhammad's message. No-one today can doubt Muhammad's sincerity. Therefore the Christian response must be at the religious level. In conclusion Moubarac proposed that dialogue would be served best by comparing not Muhammad and Jesus but the Qur'ân and the Word of God made flesh, in other words by comparing the prophetic role of Muhammad and the Divine Sonship of Jesus, as two modes of real presence and mediation between God and man.

5) With regard to the moments of crisis in the congress occasioned by the papers of Dr. Ruiz and Dr. Borrmans the following observations could be made. Such crises are normal, unless we wish to reduce dialogue to an exchange of polite words or to a series of monologues. There is a certain risk involved in any true dialogue. Moreover one has to take into account the centuries of mistrust and misunderstanding. Who could have imagined that it would have been possible to speak about Muhammad and Jesus with such freedom, and still live in a spirit of fraternity and keep the dialogue open? Here we had a living expression of "the spirit of Cordoba." *Again such crises are inevitable, given the different backgrounds of the participants and the difference of methods and language. As one participant remarked:* "Some have come to affirm their own convictions, others to explain them in response to the questions put by their interlocutors, and yet others to compare, contrast and exchange." *Futhermore, it takes time to develop openness to and respect for the opinions of others, especially if these are contrary to our own. It should be noted that Dr. Ruiz had been asked to present the Christian point of view regarding Muhammad as a prophet. His presentation was thoroughly scientific and as the same time respectful and charitable. The same could be said of the paper of Dr. Borrmans, although his subject was difficult and delicate and more likely to stir up feelings.*

Appendix
Personal Reflections Of Two Participants

Les participants viennent de divers pays, des quatre coins du monde. Ils appartiennent à des générations qui diffèrent par leurs styles, leurs conceptions. Il y a eu, queloquefois, des interventions qui frisaient la polémique, mais toujours fraternelles, bien que vivantes et fermes. Ce qui a prédominé, du début jusqu'à la fin, est incontestablement l' engagement pour l' ouverture (de ce qui n'a été jusque là qu'entrouvert): un dialogue franc. On peut dire que «l'esprit de Cordoue » est déjà une réalité.

Une remarque cependant: il y a eu trop de conférences au détriment des dialogues proprement dits. J'espère qu'on modifiera cette méthode, les fois prochaines. Quelquefois, certains exposés donnaient l'impression qu'on cherchait un certain éclectisme (par complaisance).

"Christianity and Islam"

Quelques participants avaient la sensibilité à fleur de peau: ils ne comprenaient pas que le dialogue présuppose des partenaires *différents,* qui ont des points communs et d'autres divergents, voire opposés. C'est ce que d'autres participants ont tenu à dire, à répéter et expliquer pour dissiper les malentendus: l'autre n'est autre que parce qu'il n'est pas moi, parce que nous avons des choses qui nous séparent. le sens du Colloque de Cordoue est précisément de nous réunir pour exposer les principes de nos deux religions respectives, pour en expliciter leurs orginalités, leurs compacts doctrinaux, mais aussi les points de rencontre. Ni apologétique, ni prosélytisme: faire des concessions ou en exiger de l'autre reviendrait à trahir l'esprit du Colloque. Ce point avait besoin d'être explicité. Il l'a été, cependant il faudra encore oeuvrer dans ce sens pour le succès des prochaines rencontres.

Qu'est-ce que je garde personnellement du Deuxième Congrés de Cordoue?

J'ai appris beaucoup de choses sur le Christianisme tel qu'il est compris et vécu par les siens; des témoignagnes vivants qui ont l'avantage de l'authenticité, des témoignages par des Chrétiens pratiquants et compétents. Renseignements de première main.

Les Musulmans, eux aussi, ont été des témoins. Des exposés et des interventions sur l'Islam m'ont éclairé sur certains aspects de ma foi et de mon credo et m'ont confirmé dans certaines positions. Les dialogues ont ainsi été doublement utiles. Je suppose que les Chrétiens peuvent affirmer la même chose. Les dialogues, d'ailleurs, ne se nouaient pas seulement entre Chrétiens et Musulmans, mais également à l'intérieur de chacune des deux communautés religieuses représentées.

Le niveau était inégal (c'est un jugement personnel: je n'ai pas bien apprécié une sorte de scientisme, ni aimé une certaine forme de «ton» qui se voulait sinon agressif, du moins convaincu de détenir la Vérité absolue). Par contre, j'ai été trés sensible á la simplicié généreuse de J. Taylor (de Genève), à l'esprit fin et méthodique de 'Abd al-'Azîz Kâmil (du Caire), à l'érudition militante d'Al-Hammânî (d'Alger) et á l'exposé de Y. Moubarac qui a fait montre d'un grand coeur polarisant une raison ordonnée. On ne saurait ici reprendre toutes les conférences.

Un autre profit tiré du Congrés: les amitiés liées, les échanges de cartes de visite, de revues, de livres, de photos souvenirs prises en groupes. Ne se rencontrait-on pas lá pour se connaître et se lier d'amitié? Belle tâche qui méritait bien le déplacement et ce pélerinage à Cordoue. De tels colloques, il en faudra beaucoup encore, afin de changer des hostilités historiques (conflits sanglants, colonialisme, etc...) en amitiés solidaires et de construire ainsi une cité terrestre vivable pour tous, oú régnera la paix du monde et des âmes.

Un souhait encore? Que de pareils colloques nous aident à faire de chaque homme un messager de l'amour du prochain, dans nos pratiques quotidiennes. Puissent nos religions, nos idéologies, nos diverses cultures participer, effectivement, à cette vaste entreprise et à cette économie objective du salut commun. L'Institut égyptien des Etudes Islamiques de Madrid a apporté sa collaboration efficace pour la réalisation de ce Congrés. Efforts importants pour la traduction simultanée qui a bien facilité le travail. Merci donc à nos amis d'Espagne qui se sont donné tant de peine pour organiser ce Congrés. Les Espagnols ont été trés accueillants et ont su rendre le séjour des plus doctes et des plus sympathiques.

Mohamed Aziz Lahababi
(Université, Rabat)

The Islamic-Christian Encounter at Cordoba, March 1977, took in its planning stages the challenging and ambitious subject of "Positive Evaluation of Muhammad in Christian Theology." It was apprently the Muslims who asked that this subject be expanded to "Positive Estimates of Muhammad and Jesus in Christianity-Islam." There were serious difficulties of theological symmetry in comparing the Prophet Muhammad as channel of Divine Word with Jesus Christ as Himself the manifestation of Divine Word, but there was also a sincere will for dialogue based on the integrity of each partner. Accordingly, what had been envisaged as an "encounter" of scholars and religious leaders addressing a somewhat one-sided subject, where it might have appeared that it was always the Christians who were asked to make all the efforts of comprehension and self-criticism, thus became a more reciprocal and dialogical occasion, when both partners could witness to each other of the central points of their faith and when both partners could strive not only to be understood but also to understand.

This shift of emphasis from "encounter" to "dialogue" could involve not only a shift from polite and serene objectivity to sometimes passionate subjectivity but also an acceptance of risks that the laying down of sharp differences could once again obscure patiently and only recently reclaimed common ground. Yet it was worth taking these risks, for the ultimate experience of the conference was that fundamental issues of prophecy and revelation had been honestly, frankly and respectfully raised from both sides; despite differences of conviction about how God has spoken and still speaks to humankind, there was a common affirmation to each other and to our neighbours in the world that He has spoken and does speak; there was even, for some of us, an experience that in listening more sensitively to the way in which our fellow men and women have spoken and speak we may open our hearts more fully to what God has said and is saying to us, sometimes through our neighbours.

Despite or perhaps because of the focus of the meeting upon the historical persons of Muhammad and Jesus Christ, as well as upon their eternal significance, the discussions could not avoid touching on problems of peace and reconciliation in the contemporary world. The meeting was signally free from any political manipulations and no public statements were issued. The predominantly Mediterranean and Arab participants in the meeting, reflecting Spain's own cultural history, brought several legitimate allusions to a desire for mutually respectful cultural or religious pluralism not least in the

"Christianity and Islam"

Middle East between Jews, Christians and Muslims, recapturing the best of the heritage of Andalusia but also reinstating the traditions of tolerance ranging from Morocco to Palestine. Individual participants from Indonesia, from Mauritania and from increasingly pluralistic N. Europe reminded us of the still wider concerns to establish Christian-Muslim understanding and cooperation across the world. One might hope that further meetings in Cordoba could involve more Christians and Muslims from Asia and Africa and from other areas underrepresented at Cordoba in 1974 and 1977.

The "spirit of Cordoba," a spirit of honesty and of modesty, of realism and of hope, needs to be shared more widely; it is a spirit which can lead our most precious convictions to be strengthened and deepened as we open them to the risks of challenge, correction and communication. The recent conference demonstrated that Christians and Muslims do not come together simply out of socio-political opportunism but out of thirst and the thirst of the whole world. Dialogue on theological and spiritual issues is not easy. It is not an evasion of socio-political concerns and can make a deep contribution towards reconciliation in society, just as continuing ignorance and prejudice can breed fanaticism and hostility. But dialogue on theological issues, as the participants in Cordoba found, can illuminate our own self-knowledge not only in terms of our shared — and separated — cultural histories but also in terms of our personal and communal growth in relation to each other and in relation to God.

The intellectual exchange and the shared community of Jews, Christians and Muslims in mediaeval Spain need not remain as the nostalgic memory of scholastic theologians or political scientists. It can become a model for the culturally inter-penetrated and politically inter-dependent societies of today.
John B. Taylor
(World Council of Churches, Geneva)

Bibliography
(Of the many articles in Spanish on the congress, the following are perhaps the most significant) Jose A. Carro Celada, *Cordoba, Mezquita y catedral*, in A.B.C. (19-3-77).
A. Gil, *Cordoba: Mahoma, profeta e fundador de una gran religion*, in *La Vanguardia* (23-3-77) *Cordoba: el congreso islamo cristiano a la luz del Vaticano II* (declaration of Mons. José Ma. Cirarda, bishop of Cordoba) in *Cordoba* (24-3-77).
Mons. A. Briva (bishop of Astorga), *Cordoba: inquebrantable fidelidad de los Musulmanes a su fe*, in *La Vanguardia* (25-3-37).
El dialogo interconfesional, fruto de los congresos islamo-cristianos (declaration of Mons. A. Briva), in *Cordoba* (27-3-77).
Gregorio Ruiz, *Limites y esperanzas en el dialogo islamo-cristiano*, in *El Pais* (8-4-77).
Mikel De Epalza, *España, primer lugar mundial de encuentro entre Musulmanes y Cristianos*, in *La Vanguardia* (22-4-77).
El espiritu de Cordoba (Editorial) in *Vida Nueva* (2-4-77).

The Second International Congress of Cordoba

Juan Lorente, *Se ha terminado la reconquista contra los musulmanes*, in *Vida Nueva* (2-4-77).

La Iglesia de Cordoba toma parte activa en el II Congreso Islamo-Cristiano, (declaration of Mons. José Ma. Cirarda), in *Cordoba* (24-3-77).

Antonio Gil, *Cordoba: gran cordialidad en el congreso islamo-cristiano*, in *La Vanguardia* (22-3-77).

Alcor, March-April 1977 (special issue on the congress).

Boletin informativo (Secretariat of the Spanish Episcopal Conference for interconfessional relations) no.s 1 and 2 (March and April 1977).

II Congreso Islamo-Cristiano de Cordoba, special issue of *Mundo Arabe*, April 1977, 162 p. (It contains an introduction and eight of the most important conferences during the congress).

España-Cordoba: II Congreso International Islamo-Cristiano de Cordoba, in *Bulletin. Secretariatus pro non christianis*, Vatican, 1977 - XII/1-2 no. 34-35, pp. 86-87.

Antonio J. Molina, *Cita islamo-cristiana en Cordoba*, in *Tercer Mundo*, no. 73, mayo 77, pp. 32-33.

Le IIème Congrès islamo-chrétien de Cordoue: lecon inaugurale du Cardinal Tarancon, in *La Documentation catholique*, Paris, no. 1720 (15-5-77), pp. 480-483. (In note is to be found the article of Michel Lelong which appeared in *La Croix* (26-4-77).

'Ulamâ' al-lâhût yudâfi'ûna 'an Muhammad wa-ya'tarifûna bi-nubuwwati-hi (The theologians defend Muhammad and recognize his prophetic charac-ter) in *al-'Arabî*, Kuwayt, no. 223 *(ĝumâdâ al-tâniya* 1397/June 1977) pp. 40-51.

Min al-mu'tamar al-islâmî al-masîhî (from the Muslim-Christian Congress) in *al-Hidâya*, Tunis, 4th year, no. 5, (ĝumâdâ al-ûlâ 1397/May 1977):

—, *Risâlat Muhammad wa-dustûru-hâ l-ḫâlid* (The mission of Muhammad and its eternal constitutive value) by al-Tuhâmî Nagra, pp. 50-54 and 79.

—, *Naŝât al-wafd al-tûnusi* (The activity displayed by the Tunisian delega-tion) p. 55.

—, *al-Islâm din al-uhuwwa wa-l-salâm* (Islam, religion of brotherhood and peace), the Friday ḫuṭba of ŝayḥ Muṣṭafa Kamâl al-Tarzî, pp. 56-58.

Christian-Muslim Dialogue

By JOHN B. TAYLOR

Colombo, Sri Lanka, 30 March - 1 April 1982

The international meeting between Christians and Muslims held 30th March to 1st April 1982 in Colombo, Sri Lanka, on the theme "Christians and Muslims Living and Working Together: Ethics and Practices of Humanitarian and Development Programmes" was the first such meeting jointly sponsored by international Christian and Muslim organizations. It was distinguished by an unusually long and careful process of joint planning and it is to be hoped that it may lead to further cooperation in liaison and planning between Christians and Muslims. The subject of the meeting points to the need for Christians and Muslims to work together in society and this clearly involves not only international but also regional, national and local levels, all of which were involved and reflected in the meeting.

John B. Taylor, born in Birmingham (U.K.) in 1937, is Director of the Programme for Dialogue with People of Living Faiths and Ideologies in the World Council of Churches, Geneva, and has travelled widely, giving lectures, organizing and attending conferences and committees between Muslims and Christians all over the world. He is a Ph.D. (Islamics) of McGill University, Canada (1972) with a thesis on the Concepts of Social Morality in Post-Ilkani and Pre-safawi Iran. *Author of* Thinking about Islam, *Lutterworth 1971, 3rd revised ed. 1982. This essay is taken from* Islamochristiana. *Vol. 8, 1982, pp. 201-217 and is reprinted with permission of the publishers.*

"Christianity and Islam"

1. Background

It had been nearly ten years since the World Council of Churches held a properly international Christian-Muslim dialogue, at Broumana, Lebanon, in 1972. That meeting had been planned by a group of Christians and Muslims, including His Excellency Tunku Abdu Rahman, then General Secretary of the Islamic Foreign Ministers Conference; but participants, including on the Muslim side a Shaykh from al-Azhar, had essentially come as individuals at the invitation of the World Council of Churches. A similar policy of individual non-representative invitations to Muslim was followed when the World Council of Churches sponsored its regional meetings in West Africa (Accra, June 1974) and south-east Asia (Hong Kong, January 1975), and its meetings on particular subjects ("Mission and Da'wah" at Chambésy, July 1976, and "Faith, Science and Technology and the Future of Humanity" at Beirut, November 1977).

At the World Council of Churches Assembly in Nairobi in December 1975 the World Muslim Congress had accepted an invitation to nominate its representative in Kenya, Dr. Yusuf Eraj, as a "visitor" to the Assembly. He met with several staff, advisers and delegates and helped to prepare for official participation by the World Muslim Congress (as also by the World Muslim League and the Organization of the Islamic Conference) at a planning meeting of Christians and Muslim held at Cartigny in October 1976 (See *Christians Meeting Muslims*, Geneva 1977, pp. 143-155); the Vatican Secretariat for Non-Christians was represented at that meeting by Fr Abou Mokh. Certain issues of "dialogue on socio-political issues" were described as in need of further clarification.

a) Faith and politics in Islamic and Christian thought

Muslims and Christians live in differing contexts across the world. Sometimes they are a majority and sometimes a minority, perhaps in an Islamic state, perhaps in a secular state, perhaps in a democratic state, perhaps in a totalitarian state. How far are they victims of structural violence whether from the weight of history, the international environment or the mass media? How do they envisage ways to regulate and construct their society in accordance with the teaching of their faith?

What is the role of Islam and, in particular, what is the role of Ijtihad (disciplined interpretation) in the formulation and application of the principle of equal rights and opportunities to all citizens in the state? Especially where Christians live with Muslim majorities they should ask themselves how they envisage their role as citizens. How far are both Muslims' and Christians' faiths challenged by and how far may they both act as a challenge to modern society?

b) Social justice and development

How can Christians and Muslims act together in order to realize throughout their societies the Christian and Islamic ideals of social justice and integral

186

human development? How can they engage in non-violent struggle against unjust forces and how can they narrow the widening gulf between rich and poor groups and nations? Can Muslim and Christian scholars cooperate in defining the rights of individuals and groups to enjoy social and political justice?

It was further recommended, in the context of developing countries, that:

Especially in Asian and African developing countries Christians and Muslims should discuss together the conception and construction of a community based on social justice and integral human development. They should together initiate and administer projects for the benefit of all their neighbors; in order to do this, they will need to find ways to share resources and work together and thereby to foster a just and participatory society.

The suggestion that was made in 1976 was pursued in subsequent regional and local meetings and in official visits by World Council of Churches staff, for example to the secretariat of the Organization of the Islamic Conference in Jiddah in February 1977 when the former General Secretary, Dr. Abdul Karim Jaye, expressed particular interest in pursuing the practical and humanitarian aspects of Christian-Muslim cooperation.

At a subsequent planning meeting of Christians and Muslims held at Chambésy in March 1979 with representatives of the World Muslim Congress and the Organization of the Islamic Conference among other Muslims and with Fr. Michel Lelong representing the Secretariat for Non-Christians, it was agreed to promote a discussion on "The ethics and practices of economic aid programmes in humanitarian assistance" (see *Christian Presence and Witness in Relation to Muslim Neighbours*, Geneva 1981, pp. 84-88).

It was already in the summer of 1979 that the World Council of Churches submitted the project for an international conference on this theme through the Primate's World Relief and Development Fund of the Anglican Church in Canada to the Canadian Development Agency. They generously assured financial support for approximately half the cost of such a meeting on the assumption that a good number of both Muslim and Christian participants should be people working in local situations where they could not count on financial subsidy for international travel.

At the end of 1979 a group of one hundred Christians (including some twenty-five Roman Catholics) met at Mombasa to discuss "Christian Presence and Witness in Relation to Muslim Neighbours." Among their recommendations, which were modified and commended to the churches the following summer by the Central Committee of the World Council of Churches, was the holding in 1981 of an international consultation on the theme "Christians and Muslims Living and Working Together." During the autumn of 1980 invitations were sent to the World Muslim Congress, the Organization of the Islamic Conference and the World Muslim League to confirm their interest in such a meeting. The World Muslim League conveyed a reply that Christian churches' involvement in missionary activities among Muslims made impossible, for the time being, such partnership in discussion. The Organization of the Islamic Conference, however, expressed friendly interest in the meeting. It was the staff of the World Muslim Congress in Karachi, however, who, in December 1980, agreed that the proposed meeting might benefit by joint sponsorship from both Muslim and Christian sides. They suggested that it might be possible to offer hospitality for the meeting in Pakistan, thus helping to share the expenses of the meeting; most important, they agreed to choose the participants on the Muslim side and to pursue liaison with other Islamic international organisations.

The visit of the General Secretary of the World Muslim Congress to the headquarters of the World Council of Churches in Geneva at the time of the World Council of Churches Executive Committee in February 1981 was a good opportunity for a planning meeting for the proposed conference. Dr. T.B. Simatupang and the late Bishop Samuel of Egypt took part in these discussions. It was possible for the Secretariat for Non-Christians to be represented by Fr. Schotte of the Justice and Peace Secretariat. A programme for the meeting was mutually agreed and plans were laid to hold the meeting in Pakistan in the autumn of 1981. These plans were further confirmed when World Council of Churches staff visited the World Muslim Congress headquarters in Karachi in the course of 1981; in June 1981 it was possible to include in these discussions Dr. Marouf al Daoualibi, President of the World Muslim Congress, and to gain his approval for the meeting despite certain pressures from some Muslims that the time was not ripe for such a meeting. However, various other factors led the World Muslim Congress as co-sponsors to request postponement of the meeting until March 1982 at which time they would have a widely international and influential group of Muslims together for their Council meeting and for a seminar on "The Universality of Islam" to be hosted by the Sri Lankan government.

It was agreed that Sri Lanka would be a suitable place for the meeting; Christians and Muslims are both in a minority in that country and this provides a salutary reminder that Christians and Muslims are outnumbered throughout the world by fellow humans with other religions, and ideological convictions. The host country provided excellent facilities for the conference in the Bandaranaike Conference Centre; local staff, particularly from the local branch of the World Muslim Congress and from the Ministry of Muslim Affairs, provided generous and untiring help. It was good to have this evidence of the World Muslim Congress as a decentralized and locally based worldwide organization drawing support from "laity" and "clergy," from men and women in the local communities. It was also valuable to have contacts arranged by them with local Buddhist leaders, both monks and laity. Local Christians in Sri Lanka encouraged the meeting by sending their representatives to plenary sessions and by facilitating, through the Sri Lanka Council of Churches, a special meeting for the Christian participants to review, in the days that followed, the experience of the "dialogue."

2. The meeting: participation and style

An international meeting is always open to dangers of artificiality. Splendid

Colombo Christian-Muslim Dialogue

conference facilities, the gift of the Chinese government to the people of Sri Lanka, may be welcome to long distance travellers and may help rapid progress with a crowded agenda; on the other hand and there is also an unwelcome sense of being insulated from the urban or rural life where actual dialogue of word and action must take place. The Christian and Muslim participants, however, were taking only a short break away from their offices, classrooms, hospital wards, or farms in some forty countries.

Among the thirty Christians from twenty-six countries were eight participants from Africa, eight from Asia, three from the Middle East (three others having unfortunately apologized at the last moment), two from North America and one from Europe. Some came from countries like Pakistan, Egypt, Algeria, Indonesia, the Gambia or Sudan where Muslims are a significant majority; others came from countries where Christians are in a majority as in Kenya, Uganda, USSR, Philippines or European and North American countries. Others came from countries like Sierra Leone, Chad, Ethiopia or Lebanon where numbers of Christians and Muslims are more balanced. Among both clergy and laity were teachers, doctors, social workers and aid agency administrators; among the clergy were bishops and parish priests. There were six Roman Catholics, including a representative of the Secretariat for Non-Christians and Bishop Henri Teissier, a vice-President of Caritas Internationalis. There were unfortunately only three women among the Christian participants including one Roman Catholic sister.

Muslim participants from twenty-two countries numbered thirty-three persons, including two women to whom belated invitations had been sent in order to match the Christian participation (satisfaction was expressed at this by several influential Muslim participants.) The Muslims came from nine countries in Asia, two in Africa, seven in the Middle East, two in Europe and two in North America; half of these countries are ones where Muslims live as minorities, ranging from Japan and Philippines, Singapore and India, South Africa and Uganda to West Germany and USA the other half were from Muslim majority situations ranging from Tunisia and Morocco, Saudi Arabia and Afghanistan, to Pakistan and Indonesia; some came from countries like Lebanon, Singapore or Sri Lanka where numbers of Muslims and Christians are similar. The Muslims included religious and political leaders, educationalists, doctors, journalists, social workers, those responsible for aid programmes and representatives of international organizations such as the Organization of the Islamic Conference and UNESCO; some were in high positions but others were working at the "grass roots" for example with migrant workers in Europe or with refugees in south-east Asia.

The hosts had arranged for Muslim and Christian participants to sit on separate blocks, facing each other. It was quickly suggested that we might be more comfortable sitting in a random, or deliberately alternating, seating, but this did not find favor with the local organizers. However, in the numerous social functions and in the coffee breaks and meals taken together there was the opportunity of mixing up the groups. In fact the majority of participants had already met on the day before the dialogue began during an all-day excursion arranged by the Sri Lanka hosts to Kandy.

A certain formality persisted in the overall conduct of the meeting. There were two moderators — Dr. D.C. Mulder, Moderator of the DFI Working Group, and Dr. Vigar Hamdani, of the New York office of the World Muslim Conference (in place of Dr. Inamullah Khan who was undergoing heart surgery in London and whose presence was sorely missed for it had been he who had pioneered the meeting on the Muslim side). There were also two "presidents" — Dr. Marouf al-Daoualibi, President of the World Muslim Congress, and Dr. T.B. Simatupang, Joint President of the World Council of Churches. The first day there were numerous official messages received and this inevitably took up a lot of time; however, the content of the messages was particularly positive. Mention should be made of the greetings from the Secretariat for Non-Christians and from UNESCO and also of the substantial and encouraging paper delivered by Mr. Ahmad Kamal, representing Dr. Habib Chatty, General Secretary of the Organisation of the Islamic Conference.

There was regrettably little time for any plenary discussion of the main addresses or introductory papers and these were therefore relayed to the two main mixed groups which reviewed the first days' presentations and, after further discussion, prepared recommendations which were the basis of the final report.

The mood and atmosphere of the meeting varied widely in the relatively short time available since the working schedule had had to be reduced from five to three full days. The Muslim President felt that no progress could be made unless a frank description was given of the various grievances felt by many Muslims, especially by those who had refused to attend such a dialogue. The main complaints centered on a close identification of the Christian Church with the Western world of imperialism, colonialism and neo-colonialism; within this analysis Christian mission was seen as an aggressive and culturally destructive phenomenon. He called for much greater discipline and control in the exercise of mission, especially by Christians. Christian participants avoided too defensive replies but bore witness to the international and multi-cultural facets of the Church and also pointed to the duty for proper exercise of mission in the context of repentance for abuses of mission.

Other times in the meeting were less contentious, especially as we faced together the human tragedies of refugees and victims of underdevelopment around the world. Here it was possible to listen to each other's visions and to join in the preparation of a mutually agreed report which charted common action for the future. It may be noted that the work of the whole conference was unfortunately somewhat formal, partly because the conference facilities and official patronage, including that of the Sri Lanka government, inhibited more intimate exercises. Muslims' ritual prayer was observed in a room apart; sessions and speeches opened with ritual invocations, blessings, scripture quotations or moments of silence. For a future meeting it might be desirable to build into the programme deliberate periods of shared silence and meditation, and more opportunity for discussion and conversation.

3. The content of the meeting

The main conclusions of the meeting are reflected in the mutually accepted "report" but it is useful to realize the background and input. The programme was constructed to be conducted under joint or alternating presidency and moderatorship of a Muslim or a Christian. Each subject was addressed by both a Christian and a Muslim. Formal speeches of welcome included that from the Minister of Muslim Affairs of the government of Sri Lanka who "hosted" the meeting. The two "keynote addresses" were given on the main theme by Dr. Simatupang and by Dr. Marouf al-Daoualibi. While Dr. Simatupang took serious account of tensions between Christians and Muslims especially in the colonial era, he emphasized the greater freedom and independence of the present day and the duty of Christians and Muslims to cooperate not only for each other's sakes but for the sake of their other neighbours in the world. Dr. Daoualibi reviewed the many obstructions to a fruitful dialogue but also spoke of Muslims' openness to cooperate in truly open endeavors freed of hidden or brazen attempts at proselytism and dedicated to human rights and to the service of God.

The first group of presentations on the theme "Working together in relief and rehabilitation" was given on the Christian side by Mgr. Grégoire Haddad of Lebanon, who kindly took over at the last minute when Bishop Athanasios of Egypt was unable to come. He spoke of the need to live and work together in terms of scriptural imperatives in both traditions; he insisted that orthodoxy must be expressed as orthopraxy and then described patterns of social and political cooperation where religion really inspires and is not merely a label for each partner. Especially in emergency aid and rehabilitation human rights and dignity must be respected and proselytism must always be rejected. Dr. Imtiazi, Minister of Religious Affairs in Pakistan, spoke on the same subject emphasizing respect for life, the upholding of religious faith in face of so much unbelief; we should abjure merely cosmetic methods and proselytism and work for local communities to take responsibility themselves in administering relief supplies and development materials.

The second group of presentations was on the theme of "Refugees". Mr. Fadlullah Wilmot, of the Regional Islamic Da'wah Council of Southeast Asia and the Pacific, gave many vivid illustrations of the work initated by Muslims especially in Malaysia to relieve "boat people" some of whom are Kampuchean Muslims. Mr. Kodwo Ankrah of the Planning, Development and Rehabilitation Programme of the Church of Uganda, and with long experience in Sudan and other parts of Africa, spoke of Christian involvement in refugee work, especially in Africa. These two presentations were important preparations for detailed recommendations which were eventually jointly agreed.

The third group of presentations on the theme "Planning and realizing community development" was given by Dr. Khurshid Ahmad (a former Minister of Planning in the government of Pakistan, and one who had been active in Christian-Muslim relations especially through the Islamic Foundation, Leicester, United Kingdom) and by Mgr. Henri Teissier (Roman Catholic Bishop Coadjutor of Algiers and active over many years in Christian-Muslim dialogues). Professor Khurshid Armad spoke of our duty as believers to undertake dialogue and to promote development in an atmosphere of respecting cultural pluralism in a framework of legal and political rights for all. All misinformation and exploitation should be eschewed, mission/da'wah should not be abused by either side, common humanitarian concerns should be tackled together and channels of cooperation and consultation should be established at every level. Bishop Teissier gave examples of fruitful cooperation between Christians and Muslims in the Maghreb, working together for the human development of handicapped people in Algeria, and for national development in Mauritania. He recognized various obstacles such as the "confessional" structures of much aid activity, and, worse, the abuse of aid for proselytism and propaganda in some instances. He emphasized the need to struggle together for justice in common obedience to God with the possibility of discovering true human values together.

The fourth set of presentations were more in the nature of case studies and personal testimonies on the theme "Religious minorities." On the Christian side Rev. Ian Roach spoke of the situation of Christians and Muslims cooperating in national building in the Gambia, especially in the aftermath of the abortive coup, while Bishop Alexander Malik of Pakistan spoke of Christians' co-citizenship with Muslims in Pakistan, emphasizing the role that a minority can play for example in education. Mr. Mohammed Abdullah spoke of the situation of dialogue in the Federal Republic of Germany; he spoke of the need for mutual respect and confidence and the desire for a new start in cooperation against materialism. Mr. Ahmad von Denffer, a German working in England at the Islamic Foundation, contrasted what he saw as a position of influence for the Christian minority in Indonesia with the marginalization of Muslims in Europe, especially in the legal and education fields.

4. Conclusions

It is perhaps best to let the conclusions of the meeting, as jointly expressed by the participants in the Final Report, speak for themselves. To this one may add the confirming and endorsing words of the Christian participants who met in the days immediately following. It should be noted that the recommendations are those of a conference and, in the second case, of a group of participants. Both reports will be submitted on the side of the Council of Churches to the relevant bodies, notably the Central Committee of the WCC meeting in July, 1982 in Geneva. It is to be hoped that they may endorse these recommendations and that similar action on the World Muslim Conference side, and in other Christian and Muslim bodies, may lead to the earnestly desired establishment of regular liaison and planning processes.

Colombo Christian-Muslim Dialogue

CHRISTIANS AND MUSLIMS LIVING AND WORKING TOGETHER
ETHICS AND PRACTICES
OF HUMANITARIAN AND DEVELOPMENT PROGRAMMES

FINAL REPORT

At the invitation of the Hon. Minister of Transport and Muslim Affairs of the Republic of Sri Lanka, and through the hospitality of the Government of that friendly country, a conference of Muslim-Christian dialogue was convened in Colombo, 30 March - 1 April, 1982, on the theme "Christians and Muslims Living and Working Together: Ethics and Practices of Humanitarian and Development Programmes."

Initiated and organized cooperatively by the World Muslim Congress, Karachi, and the World Council of Churches, Geneva, the conference was attended by 33 representatives from the Muslim world and 30 from the Christian churches. Messages and observers were sent from the Secretariat for Non-Christians, Vatican City; the Organisation of the Islamic Conference, Jeddah; and UNESCO, Paris.

Presided over by the Hon. Mohammed Haniffa Mohammed, Minister of Transport and Muslim Affairs of Sri Lanka, together with H.E. Dr. Marouf Daoualibi, President of the World Muslim Congress and Dr. T.B. Simatupang, one of the Presidents of the World Council of Churches, the conference was moderated by Dr. Viqar Hamdani, World Muslim Congress representative to the United Nations, New York, and Dr. D.C. Mulder, Moderator of the World Council of Churches' Dialogue with People of Living Faiths and Ideologies.

Both parties agreed on the need to discuss the conference theme in a world threatened by materialism and loss of faith, and disfigured by injustices and violations of human rights that have been especially destructive in the context of situations of invasions and displacement of peoples. It was recognized that there are still numerous obstacles in the way of fuller cooperation between Christians and Muslim and there was frank discussion of the suspicions promoted by restriction of cultural and religious rights of any peoples whether majorities or minorities. Both sides expressed concern about the abuse of some humanitarian work when force or false persuasion is used for conversion and proselytism.

The Muslim participants emphasized that cooperation deserves to be built on the foundations of removing obstacles and supporting the victims of aggression and persecution. They stressed the need for:

a) unequivocal condemnation of agression against the people of Palestine, who had been dispossessed from their homeland and are being subjected to oppression and persecution, of the invasion of Afghanistan, and of the persecution of Muslims in different parts of the world especially in the South ern Philippines;

b) sympathetic appreciation of Muslims' commitment to develop their communities and societies on the basis of their faith and law (Shari'ah) on the part of their Christian neighbours and other believing communities, as Muslims struggle to establish the Islamic social order in places where they enjoy political sovereignty;

c) implementation of principles agreed upon in earlier dialogues, particularly that at Chambésy in 1976, in order to remove obstacles to Christian-Muslim cooperation.

While sharing many of the preoccupations expressed by the Muslims, the Christian participants, both in plenary addresses and discussions, emphasized their desire that they might work more closely with Muslim neighbours in nation building and in community development. In some places Christians felt that they were not accepted as full citizens by their Muslim neighbours, while in other places Christians acknowledged their responsibility for having left Muslims with analogous feelings. But the major preoccupation of the Christians was not to allow the suspicions or caricatures of the past to disfigure the present and the future. Determined efforts should be undertaken for closer understanding and more effective partnership with their Muslim neighbours.

Recommendations of the Conference lay in three major areas:

A. Recommendations on Christian-Muslim Cooperation

The participants, having discussed issues of "Cooperation in Relief and Rehabilitation" and "Planning and Realising Community Development," recommended that:

The World Muslim Congress and the World Council of Churches be requested to establish a Joint Standing Committee with a view to:

1. working out the targets, forms and modalities of Muslim-Christian dialogue in a manner that would ensure authentic participation from both communities and lead to better understanding and greater cooperation among them;

2. identifying obstacles to and difficulties in the healthy pursuit of dialogue and cooperation between the two communities, and using their good offices to redress any such obstacles and difficulties.

3. responding to the challenges of development;

4. giving to human existence its transcendent dimension, which is obstructed by all the forms of misunderstanding of faiths, whether these forms are encouraged by materialist ideologies or inspired by a narrowly scientific interpretation of the achievements of science and technology;

5. undertaking everything possible to promote a form of education that situates knowledge in a truly human perspective where faith and knowledge give each other mutual reinforcement and seek inspiration from divine revelation;

6. studying and examing the possibilities of deepening dialogue on practical action to be undertaken in common and with clear and precise conditions laid down by the Joint Standing Committee; these should reflect the notion of

development in the context of justice and as a way of full realisation of human potential; there should also be examination of the methods to be used for implementing moral and cultural values in the process of development;

7. instituting joint study groups and holding seminars on Muslim and Christian approaches to the solution of major problems jointly faced by them in their search for a just social order; in this respect the Joint Standing Committee is requested to constitute working groups on the problems of 'law (*šarī' ah*) and Life'. 'The role of the State' and 'human and Religious rights', from the Islamic and Christian points of view;

8. trying to bring into the Joint Standing Committee representatives of other international Islamic organisations and the Roman Catholic Church.

B. Recommendations on refugees

The participants discussed the world refugee problem. Because of internal conflicts and the systematic and flagrant violation of human rights in many countries, the number of refugees has dramatically increased in recent years. This trend was noted with grave concern. The living conditions borne by most of these refugees strike at their dignity and rights as human beings. The participants, therefore, recommended that:

1. since work for refugees is a field in which both Christians and Muslims can cooperate fruitfully together, Christian-Muslim cooperation in alleviating the plight of refugees on international, regional and local levels should be developed; further, Christian churches and Muslim organisations should come together to study the causes of the refugee problem as well as methods of preventing it;

2. Christian churches and Muslim organisations should attempt to convince the appropriate authorities to allow refugees to return to their homeland with guarantee of security of life, property, and fundamental human rights;

3. noting the enormity of the refugee problem and the fact that over three-quarters of the world's refugees are Muslims, the Muslim participants appeal to the Organisation of the Islamic Conference (OIC) to establish a unit to deal with all aspects of the refugee problem; such a unit should cooperate with the existing organisations dealing with refugees;

4. services for refugees should not serve as means for conversion or proselytism and should be made available to all without discrimination;

5. Christian churches and Islamic organisations should encourage the peoples and governments of their respective countries to accept refugees, to have sympathy for their plight, and to adhere to international conventions governing assistance to refugees and the granting of asylum to them.

C. Recommendations on minorities

The participants came to a deeper awareness of the fact that Christians and Muslims share the same experience in living both as a majority and as a minority. They are convinced that Christians and Muslims can live together in harmony, but recognized that there is a need to overcome the tensions that exist in some countries. The participants agreed that:

1. each religious group should be enabled to live according to the teachings of its faith with the right to perpetuate itself; in order to do this, full freedom of worship should be guaranteed;

2. particularly where Christians and Muslims are both in the minority they should cooperate with each other to obtain and maintain their freedom of worship and practise their religion;

3. there have been and are persistent and serious violations of the fundamental human rights of religious minorities in many countries; these acts and the governments responsible for them were condemned and it was agreed that the Joint Standing Committee should be asked to study instances of discrimination and persecution and to take appropriate action;

4. marriage, divorce and inheritance and charitable trusts are regulated in a specific manner for Muslims and for some Christian confessions and these provisions should be respected; a serious diaglogue should be undertaken to find appropriate ways of maintaining or creating legal safeguards in these matters;

5. multi-religious, multi-cultural and multi-linguistic communities offer new methods of living and working together; these need further study.

Conclusion

The experience of the Christian-Muslim dialogue in Colombo, with its frank and open discussion, has fostered a clear understanding of each other and the determination to work together in the interests of peace, justice and humanity, thus exemplifying Muslims' and Christians' united commitment to achieve God's purpose for humanity.

REPORT OF WCC DELEGATION TO CHRISTIAN-MUSLIM DIALOGUE

In the three days following the Christian-Muslim dialogue, held under the joint auspices of the World Council of Churches and the World Muslim Congress, in Colombo, Sri Lanka, the Christian participants evaluated the meeting and agreed upon the following report:

We, the delegates appointed by the World Council of Churches to participate in the Christian-Muslim dialogue on "Living and Working Together", have met following that dialogue, on 3rd - 5th April, 1982, in Colombo. After studying the document presenting the final report of the dialogue, we offer the following recommendations to the World Council of Churches and its constituent member churches.

I. Regarding future structure for continuing dialogue, we recommend:

1. that the WCC work toward the establishment of a Joint Standing Committee with the World Muslim Congress (WMC);

2. that in the first phase this committee have the status of a liaison and planning committee;

3. that as soon as possible efforts be made to bring the Roman Catholic Church and other international Islamic organisations into the Joint Standing Committee;

4. that possible membership for the committee be up to 20, with up to 10 on either side, and a limited number of ad hoc advisory observers;

5. that Christian membership of the committee include experts in different fields and be largely made up of people who live in the Muslim world or who work with Muslims.

II. *Regarding relief and rehabilitation, we recommend:*

1. that the WCC and its constituent member churches reaffirm that *diakonia* is the expression of God's love to all those in need, regardless of religion or nationality, with no intention of proselytism or benefit to those practising such *diakonia*, though not hiding that we are Christians;

2. that the WCC, its member churches and related agencies study whether, in certain special circumstances, the provision of resources for relief and rehabilitation should preferably be channelled through other humanitarian organisations;

3. that the churches continue to pay special attention to the task of transforming relief and first-help service into a long-range process of rehabilitation and development, and encourage cooperation between Christians, Muslims and other communities in this task.

III. *Regarding development, we recommend:*

1. that, in the continuation of the dialogue, attention be given at the earliest opportunity to reflection on the challenges of development, and that for this purpose the WCC call upon the special competence of CCPD and its staff;

2. that Christian-Muslim dialogue regarding development be encouraged at the national and local levels, taking into consideration the political, economic and social context within each nation and community;

3. that a study be made of particular development projects in which Christians and Muslims are cooperating, with a view to learning which methods are effective and which are not, and to sharing those models which may be adapted elsewhere;

4. that the WCC and churches in the industrialized countries call upon the governments of the industrialized countries to hear the appeal of the nations of the South to establish a new international economic order, and to share a larger proportion of their Gross National Product in development assistance to poorer countries, working toward the goal of 0.7% of GNP called for by the United Nations, in order to share in their struggle for justice;

5. that churches around the world be called upon to share a larger proportion of their resources for development programmes in developing countries, with a view to struggling together with the peoples of those nations for a more

just, participatory and sustainable global society to the glory of God and the fulfilment of the potential of his creation.

IV. *Regarding refugees, we recommend:*

1. that the WCC heartily endorse the five recommendations regarding refugees which appear in the Final Report of the dialogue;

2. that the WCC and its member churches reaffirm clearly our Christian practice of serving all refugees regardless of their religion, and continue to study and analyse the causes of refugee situations which are often complex and of a socio-political, religious and racial character;

3. that the WCC encourage cooperation wherever possible at the national and local level between Christians, Muslims and all other institutions in meeting the immediate and long-range needs of refugees, working within the context of the policies of the receiving countries;

4. that the WCC express its readiness to consult with apropriate Islamic organisation to consider all aspects of the refugee problem, with the understanding that such consultation be carried out within the context of international agencies dealing with refugee issues, such as UNHCR, and on the part of the WCC within the existing structures of church work for refugees;

5. that, in view of the fact that many of today's refugees in the world are of Muslim religion, the WCC express its readiness to discuss the deeper complex issues which have led to this alarming phenomenon and to undertake whatever action or initiative may be appropriate;

6. that the WCC reaffirm that the ultimate goal of work among refugees is repatriation to the country from which they have fled, and failing this refer to WCC resolutions dealing with other possible solutions.

V. *Regarding minorities, we recommend:*

1. that the WCC affirm the recommendations on minorities, while recognizing that the whole concept of majority and minority needs further study;

2. that the question of minorities be further discussed in the framework of human rights, recognizing that basic human rights are of three categories, individual rights, rights of smaller communities (including those cases where identity is based on religion), and the rights of the larger society. In emphasizing the rights of the smaller communities, it is recognized that this may conflict with individual rights, and might in turn force groups and individuals into ghetto-like situations. Thus, a balance has to be sought between individual rights, the rights of the smaller communities, and the unity and ethos of the wider society;

3. that in the continuing dialogue on minorities, the tensions mentioned in the preamble of the report on minorities should be expected to include:

a) tensions between different historical perspectives and theological perceptions;

b) tensions between ideals and realities;

c) tension between the different realities.

VI. *Comments for future implementation of Christian-Muslim cooperation:*

Colombo Christian-Muslim Dialogue

1. In order to give support to the DFI and the WCC at large in facing the ongoing dialogue with the Muslim partners, it is essential that a network of Christian consultants be established which can be drawn upon for information and expertise.

2. It is important that Christians identify and make known their preoccupations in pursuit of dialogue. It is urged that studies continue with regard to the issues of legitimate diakonia and evangelism, and the misuse of diakonia and evangelism as a form of proselytism.

3. Several points in the Final Report of the dialogue should be read against the background that Christians should be sensitive to the desire of many Muslims to relate common projects to a mutual understanding of the whole philosophy of development.

4. It would be important to make an effort to bring the findings of the WCC in the field of development, and the relation between science and revelation, reason and faith into relation with the dialogue with our Muslim partners and where possible to bring their ideas into our own focus, as well as our ideas into their focus.

5. With regard to recommendation A(7) of the Final Report of the dialogue, we are convinced that the problems mentioned there are of utmost importance to both parties. We support the idea of constituting bilateral working groups on the topics mentioned. We would urge very strongly that DFI cooperate with other WCC sub-units in promoting as soon as possible a thorough study from the Christian side on these problems. We are deeply convinced of the necessity of preparing Christians for dialogue with Muslim partners, and we call on church authorities, national and regional councils of churches, Christian study centers, and the WCC to promote such preparation.

LIST OF PARTICIPANTS

Christians

Delegates

Mr. Kodwo Ankrah (Uganda)
Dr. John Berthrong (Canada)
Pasteur Roby Bois (France)
Fr. Angel Calvo (Philippines)
Dr. James Cogswell (USA)
Mrs. Mary Fadel (Egypt)
Sr. Fatima Prakasam (India)
Mrs. Margaret Greene (Sierra Leone)
Bishop Grégoire Haddad (Lebanon)
Dr. Ihromi (Indonesia)
Rev. Stanley Jeyaraj (Sri Lanka)
Fr. Michel Lelong (France)
Dr. U.N. Malakar (Bangladesh)
Bishop Alexander Malik (Pakistan)
Fr. Tom Michel (Vatican)

"Christianity and Islam"

Dr. D.C. Mulder (Netherlands)
Dr. Jürgen Micksch (Federal Republic of Germany)
Fr. Augustin Nikitin (USSR)
Mr. Cees van der Poort (Netherlands)
Rev. Ian Roach (The Gambia)
Rev. E. Ramtu (Kenya)
Mr. Elie Romba (Chad)
Dr. Olaf Schumann (Federal Republic of Germany)
Dr. T.B. Simatupang (Indonesia)
Rev. F. Suleiman Greis (Sudan)
Rev. Tan Chi Kiong (Malaysia)
Bishop Henri Teissier (Algeria)
Fr. A. Tilahun (Ethiopia)
Rev. R. Ward (Kenya/Canada)
OKR Klaus Wilkens (Federal Republic of Germany)

Observers

Sus Abharatna
Mrs. T.B. Irving
Mrs. K. Wilkens

Secretariat

Dr. John B. Taylor
Mr. J. Fischer
Mr. G. Rubeiz
Mrs. J. Spechter

Interpreters

Mrs. Nicole Fischer
Mr. H. Birchmeier

Muslims

Delegates

H.E. Dr. Marouf Al Daoualibi (President, World Muslim Congress)
Hon. M. Haniffa Mohammad (Minister, Sri Lanka)
Sayed Haider Al-Hussieni (Deputy S.G.)
Dr. Ahmed D. Alonto (Philippines)
Mr. Abdus Salam Morita (Japan)
Mr. Yunus Saleen (India)
Sheikh Hashim Al-Mojaddedi (Afghanistan)
Sheikh Eisa Bin Nasser (United Arab Emirates)
Mr. B. Tarzi Kamel (Tunisia)
Dr. Aboubakrel Kadiri (Morocco)
Hon. Abubakar Mayanja (Uganda)
Mr. Haji Mohamed Khan (Singapore)
Dr. Rifat M. Yucelten (Motamar-Cyprus)
Dr. A.H. Tabibi (Motamar-U.N.-Switzerland)
Dr. Viqar Hamdani (Motamar-U.N.-USA)
Mr. I. Ahmed Imtiazi (Pakistan)

Colombo Christian-Muslim Dialogue

Mr. Ahmed Kemal (World Muslim Congress)
Mr. M.H. Farugi (Impact Institute-UK)
Dr. A. Fuad Sahin (Canada)
Dr. T.B. Irving (USA)
Dr. Kalil Abdel Alim (Indonesia)
Professor Ahmad Saddali (Indonesia)
Mr. Ahmad Sahirul Alim (Indonesia)
Mr. Fadlullah Wilmot (Regional Islamic Da'wah Court of Southeast Asia
  and the Pacific
Mr. A. Sinaceur (UNESCO)
Professor Abdul Majid Mackeen (Sri Lanka)
Dr. Badrivaal Aawadhi (Motamar)
Dr Roqaiya Vi Mangalett (Philippines)
Dr. Mohamed I. Momoniat (South Africa)
Dr. Y. Najmuddin (India)
Professor Khrusheed Ahmed (Islamic Foundation-UK)
Mr. M.A. Abdullah (Federal Republic of Germany)
Mr. Ahmed Von Denffer (Islamic Foundation-UK)

Observers

Hon. M.L.M. Aboossally (Sri Lanka)
Mr. Moulana Jamal Mian (Motamar)
Mr. Khalid Ikramullah Khan (World Muslim Congress)
Mr. R.J.M. Ariff (Sri Lanka)
Mr. Djailan (Indonesia)
Dr. Hisham Ahmed (Canada)
Mr. Ustad M. Alouini (Belguim)

Secretariat

Mr. S.I. Jafferjee
Dr. Hasonnah
Mr. M.I. Kaleel

XI

From Tolerance to Spiritual Emulation
An Analysis of Official Texts on
Christian-Muslim Dialogue

By Lucie Provost

I n the Catholic Church, since the time of the Second Vatican Council, the way towards dialogue between Christians and Muslims has been marked out by texts and official declarations originating from the highest levels of the hierarchy. One of these texts can be considered equivalent to a basic principle. This is the conciliar declaration *Nostra Aetate* (28 October 1965), a document of capital importance in this field. This declaration however should be seen within the context of a number of other documents, of which some prepared the way for it from 1963, and others followed it.[1]

A number of these texts owe their origin to the Council.[2] Others, such as encyclicals, allocutions and messages, express the mind of two popes, Paul VI[3] and John Paul II.[4] All of the texts look beyond the confines of the Catholic Church. It is true that some of them are directed in the first place to those who exercise authority in the Church, to the Christian world. This is so in the case of the encyclicals, the acts of the Council, and certain allocutions. Yet, in fact, they are destined to be heard or read by all who are interested in mutual encounter. This openness appears implicitly in messages addressed to particular faith communities. Thus a Christian community living in a country with a Muslim majority is invited to « *give the reasons for its hope* »[5], and such

This article first appeared in French in Panorama Inter-Eglises 1980, *supplement to* Lettre Inter-Eglises, *no. 18 (October 1980). It is reproduced here by courtesy of the Centre de Recherche Théologique Missionnaire, Paris (English translation by M.L. Fitzgerald and that of* Islamochristiana. (5, 76, p. 1-9) *and reprinted here by permission of the publisher.*

a Muslim community finds its martyrs for the faith praised together with Christian witnesses.[6]

Sometimes the destination is explicitly stated to be universal, as when, over and above Christians and « *whoever professes monotheism* », the message is addressed to the whole world.[7]

This corpus of texts, covering a period of eighteen years, presents a doctrine of dialogue. It can be seen how this doctrine was gradually elaborated. A brief survey makes it possible to bring out the main lines. It can be shown that there is great continuity in the thinking with, at the same time, an evolution in the language used and in the manner of encounter with the non-Christian, and particularly with the Muslim. These characteristics can be observed at two levels, that of knowledge of other people and that of the practice of dialogue.

1. Knowing about others.

Immediately after his election Paul VI stressed that it was necessary for Christians to open up to knowledge of other religions and to enter into dialogue with non-Christians. All the documents which followed the pope's first address to the Vatican Council (29 September 1963) insist on this need. Its theological foundation, clearly expressed in the encyclical *Ecclesiam Suam*, is the Incarnation. The dialogue between God and mankind is at the same time the norm and the source of Christians' dialogue with other people. God the Father took the initiative of the encounter with humanity in various different ways and, "*in our own time, the last days,*" through the mediation of Christ (cf. Heb. 1, 1-2). He thus inaugurated with humanity the dialogue of salvation. In the same way it behoves Christians to take "*the initiative in extending to men this dialogue without waiting to be summoned to it.*" At the same time they must "*take cognizance of the slowness of psychological and historical maturation*" without however wanting to "*postpone all for tomorrow what it can accomplish today.*"[8]

Two things follow from this theological foundation: a vision which passes beyond the Church, and the discovery of the faith of others. A close reading of the texts can bring out the evolution in the thinking and the language on these two points.

(A) In the beginning it is noticeable that the vision has a centre as its point of departure. "*The Catholic Church looks further still, beyond the confines of the Christian horizon,*" looking "*beyond her own sphere towards the other religions.*"[9] For, "*those who have not yet received the Gospel are related in various ways to the People of God.*"[10] The same vision, broadening out in concentric circles, if found in both *Lumen Gentium* and *Ecclesiam Suam*.

Yet the language used already bears the seeds of its own transformation. The idea comes through of a community of destiny and life, having its foundation in an analogous faith. For this circle in fact "*is made up of the men who above all adore the One, Supreme God, whom we too adore.*" The encyclical lists these people who are brought together by monotheism but who are distinct on account of their knowledge of God: "*We refer to the children of the Hebrew people ..., then to the adorers of God according to the conception of monotheism, the Muslim religion especially ... and also to the followers of the great Afro-Asiatic religions.''*[11] Although the reverse order is found in *Nostra Aetate*, the Church is always at the centre of the circle. Yet the text describes the elements of a community of faith, leading Christians and Muslims to unite in their efforts to transform a world which is theirs in common.

These seeds of a transformation of the vision can be seen to develop gradually in several of Pope Paul's allocutions in which he talks about the relations between Catholic and non-Christian religions. This is particularly evident in his allocution, in Bombay, in December 1964. *''We should meet not as mere tourists, but as pilgrims who seek God, not in stone buildings but in human hearts.''*[12] In 1969, the Pope goes well beyond the vision of concentric circles when he expresses to the Muslim communities of Uganda his ''hope'' *''that what we hold in common may serve to unite Christians and Muslims ever more closely, in true brotherhood.''*[13]

These words show that no longer is one thinking in terms of ''Christendom,'' which seemed to be the core in the texts of 1963 and 1964. From now on the representative of the Catholic Church is addressing a pluralistic world, a world where people of different religions live together in the same nation and sometimes in the same family. The idea of ''Christendom,'' disappears altogether in the allocution of John Paul II of 19 November 1979 to the Christian community in Ankara, a diaspora living *''in the framework of a modern state,''* together with *''fellow citizens who have a different faith.''*[14]

(B) The invitations to discover the content of the Islamic faith give evidence of the same type of evolution as regards the language used and the thought expressed. Here again the point of departure is simply a description, sometimes couched in comparative terms, before engaging progressively in the directions of a serious search for that which unites.

The description which is a fruit of the way in which the Church ''looks upon'' other religions is always expressed in terms of ''esteem.'' *''The Church ... cannot exclude them from her thoughts and would have them know that she esteems what they contain of truth and goodness and humanity.''*[15] In 1967, Paul VI addressing the President of Turkey and the Mufti of Istanbul, echoes the manner of speaking in use since *Nostra Aetate*, saying: *''We wish to tell you of Our esteem for Muslims ... so well-expressed by the recent Council.''*[16]

The basis of this esteem would seem to lie essentially in the content of the faith of Muslims and in the fact that they worship God. Thus the ''pillars'' of the Islamic creed are mentioned by the documents being analyzed here, either by means of a general definition of abrahamic monotheism, or as constitutive elements of a particular religion, namely Islam. So *''The Church looks ...''* towards *''the other religions which preserve the sense and notion of the One, supreme, transcendent God, Creator and Sustainer,''*[17] *''the one and true God, the living God who is supreme, the God of Abraham, the All-High.''*[18]

"Christianity and Islam"

To these general elements *Nostra Aetate* adds more precise details drawn from the way Muslims speak about God: *"One God, living and enduring, merciful and all-powerful, Maker of heaven and earth, and Speaker to men,"* who *"will give each man his due after raising him up."* Moreover Muslims *"strive to submit wholeheartedly to this inscrutable decrees, just as did Abraham."*[19]

It is true that the first pontifical declarations, when speaking about non-Christian religions in general, mention *"omissions, insufficiencies and errors which cause her* (the Church) *sadness."*[20] So *"obviously we cannot share in these various forms of religion nor can we remain indifferent to the fact that each of them, in its own way, should regard itself as being the equal of any others and should authorize its followers not to seek to discover whether God has revealed the perfect and definitive form, free, from all error, in which He wishes to be known, loved and served."* For, *"there is but one, true religion, the religion of Christianity,"*[21] *"The religion of Jesus ... our religion effectively establishes a real and loving relationship with God which the other religions do not succeed in doing, though they constantly lift their arms to heaven, as it were."*[22]

Despite these warnings against being too quick to see equivalences, later documents bring out with less and less timidity a certain convergence between the different monotheistic religions, especially Islam, and Christianity. Besides Christians, *"the plan of salvation also includes those who acknowledge the Creator. In the first place among these are the Muslims, who, professing to hold the faith of Abraham, along with us adore the one and merciful God, who on the last day will judge mankind."*[23] From as early as 1965 the Decree *Ad Gentes* has been inviting Christians *"gladly and reverently* (to lay bare) *the seeds of the Word which lie hidden"* in non-Christian religious traditions.[24] Granted, the apostolic exhortation *Evangelii Nuntiandi* is still underlining in 1975 the incomplete nature of the quest for God in which non-Christian religions have been engaged for thousands of years. Yet at the same time it states that these religions are all *"strewn with innumerable 'seeds of the Word,' and can constitute a true 'proposition from the Gospel.'"*[25]

Though wishing to be extremely respectful of non-Christian religions this type of language shows a certain condescension. For while non-Christian religions *"bear within them the reflection of thousands of years of searching for God,"*[26] this search is judged to be incomplete. Such a formulation runs the risk of giving serious offence to the people outside of Christianity and particularly in Islam, who have had an authentic and deep spiritual experience whose degree of completeness cannot be judged by anyone in this world. This is why it is fitting to call attention to more positive statements where the *"common faith in the Almighty"* is fully recognized.

This faith can find concrete expression in common witness, in Uganda for example, where Paul VI paid tribute to: *"those confessors of the Moslem faith who were the first to suffer death in 1875, for refusing to transgress the precepts of their religion."* The Pope unites Christians and Muslims in his prayer to the Glory of God: *"May the shining sun of peace and brotherly love rise over this land, bathed with their blood by generous sons of the Catholic, Christian and Moslem communities of Uganda, to illuminate all of Africa."*[27]

John Paul II[28] does not hesitate to apply to the faith of Muslims the words which, during the first century of the Church, St. Peter addressed to the Christians scattered throughout the regions which correspond to present-day Turkey: *"Today, for you Christians living here in Turkey, your lot is to live . . . with persons who, in their great majority, while not sharing the Christian faith, declare themselves to be 'obedient toward God,' 'submissive to God,' and even 'servants of God' according to their own words which match those of St. Peter already quoted (cf. 1 Pet. 2,16)."*

The Pope also establishes a parallelism between the statements of the Bible and the Qur'an on man, creation, and the proscription of idols: *"As a consequence of this faith in God the transcendent Creator ("faith in God, which the spiritual descendents of Abraham, Christians, Moslems and Jews profess") man finds himself at the summit of creation. He has been created, the Bible teaches, 'in the image and likeness of God' (Gen. I, 27). For the Qur'an, the sacred book of Moslems, although man is made of dust, 'God has breathed into him his spirit and endowed him with hearing, sight and heart,' that is with intelligence. (Q. 32, 8) . . . Insofar as he is a creature of God, man has rights which may not be violated, but he is also bound by the law of Good and evil which is based on the order established by God. Thanks to this law, man will never submit to any idol. The Christian abides by the solemn commandment: 'You shall not have any other God but me' (Ex. 20, 30). For his part, the Moslem will always say: 'God is the greatest.'"*

The language used by John Paul II would seem to follow exactly the line of preceeding texts and declarations. Yet it is easy to detect a break in continuity. For John Paul II in fact adopts a universalistic manner of speaking which explicitly makes use of Jesus' admiration of the Centurion of Caphernaum (Mt. 8, 10): *"A Christian finds it of the highest interest to observe truly religious people, to read and listen to the testimonies of their wisdom, and to have direct proof of their faith to the point of recalling at times the words of Jesus: "Not even in Israel have I found such faith.'"*[29]

The Pope goes so far as to express a certain reversal of the triumphalist vision current previously. He is not afraid to upbraid Christians for their lack of faith: *"Does it not sometimes happen that the firm belief of the followers of non-Christian religions – a belief that is also an effect of the Spirit of truth operating outside the visible confines of the Mystical Body – can make Christians ashamed of being often themselves so disposed to doubt concerning the truths revealed by God and proclaimed by the Church and so prone to relax moral principles and open the way to ethical permissiveness."*[30]

It will be noticed that as far as making comparisons is concerned, there has been a transfer from the plane of the content of faith to that of moral conduct which should flow from it. In this regard the omissions are no longer attributed to non-Christians, but more generally, and independently of belonging to any particular religion, to everyone who *"loses certitude about one's own faith or weakens the principles of morality the lack of which will soon make itself felt in the life of whole societies, with deplorable consequences besides."*[31]

By means of its most qualified representative the language of the Catholic Church is visibly opening up to the fresh air of contemporary religious pluralism. The value of this pluralism is fully recognized from the moment encounter brings the discovery of an aspect of the infinite face of God which he reveals to mankind through his prophets. This openness must necessarily lead to a religious dialogue which is loyal and constructive.

II. The Practice of Dialogue

An evolution can also be noted in the language and the thought of the Church concerning the practice of dialogue. This evolution is at one and the same time similar to and different from that described above. With regard to the Islamic faith there is an ever more noticeable movement towards common action, while at the same time there emerges anew the need to affirm one's faith in Christ.

(A) Up to the declaration *Nostra Aetate* (1965), the texts simply express respect and esteem. The declaration opens up new horizons. The Council exhorts Christians and Muslims to unite: *"On behalf of all mankind, let them make common cause of safeguarding and fostering social justice, moral values, peace and freedom."*[32] Paul VI will recall the importance of this common vocation in his 1967 allocution to the Turkish authorities. After quoting the conciliar declaration he continues: *"All those who adore the one, the unique God, are called to establish an order of justice and peace on the earth."*[33] We have here a social dimension of dialogue. It can be seen what importance the Church of Vatican II attached to the development of nations.

Redemptor Hominis proposes a new level in the practice of religious dialogue. John Paul II does not exclude the development dimension, but nor does he speak about it. He proposes a practice of dialogue which will also find expression *"through contacts, prayer in common, investigation of the treasures of human spirituality."*[34]

The Pope insists once more on this aspect of dialogue at Ankara in 1979, in order to give a new elan to the directives contained in *Nostra Aetate*: *"I wonder whether it is not urgent, precisely today when Christians and Moslems have entered a new period of history, to recognize and develop the spiritual trends which unite us in order to 'safeguard and foster, on behalf of all mankind – as the Council invites us to do – social justice, moral values, peace and freedom.'"*[35] John Paul II goes on to invite his brothers in Christ to: *"consider each day the profound roots of the faith in God in whom your Moslem fellow-citizens also believe, to draw from it the principle of a collaboration with a view to the progress of men, to emulation in doing good, to the extension of peace and brotherhood in the free profession of the faith proper to each."*[36]

(B) Yet John Paul II does not play down to duty that disciples of Christ have *"to give the reason for the hope that is in them."* Here again his language has a rather new ring. In point of fact never, since the Council, had the Church affirmed the necessity of their witness for Christians living with Muslims. The same is not true of the relations with those who follow African or Asian religions other than Hinduism and Islam. This difference appears clearly in the Declaration *Nostra Aetate.* In the second section, concerning non-Christian religions, a title which covers neither Islam nor Judaism, the Church exhorts: *"her sons prudently and lovingly... and in witness of Christian faith and life, (to) acknowledge, preserve, and promote the spiritual and moral goods found among followers of other religions."*[37] It is in a similar context that the Exhortation *Evangelii Nuntiandi* (1975) notes that *"neither respect and esteem raised for these religions nor the complexity of the questions raised is an invitation to the Church to withhold from non-Christian the proclamation of Jesus-Christ."*[38] John Paul II, in April 1979, again states: *"the Christian has the tremendous responsibility and the immense joy of speaking to these people with simplicity and openness... of 'the mighty works of God.' "*[39]

At Ankara, once more, a decisive step is taken. Taking again as his starting point the First Letter of Peter, the Pope invites the Christians who live in these regions to be attentive to one of its exhortations: *"Should anyone ask you the reason for this hope of yours, be ever ready to reply, but speak gently, and respectfully, in possession of a good conscience' (1 Pet. 3, 15-16). These words are the golden rule for the relations and contacts that the Christian must have with his fellow-citizens who have a different faith"*[40] i.e. in this case, Muslims. There is no question here of aggressive proselytism, but rather of a dialogue based on the witness of faith in Christ by whom all men are saved.

To be sure there is a certain continuity with the ideas expressed in the Decree *Ad Gentes: "For wherever they live all Christians are bound to show forth, by example of their lives, and by the witness of their speech, that new man which they put on at baptism, and that power of the Holy Spirit by whom they were strengthened at Confirmation. Thus, other men, observing their good works, can glorify the Father, and can better perceive the real meaning of human life and the bond which ties the whole community of mankind together."*[41]

Yet the thought develops into a new attitude, that of moving ahead together. To this the Pope has alluded in the most recent of the documents to be analyzed here. Addressing the representatives of the Muslim community in France, on 31 May 1980, John Paul II expresses the need for emulation: *"The ideal we have in common is that of a society in which men recognize one another as brothers, walking in God's light to emulate one another in goodness."*[42] The formulation used is very close to a Qura'nic verse frequently referred to by those who desire to promote authentic Christian-Muslim dialogue: *"If God had pleased, He had surely made you all one people... be*

"Christianity and Islam"

emulous, then, in good deeds. To God shall you all return'' (Q. 5, 48). Should not this emulation between believers of different religions lead to the spread of divine light among the nations? *"Your light must shine in sight of men so that, seeing your good works, they may give the praise to your Father in Heaven* (Mt. 5, 16).

This article first appeared in French in Panorama Inter-Eglises 1980, *supplement to* Lettre Inter-Eglises, *no. 18 (October 1980). It is reproduced here by courtesy of the Centre de Recherche Théologique Missionnaire, Paris (English translation by M. L. Fitzgerald and that of* Islamochristiana. (5, 76. p. 1-9)

1)   For the background to the elaboration of the Declaration Nostra Aetate *see R. Caspar,* Le Concile et l'Islam, *in* Etudes, *janvier 1966, pp. 114-126.*
2)   *Constitution* Lumen Gentium, *No. 16; Decree* Ad Gentes, *No. 10 and 11. Conciliar documents are quoted according to the translation given in Walter M. Abbott,* The Documents of Vatican II, *London, Geoffrey Chapman, 1966.*
3)   Address at the opening of the Second Vatican Council, *29 September 1963, in Xavier Rynne,* The Second Session, *London, Faber and Faber, pp. 347-363;* Message from Bethlehem to Christians and to the world, *January 1964; Encyclical letter* Ecclesiam Suam, *6 August 1964, Tipografia Poliglotta Vaticana, 1964;* Address to the President of Turkey and to the Mufti of Istanbul, *July 1967;* Address to the leaders of Muslim communities, *Kampala, Uganda, August 1969, in* Bulletin. Secretariatus pro non Christianis *12 (1969) p. 157; Apostolic exhortation* Evangelii Nuntiandi, *8 December 1975, English translation by the White Fathers' Documentation Service, Rome; for a fuller study of the thought of Pope Paul VI see M. Borrmans,* Le Pape Paul VI et les Musulmans, *in* Islamochristiana, *4 (1978), pp. 1-10.*
4)   *Encyclical letter* Redemptor Hominis, *15 March 1979, English translation in* The Tablet, *17.3.1979;* Discourse to the participants in the Plenary Meeting of the Secretariat for Non-Christians, *27 April 1979, in* Bulletin. Secretariatus pro non Christianis *41-42 (1979) pp. 79-81.* Discourse to the Catholic Community in Ankara, *29 November 1979, in* Bulletin. Secretariatus pro non Christianis *43 (1980), pp. 2-5.*
5)   *John-Paul II,* Discourse to the Catholic Community in Ankara, *1979.*
6)   *Paul VI,* Address to the leaders of Muslim communities, *Kampala, 1969.*
7)   *Paul VI,* Message from Bethlehem, *1964.*
8)   Ecclesiam Suam *nos. 74 and 79.*
9)   *Paul VI,* Address at the opening of the Second Vatican Council, *1963.*
10)   Lumen Gentium *no. 16.*
11)   Ecclesiam suam *no. 111; cf.* Lumen Gentium *no. 16.*
12)   *Paul VI,* Address to representatives of non-Christian religions in India, *1964.*
13)   *Paul VI,* Address to the leaders of Muslim communities, *Kampala, 1969.*
14)   *John-Paul II,* Discourse to the Catholic Community in Ankara, *1979.*

15) *Paul VI,* Address at the opening of the Second Vatican Council, *1963.*
16) *Paul VI,* Address to the President of Turkey, *1967.*
17) *Paul VI,* Address at the opening of the Second Vatican Council, *1963.*
18) *Paul VI,* Message from Bethlehem, *1964.*
19) Nostra Aetate *no. 3; cf. R. Caspar,* La Religion musulmane, *in* Vatican II, Les Relation de l'Eglise avec les Religions non-chrétiennes, *Paris, le Cerf (Unam Sanctam 61), 1966, pp. 201 sq.*
20) *Paul VI,* Address at the opening of the Second Vatican Council, *1963.*
21) Ecclesiam Suam, *no. 111.*
22) Evangelii nuntiandi, *no. 53.*
23) Lumen Gentium, *no. 16.*
24) Ad Gentes, *no. 11.*
25) Evangelii nuntiandi, *no. 53.*
26) Ibid.
27) *Paul VI,* Address to leaders of Muslim communities, Kampala, *1969.*
28) *John-Paul II,* Discourse to the Catholic Community in Ankara, *1979.*
29) *John-Paul II,* Discourse to the Secretariat for non-Christians, *1979.*
30) Redemptor hominis, *no. 6.*
31) Ibid.
32) Nostra Aetate, *no. 3.*
33) *Paul VI,* Address to the President of Turkey, *1967.*
34) Redemptor hominis, *no. 6.*
35) *John-Paul II,* Discourse to the Catholic Community in Ankara, *1979.*
36) Ibid.
37) Nostra Aetate, *no. 2.*
38) Evangelii nuntiandi, *no. 53.*
39) *John-Paul II,* Discourse to the Secretariat for non-Christians, *1979.*
40) *John-Paul II,* Discourse to the Catholic Community in Ankara, *1979.*
41) Ad Gentes, *no. 11.*
42) *John-Paul II,* Discourse no. 6 ter, *31 May 1980; cf. Jean-Paul II,* «France, que fais-tu de ton baptême?», *Paris, Centurion, 1980, p. 94.*

"Christianity and Islam"

XII

World Council of Churches (W.C.C.)

Christian Presence and Witness in Relation to Muslim Neighbours (Mombasa, December 1979).

Here are the recommendations of a conference on «Christian presence and witness in relation to Muslim neighbours», held at Kanamai, Mombasa, Kenya, 1-7 December 1979. This meeting of 100 Christians from 40 countries was organized by the sub-unit on Dialogue with People of Living Faiths and Ideologies (DFI) of the World Council of Churches. Participants, who included 25 Roman Catholics as well as Orthodox, Protestants and others from member and sister churches of WCC, shared their varied experiences in relating to their Muslim neighbours, and made several recommendations concerning the churches' attitudes to dialogue with Muslims.

Christian communities, such as those in the Middle East, have lived in close proximity with Muslims for centuries. Now, the churches in many western countries are also having to face the problems and opportunities arising from the growing number of Muslims who have settled there. These circumstances call for dialogue in order to live together in religious maturity. Yet too many churches are ill-prepared for such a «dialogue in community».

Among its recommendations, the conference encouraged Christians to view the movement of «renewal» in the Muslim world with an open but discerning mind; and to promote mutual encounter, communication and

This WCC statement is taken from ISLAMOCHRISTIANA, Vol. 6, 1980, pp. 46-48 and is reprinted here by permission of the editors.

"Christianity and Islam"

collaboration with Muslims in shared spiritual concerns. The several study centres and programmes specializing in the field of Islam and Christian-Muslim relations should be strengthened and encouraged to develop their activities to meet the needs of Christian-Muslim dialogue in the 1980's. The report is available in *Wcc Exchange (a Bi-monthly Documentation Service from the W.C.C.)*, No. 6, December 1979.

Recommendations

The above report was received and discussed by participants in the Mombasa conference. They requested the appropriate bodies of the WCC, its member churches and all fellow Christians to study the report and to take up the following recommendations:

1. Attitudes in dialogue.

We recommend:

—that Christians understand dialogue with Muslims as a mode, a spirit, an attitude which may appear new, but which is in fact integral to the theology and the history of our respective faiths.

—that Christians view the movement of «renewal» in the Muslim world with an open but discerning mind, and be encouraged to seek mutual encounter, communication and collaboration with Muslims in shared practical and spiritual concerns.

2. Preparations for dialogue.

We recommend:

—that churches study and make known the WCC publication *Christians Meeting Muslims: WCC papers on 10 years of Christian-Muslim dialogue* (Geneva 1977) and the Vatican Secretariat for Non-Christians' *Guidelines for a Dialogue between Muslims and Christians* (under revision).

—that churches undertake catechetical preparation and pastoral training of people both young and old, laity and clergy, many of whom are not ready for encounter with people of other living faiths and ideologies.

—that the several study centres and programmes specializing in the field of Islam and Christian-Muslim relations be strengthened and encouraged to develop their activities to meet the needs of Christian-Muslim dialogue in the 1980's and beyond; people should be encouraged to give themselves to the task of Christian and Islamic theological reflection, interpretation, and witness, recognizing that effective theology and witness are not however the exclusive domain of experts.

—that the WCC, the Vatican and Muslim world bodies but also Christian and Muslim regional and local bodies be encouraged to continue planning formal dialogue conferences, planned and executed on a cooperative basis; that further consideration be given to the possibility of arranging multilateral dialogues between Muslims, Christians and others; and that real attempts should be made to involve young people of both sexes in such meetings on an equal footing with adults.

3. Relationships between Christians and Muslims.

We recommend:

—that Christians and Muslims spare no effort to live and work with each other, and with others, towards reconciling conflicts and helping grassroot level communities to act upon their own choices in self-development towards a more just, participatory society.

—that with the cooperation of the WCC sub-units of DFI and CCIA a joint Christian-Muslim commission be established with responsibility as a monitoring and mediating body in situations of grievance between Muslims and Christians.

4. Human rights and legal and pastoral issues.

We recommend:

—that, following the WCC stand on human rights and religious freedom, most recently enunciated at the Nairobi General Assembly and at the Geneva 1979 Executive Committee of the WCC, exact information should be communicated to other churches and religious organizations through the WCC, the Vatican and Patriarchates, about situations where religious freedom is violated, but also where it is being safeguarded and promoted. Joint efforts might be also undertaken by the WCC, the Vatican, World Muslim Congress, World Muslim League, in cooperation with international organizations like the United Nations, for organizing an International Year of Religious Freedom.

—that, in situations where marriages between persons of different religions create tensions and difficulties, churches should exercise special pastoral care for the partners and their families.

5. Theological engagement.

We recommend:

—that more theological reflection about Islam take place in coming years among Christians on a widely ecumenical basis; we covet a further theological consultation among Christians about Islam; Christians' varying theological presuppositions and cultural experiences concerning Islam might wherever possible be observed and collated at the level of national and regional councils of churches and then contributed for international sharing among Christians, and perhaps among Muslims too.

—that a major international consultation between Christians and Muslims be held in 1981 on the theme «Christians and Muslims Living Together» and that matters of theological concern should be included in Christian proposals to those Muslims who will share in the planning.

—that eventually and after careful preparation a joint Christian-Muslim theological commission be created to undertake rigorous study and reflection in the areas of theological concern mentioned in this report, and in such other areas of theological concern as Muslims might wish to propose.

6. Mutual witness between Christians and Muslims, and their mutual witness to the world.

We recommend: .

—that the possibility of mutual witness between Christians and Muslims, and their mutual witness to the world, raised in an exploratory fashion in this report, should continue to receive critical examination as the WCC's programmes for Christian-Muslim dialogue develop in the future.

Index

Index

Index

Index

Index

Index

Index

Index

Mosos, 15
Mosques, 81
Moubarac, Y., 66
Moubarac, Yoakim, 173
Movements, 6
Mozarabic, 177
Mt 25:21, 41
Mt 25:32, 41
Mt 5:16, 210
Mt 5:44-48, 44
Mt 6:5, 42
Muhammad, ii, iii, x, xv, xvi, 2, 11, 68, 163, 165, 166, 167, 169, 170, 171, 173
Muhammad, Murtala, 117
Mulder, D.C., 190
Muslim, 1
Muslim Educational Trust, 83
Muslim Women's Association, 85
Muslim World, 120
Muslim-Christian Relations, 12
Muslims, 9
Muslims, Shiite, ix
Mystery, 36
Mystical Knowledge, 150
Myths, 60
Nadeau, L., 121
Nahda, 18, 54, 57, 63
Nairobi, 186, 215
Naked, 43
National, 45
National Interfaith Conference, vii
Nations, Community of, 47
Nigeria, 111
Nigerian Dialogue, 123
Nigerian Journal of Islam, 124
Nogales, Gomez, 162
Nostra Aetate, 40, 41, 42, 44, 65, 95, 203, 209, 205, 206
Nubian, 112
Nussle, Henri, 59
Obedience, 21, 173

Odyssey, Spiritual, 60
Official Positions, xvi
Ojukwu, Chukwumeka, 115
Old Testament, 16
Oneness of God, iv
OPEC, xiv
Opposition to Progress, 21
Oraison, Marc, 56
Organized Dialogue, 137, 142, 145
Oriental Heresies, 9
Orientalism, Christian, 140
Orientalist, 144
Orientalists, 19
Original sin, 35
Orthodox, 147, 213
Orthopraxy, 191
Outbah, 175
Pakistan, 90, 187, 189, 192
Pakistan Islamic Society, 85
Pakistanis, vi, xv, 83
Palestine, 6
Palestinian Heritage, 11
Paradise, 41
Pardon, 45
Patienco, 27
Paul, Saint, 35, 41
Paul VI, 22, 24, 27, 203, 204, 205, 206, 209
Peace, 45, 47
People of the Book, 146
Personal Reflections, 179
Phil 4:8, 152
Philippines, xv, 17, 189
Pignedoli, Archbishop Sergio, 121
Pignedoli, Cardinal, 23, 137, 143
Pilgrimages, 151
Plateau, 113
Platitudes, 6
Pluralist Society, 132
Polemical, 59, 143
Polemics, v, 61, 115
Politics, 47
Poor, 187

225

Index

Index

Index

Index